GREAT QUESTIONS IN POLITICS SERIES

A Divider, Not a Uniter

George W. Bush and the American People

D0070715

GARY C. JACOBSON
UNIVERSITY OF CALIFORNIA, SAN DIEGO

GEORGE C. EDWARDS III, *SERIES EDITOR*
TEXAS A&M UNIVERSITY

PEARSON
Longman

New York   Boston   San Francisco
London   Toronto   Sydney   Tokyo   Singapore   Madrid
Mexico City   Munich   Paris   Cape Town   Hong Kong   Montreal

Executive Editor:	Eric Stano
Senior Marketing Manager:	Elizabeth Fogarty
Production Manager:	Denise Phillip
Project Coordination, Text Design, and Electronic Page Makeup:	WestWords, Inc.
Cover Design Manager:	Nancy Danahy
Cover Designer:	Base Art Co.
Cover Image:	© Corbis
Manufacturing Manager:	Mary Fischer
Printer and Binder:	R. R. Donnelley and Sons
Cover Printer:	Phoenix Color Corporation

Library of Congress Cataloging-in-Publication Data
Jacobson, Gary C.
  A divider, not a uniter : George W. Bush and the American people / Gary C.
Jacobson. — 1st ed.
      p. cm.
  Includes index.
  ISBN 0-321-41699-6
  1. United States—Politics and government—2001– 2. United States—Foreign
relations—2001– 3. Iraq War, 2003– 4. Bush, George W. (George Walker),
1946—Influence. 5. Bush, George W. (George Walker), 1946—Public opinion. 6.
Bush, George W. (George Walker), 1946—Political and social views. 7.
Polarization (Social sciences) 8. Political participation—United States. 9.
Political parties—United States. 10. Public opinion—United States. I. Title.
  E902.J33 2006
  973.931092—dc22

                                                      2006003620

Please visit us at www.ablongman.com

ISBN 0-321-41699-6

1 2 3 4 5 6 7 8 9 10—DOH—09 08 07 06

For Lynne and Wendy

Contents

Preface

This book aims to explain why George W. Bush's presidency has provoked the widest partisan divisions ever recorded in the more than 50 years that surveys have regularly gauged the public's assessment of presidential performance. The idea of writing it occurred after I had already done a good deal of the research in the course of other projects on party polarization in Congress and the electorate, electoral politics, and mass opinion. I had initially been investigating the political consequences of polarized views of the president, but that naturally raised the question of why partisans reacted to the president as they did. I began to address this question in a series of talks and seminars I gave around the country during the 2004–2005 academic year, most of them as part of my service as a Phi Beta Kappa Visiting Scholar. At the end of the year, I realized that the question deserved a more thorough treatment than I could give it in a lecture or journal article, and the result is in your hands.

I incurred more than the usual number of obligations in completing this project. Jim Caraley, David Brady, Fred Greenstein, George C. Edwards III, Susan Webb Hammond, Mat McCubbins, and Michael Nelson were all instrumental in stimulating and helping to publish research studies from which some of the evidence and arguments in this book are drawn.[1] I greatly appreciate their encouragement and suggestions. As will be immediately apparent, I rely heavily on the major media polls for essential data, and I am grateful to Richard Benedetto, Adam Clymer, Claudia Deane, Michael Dimock, Kathleen Francovic, John Harwood, Richard Morin, Jill E Darling Richardson, Brian Scanlon, and Maura Strausberg for patiently answering requests for detailed information on the results of their surveys and often for the surveys themselves; Ms. Deane deserves special thanks in this regard. I leave a more complete account of data sources for the Appendix; here I wish only to acknowledge the enormously valuable contribution made by the producers of high-quality media-sponsored surveys to the research reported in these chapters.

I am obliged also to the many people who helped arrange the various talks and seminars where I was able to explore and debate the ideas and analyses woven into the book. Kathy Navascues heads the list for arranging my itinerary as Phi Beta Kappa Visiting Scholar; there are too many deserving people at the nine campuses I visited in that guise for me to thank them all here, but I

---

[1] These works include "Congress: Elections and Stalemate," *The Elections of 2000*, ed. Michael Nelson (Washington, D.C.: Congressional Quarterly Press, 2001), pp. 185–209; "A House and Senate Divided: The Clinton Legacy and the Congressional Elections of 2000," *Political Science Quarterly*, Vol. 116 (Spring 2001):5–27; "Terror, Terrain, and Turnout: The 2002 Midterm Election," *Political Science Quarterly* 118 (Spring 2003):1–22; "Partisan Polarization in Presidential Support: The Electoral Connection," *Congress and the Presidency* 30 (Spring 2003):1–36; updated version reprinted in *Readings in Presidential Politics*, ed. George C. Edwards III (Belmont, CA: Wadsworth, 2006), pp. 69–108;"The Bush Presidency and the American Electorate," *The George W. Bush Presidency: An Early Assessment*, ed. Fred Greenstein (Johns Hopkins University Press, 2003), pp 197–227; also in *Presidential Studies Quarterly* 32 (December 2003): pp. 701–729; "The Congress: The Structural Basis of Republican Success," *The Elections of 2004*, ed. Michael Nelson (Washington, D.C.: Congressional Quarterly Press, 2005), pp. 163–186; "Polarized Politics and the 2004 Congressional and Presidential Elections," *Political Science Quarterly* 120 (Summer 2005): 199–218; reprinted in *The Meaning of American Democracy*, ed. Robert Y. Shapiro (New York: Academy of Political Science, 2005), pp. 185–204; "Explaining the Ideological Polarization of the Congressional Parties Since the 1970s," in *Process, Party and Policy Making: Further New Perspectives on the History of Congress*, ed. David Brady and Mathew McCubbins (Stanford: Stanford University Press, forthcoming).

can at least acknowledge the institutions and their uniformly hospitable Phi Beta Kappa chapters and political science faculty: Rockford College; George Washington University; Rhodes College; Wayne State University; University of North Carolina, Greensboro; Virginia Tech; Furman University; the University of North Dakota, Grand Forks; and the University of Missouri, Columbia. I am also grateful to Denis Lacorne (Paris), Chris Wlezien (Oxford), and Stephan Bierling (Regensburg) for inviting me to present some of this work internationally, and to Elizabeth Garrett, John Geer, Bruce Oppenheimer, Andrea McAtee, Russell Renko, and Richard Almeida for arranging opportunities for presentations at their institutions. The interest these colleagues and the audiences showed in the research was a major stimulus to putting it all into a book.

James Pfiffner's especially careful reading of the manuscript saved me from several embarrassing errors and pointed me in fruitful directions. I also appreciate the comments and suggestions I received from Stephan Bierling, Tom Edsall, John E. Mueller, Sam Popkin, Arthur Sanders, Joe Uscinski, Corey Cook, the data supplied by my colleague Keith T. Poole, and the support and enthusiasm that series editor, George C. Edwards III, and Longman editor, Eric Stano, have given the project.

Finally, I've dedicated this book to my sisters, Lynne H. Rosenthal and Wendy M. Reilly. It was not until a family reunion in Idaho with them and our extended families in July of 2004 that I fully realized how intensely even people without particularly strong partisan or ideological commitments had come to feel about George W. Bush.

Gary C. Jacobson

CHAPTER I

❖

Introduction

In his convention speech accepting the Republican presidential nomination in August 2000, George W. Bush pledged to be "a uniter, not a divider," offering himself as an outsider with "no stake in the bitter arguments of the last few years" who could "change the tone of Washington to one of civility and respect."[1] Bush has instead become the most divisive and polarizing president in the more than 50 years that public opinion polls have regularly measured citizens' assessments of presidents. My purpose in this book is to explain how and why.

Bush's pledge of reconciliation was well gauged to appeal to a public weary of the fierce partisanship characteristic of the previous administration, epitomized by the congressional Republicans' attempt to impeach and remove Democratic president Bill Clinton less than two years earlier. Moreover, coming from a candidate who, as governor of Texas, had worked effectively with a

---

[1] Speech to Republican National Convention, August 3, 2000, accepting the nomination.

Democratic legislature, it was credible. And indeed for a time during his first term, in the aftermath of the attacks on New York and Washington, D.C. by al Qaeda terrorists, Bush did rally virtually the entire nation, politicians and public alike, behind his leadership. But in the months before the events of September 11, 2001, had radically altered the political context, Bush had inspired the widest partisan differences in evaluations of a newly-elected president ever recorded. And by the time he sought reelection in 2004, he had become by a wide margin the most polarizing president on record.

The overall trends in public evaluations of George Bush are displayed in Figure 1.1 (in this and many subsequent figures, the trends are highlighted by Lowess smoothing).[2] Summarized briefly—I will have much more to say about these patterns later—Bush's overall approval ratings drifted in the mid-50 percent range until the September 11 terrorist attacks, and the president's resolute response to them, provoked the greatest "rally"[3] in presidential approval ever observed. Over the following fifteen months, his ratings returned gradually to where they had been before 9/11. The effects of another, more modest rally following the invasion of Iraq in March of 2003 eroded more quickly, as did

---

[2] Each point in the figure represents the proportion of respondents in a poll who responded "approve" when asked, "Do you approve or disapprove of the way George W. Bush is handling his job as president?" or some close variant. The Lowess smoothed trend (bandwidth=.05) is shown by the solid line. Data are from the CBS/*New York Times* Poll, the Gallup Poll, NBC News/*Wall Street Journal* Poll, Pew Research Center for the People and the Press Poll, *Newsweek* Poll, ABC News/*Washington Post* Poll, *Los Angeles Times* Poll, *Time* Poll, CNN/*Time* Poll, and Associated Press/IPSOS Poll reported at http://pollingreport.com/wh.htm, December 22, 2005. Only surveys that sample the entire adult population are included.

[3] The term entered the literature with John E. Mueller's *War, Presidents, and Public Opinion* (New York: John Wiley and Sons, 1973), p. 53.

FIGURE 1.1
Approval of George W. Bush's Job Performance, 2001–2005

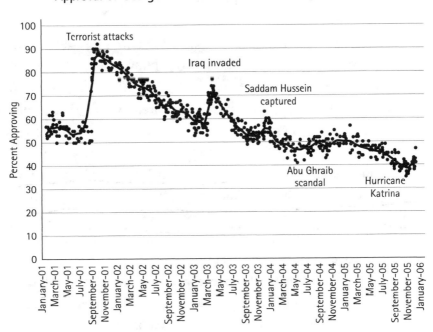

the even smaller spike in approval later that year inspired by the capture of Saddam Hussein in December. Bush's low point for 2004 coincided with the Abu Ghraib prison scandal in the spring. His ratings recovered a bit around his reelection but continued on a downward trajectory thereafter, reaching the lowest point of his presidency to date in November 2005 in the face of rising gas prices, the federal government's inept response to the devastation wrought by Hurricane Katrina, the indictment of the vice president's top aide for perjury, and continuing difficulties in Iraq. A small up tick in early December, attributed to good economic numbers and a concentrated campaign to stem the decline in support for the Iraq War, still left his approval ratings hovering a little above 40 percent.

These trends reflect, then, the signal events of Bush's presidency to date more or less as the standard literature on presidential approval would predict.[4] Far less standard is their partisan composition. When the data are disaggregated by the respondent's party identification (Figure 1.2),[5] it is apparent that independents and Democrats account for nearly all of the temporal variance in the president's job approval. Republicans' approval rates have been very high from the start and have moved comparatively little in response to changing circumstances and events. Even at his low point in the fall of 2005, about 80 percent of Republicans continued to approve of Bush's performance. He received relatively low marks from Democrats until the terrorist attacks, after which they rallied to deliver the highest approval ratings ever given to a president by rival-party identifiers, reaching a record 84 percent in one October 2001 Gallup Poll. Thereafter, the steady downward trend in approval among Democrats was interrupted only temporarily by the onset of the Iraq War and later capture of Saddam Hussein and, by the beginning of 2004, had dipped below 20 percent. Democrats' approval fell further during the campaign, hitting a low of 8 percent in one October 2004 Gallup Poll. It rose a bit

---

[4] Cf. Richard A. Brody, *Assessing the President* (Stanford: Stanford University Press, 1991); Mueller, *Wars, Presidents, and Public Opinion.*

[5] Unless otherwise specified, I do not include leaners in the partisan categories; I do so not on theoretical grounds (although some, notably Warren E. Miller and J. Merrill Shanks in *The New American Voter* [Cambridge: Harvard University Press, 1996], Ch. 6, would argue that I should), but because most of the polls I examine here treat leaners as independents. Typically in these polls, a little more than a third of the respondents identify themselves as Democrats, a little less than a third call themselves Republicans, and about a third say they are independents.

FIGURE 1.2
Approval of George W. Bush's Job Performance, 2001–2005, by Party Identification

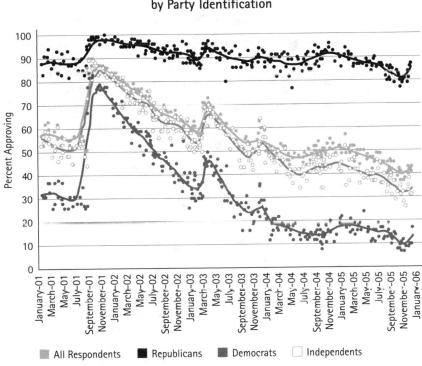

All Respondents   Republicans   Democrats   Independents

Source: 279 CBS News/*New York Times* polls.

after the election, but a year later had fallen to the lowest levels ever recorded by Gallup among rival party identifiers, reaching 7 percent in one late October 2005 survey.[6] To put this figure in perspective, it is 4 percentage points lower than Richard Nixon's worst showing among Democrats just before he resigned in disgrace in 1974.

---

[6] The 7 percent figure was matched in the November 10–13, 2005 Gallup survey.

In the course of his first term, then, partisan differences in George W. Bush's approval ratings went from the widest for any newly elected president, to the narrowest ever recorded after 9/11, and then to the widest for any president at any time by the end of his first term in office. Figures 1.3 and 1.4 provide the comparisons that confirm the historical singularity of partisan responses to Bush. Figure 1.3 shows that Bush has achieved the highest average approval ratings among his own partisans of any president since the question has been polled. His average level of approval among Republicans in the Gallup Polls taken through December

FIGURE 1.3
Presidential Approval, Eisenhower through G.W. Bush
(Quarterly Averages)

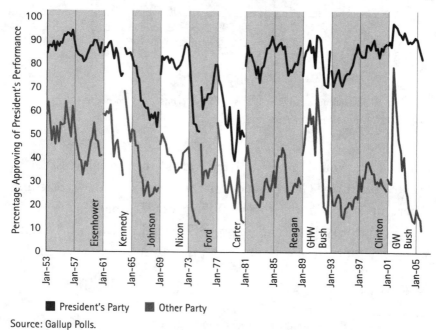

President's Party   Other Party

Source: Gallup Polls.

FIGURE 1.4

Partisan Differences in Presidential Approval, Eisenhower Through G.W. Bush (Quarterly Averages)

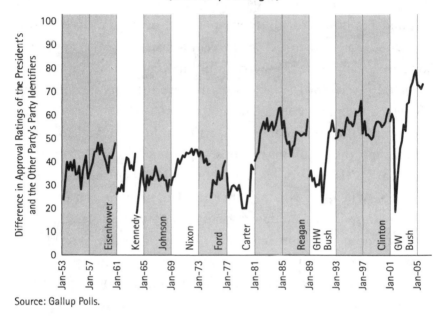

Source: Gallup Polls.

2005, 91.1 percent, exceeds the next highest, that of Dwight D. Eisenhower (87.6 percent over two terms) by a statistically significant margin (p < .001). Among the other party's supporters, his ratings have been both higher (immediately after 9/11) and lower than for any of his predecessors. Before Bush and going back to Eisenhower, the partisan difference in approval ratings had never exceeded 70 percentage points in any Gallup Poll (Figure 1.4). In the 18 Gallup Polls taken during the final two quarters of 2004, the gap never fell *below* 70, averaged 78 and peaked at 83 (94-11). The gap decreased somewhat after the election (averaging 72 points during 2005) but still remained in previously uncharted territory. The partisan divisions were deep as well as wide; in the sixteen ABC News/*Washington Post* surveys taken from the beginning of 2004 through August 2005 that asked respondents how strongly they approved or disapproved of the president, an average of 66 percent of Republicans approved strongly (comprising 75 percent of all Republican approvers), while 62 percent of Democrats disapproved strongly (comprising 78 percent of all Democratic disapprovers).[7]

Several other things are noteworthy in this historical comparison. In previous administrations, approval ratings offered by both parties' identifiers tended to move together and by similar amounts. When, for example, the president's party's approval rating is regressed on the opposing party's approval rating approval for each administration from Eisenhower through Clinton, the regression coefficient ranges from .33 to .92, with an average of .56. That is, on average in previous administrations, a 10 point shift in approval among the opposing partisans is accompanied by a 5.6 point shift among the president's partisans. For the George W. Bush administration, the coefficient is .16; a 10 point shift among Democrats would be accompanied by a 1.6 point shift among Republicans. Among Bush's own partisans, approval is not only highest on average for any president, but it is also the least volatile, with a standard deviation of only 4.1 percentage points. Among Democrats, it is the most volatile, with the standard deviation at 19.6 percentage points.[8]

---

[7]On average in these polls, 66 percent of all respondents have expressed strong approval or disapproval of the president, compared to 31 percent who said they approved or disapproved "somewhat." They are accessible at http://www.washingtonpost.com/wp-dyn/politics/polls.

[8] The opposing partisans usually display greater volatility in approval ratings; the ratio of the standard deviation of approval ratings of the opposing party to that of the president's party ranges from .97 to 2.18:1, with an average of 1.53:1. For G.W. Bush, the ratio is 4.90:1.

The data in Figure 1.4 also indicate that partisan differences in presidential approval have grown since the 1970s. From Eisenhower through Carter, the partisan gap averaged 34 percentage points. Under Reagan the average gap rose to 52 points. The partisan gap for the senior Bush was similar to that for pre-Reagan presidents, 36 points, but by the end of his presidency it was as wide as for Reagan. The average difference for Clinton was 55 points, and for G.W. Bush so far it is 59 points, the highest of any president despite the extraordinarily high level of approval he received from Democrats in the year following 9/11. I will have more to say about this upward trend in the next chapter.

Finally, returning to Figure 1.2, notice that Bush's approval level among self-identified independents has been considerably closer to that of Democrats than of Republicans. This is unusual. Although independents are usually a bit closer to opposition partisans than to the president's partisans on this measure, the difference has always been much smaller than for Bush. For example, Bill Clinton's average approval rating among independents was 27 points higher than among Republicans, 28 points lower than among Democrats. Independents were thus only about 1 point closer to one set of partisans than the other, and the average ratings of independents were virtually identical to those of all respondents combined. Bush's rating among independents has averaged 35 points lower than among Republicans, 21 points higher than among Democrats, and thus 14 point closer to the latter. If analysis is confined to polls taken since the beginning of 2004, the difference is even larger, 18 points, and his rating among independents is 6 points lower than his average among all respondents. Thus only Bush's sustained, remarkably high level of support among Republicans kept his overall support level from

falling well below 50 percent after the beginning of 2004, and
without continuing Republican loyalty, the president's numbers in
late 2005 would have been even more dismal.

Questions on G.W. Bush's handling of specific policy domains
also produce large partisan differences, with the distribution of
responses from independents again closer to those of Democrats
than of Republicans. The trends in these evaluations differ to
some extent, but all show substantial increases in partisan polarization over the course of the administration. Figure 1.5 indicates

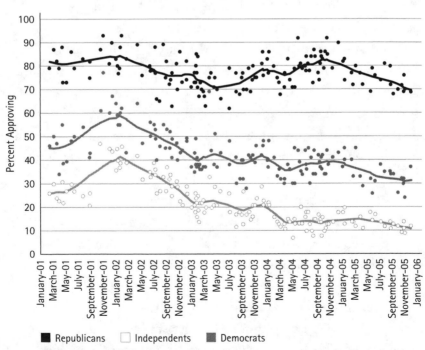

FIGURE 1.5
Approval of G.W. Bush's Handling of the Economy

■ Republicans   ☐ Independents   ■ Democrats

Sources: 139 ABC News/*Washington Post*, CBS News/*New York Times*, *Los Angeles Times*, and Pew
Center for the People and Press Polls.

that Bush's handling of the economy has always drawn rather widely divergent partisan evaluations, with the gap closing only modestly after September 11. Prior to the terrorist attacks, the partisan difference averaged 52 percentage points; for the year after the attacks, the average was down to 43 points, but by the final six months of 2004, it had risen to 68 points and has remained above 60 points since then.

Initial reaction to Bush's handling of terrorism was strongly positive regardless of party (Figure 1.6). Partisan differences

FIGURE 1.6
Approval of G.W. Bush's Handling of Terrorism

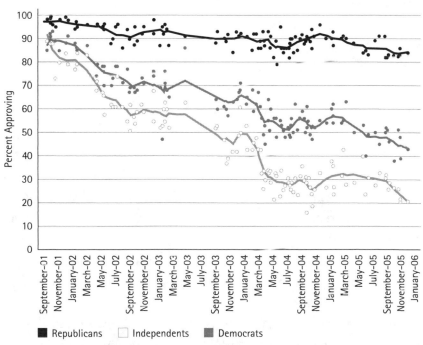

Percent Approving

■ Republicans   ☐ Independents   ■ Democrats

Sources: 139 ABC News/*Washington Post*, CBS News/*New York Times*, *Los Angeles Times*, and Pew Center for the People and Press Polls.

increased slowly during the year after the attacks but majorities of Democrats (and independents) continued to approve. The question was not asked between April and September 2003 in these polls, and when it reappeared, partisan differences had grown, reaching a peak around the November election (the gap averaging 66 percentage points in October and November). Still, Democratic approval of Bush's performance in this domain was notably higher than in other domains. From July 2004 through early December 2005, an average of 30 percent of Democrats approved Bush's handling of terrorism, a figure twice as high as approval of his handling of the economy or Iraq.

Evaluations of Bush's handling of the situation in Iraq follow yet another trend (Figure 1.7). Approval among Republicans has been high all along (though not as high as his overall ratings, and it dipped to around 70 in the late fall of 2005). Among Democrats (and independents), approval rose substantially during the administration's campaign of justification leading up to the war, peaking around the time Baghdad fell. Approval then fell off sharply until Saddam Hussein's capture in December 2003, after which it resumed its downward trajectory. Between July 2004 and December 2005 the partisan difference on this question averaged 62 percentage points. (A full discussion of partisan differences on matters relating to the Iraq War awaits chapters 5 and 6.)

Comparing trends in partisan polarization in presidential approval across domains and overall (Figure 1.8), it becomes evident that each displays its own unique dynamic, but over time, the trends have become increasingly parallel. Polarization on every domain peaks around the 2004 election—not surprising and of

FIGURE 1.7
Approval of G.W. Bush's Handling of Iraq

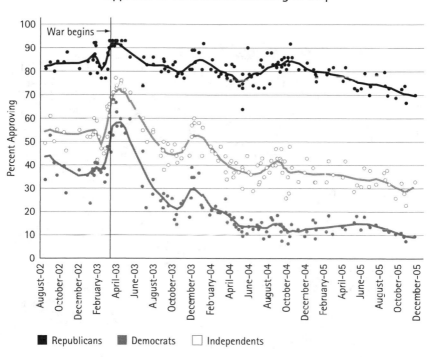

■ Republicans ■ Democrats □ Independents

which more in Chapter 7—and contracts only slightly thereafter. Notice also that, except for the year following the terrorist attacks, polarization has been consistently greatest on the general job approval question that sums up the public's overall evaluations of the president.

In retrospect, George W. Bush's pledge in 2004 to be a "uniter, not a divider" turns out to be deeply ironic, as he has, by the measures examined here, become the most divisive occupant of the White House in at least 50 years. The irony is underlined by responses to a question posed by Gallup in October 2004,

FIGURE 1.8

Partisan Differences in Approval of G.W. Bush's Performance, by Issue Domain

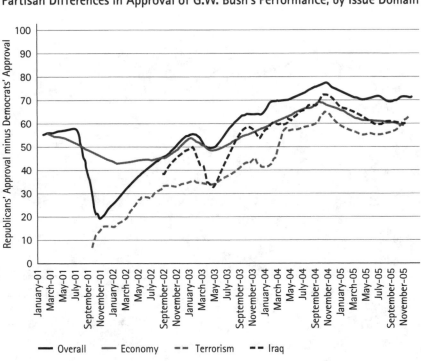

displayed in Figure 1.9. Asked if Bush has done more to unite or to divide the country, Americans as a whole divided precisely in half, 48 percent choosing each alternative; 87 percent of Republicans said that he had done more to unite the country, while 81 percent of Democrats said he had done more to divide it. This is the rare survey question that, in the distribution of responses, effectively answered itself.

This brings us to the central question I address in this book: Why has the public become so thoroughly divided along party

FIGURE 1.9

"Has George W. Bush done more to unite the country, or has he done more to divide the country?"

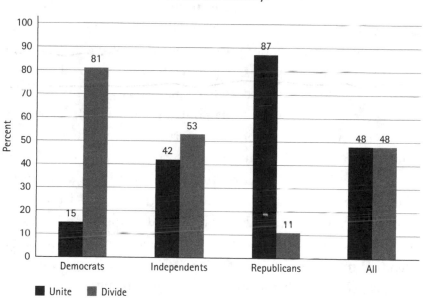

lines about this president? There is, I shall argue, no single answer, but rather a complex set of converging political forces, events, and decisions that brought public opinion on this president to its present state. Responses to Bush had been shaped by both deep, enduring historical currents and random historical accidents; they have been affected by the president's own character, policy choices, and strategies, as well as by conditions entirely beyond his (or anyone else's) control. In examining these diverse causal strands, I hope not only to explain why George W. Bush has become such a polarizing figure, but to use this exploration to illuminate some central developments in American politics over the past several decades and to address questions of interest to political scientists about the sources of mass political opinion and behavior.

I begin by putting the Bush administration in its historical context, for one obvious obstacle to Bush's becoming "a uniter, not a divider" was taking office in the wake of more than three decades of growing partisan polarization in national politics. Chapter 2 describes and seeks to explain this pervasive, widely-noted trend, arguing that it left political elites and ordinary citizens alike primed to respond in partisan terms with only the mildest provocation. Provocation, of course, came even before Bush took office, in the form of the fight over Florida's electoral votes. Chapter 3 focuses on the 2000 election and its denouement in the Supreme Court; it also analyzes the cultural and economic divisions exposed and reinforced by that election, with particular attention to the strong cultural affinity Bush had forged with religious conservatives before and during the campaign.

The fourth chapter covers the first two years of the Bush administration. It begins with an examination of the president's agenda and political strategies for implementing it; both, I argue, contributing to partisan polarization. The September 11 terrorist attacks changed everything—including the meaning of the presidential approval question—for a time. The effects persisted long enough to serve Republicans well in the 2002 election, but their use of the terrorism issue in the campaign left a residue of partisan bitterness that has yet to dissipate.

Chapters 5 and 6 delve into what I shall argue is the principal reason Bush leaped ahead of Bill Clinton and Ronald Reagan to become the most divisive president on record: the Iraq War.

Chapter 5 looks into the public's divergent views on the war, its necessity, and Bush's justifications for it prior to the invasion of Iraq in March of 2003 and through its immediate aftermath, crowned by the president's "Mission Accomplished" moment on the aircraft carrier *Abraham Lincoln* in May. Chapter 6 explores how views of the war and the president changed—or, in the case of most Republicans, did not change—as the war's basic premises, that Saddam Hussein possessed weapons of mass destruction and was in league with al Qaeda, became increasingly untenable. I show how the strikingly divergent responses of ordinary Republicans and Democrats to both factual and attitudinal questions about the war have created by far the largest partisan difference in support for a war of any in the past half century.

The Iraq War was, not surprisingly, a central issue in the 2004 presidential campaign, which is the subject of Chapter 7. Partisan polarization in attitudes toward the war and the president, along with the Bush campaign's successful strategy of mobilizing core supporters rather than reaching out to swing voters, inspired the highest level of party line voting yet observed in the 52 year history of the National Election Studies. Because of the Republicans' structural advantage in House and Senate elections (a more efficient distribution of voters), this highly partisan atmosphere produced not only a narrow Republican presidential victory, but also solidified the party's control of both houses of Congress.

Chapter 8 examines the election's aftermath. Bush continued to set new records for polarization, provoking the widest partisan gap in approval of any newly reelected president on record. I consider his prospects for leading the country as "president of half the people," arguing that he can succeed without popular or elite support among Democrats as long as his party remains united, but on issues where bipartisan support is necessary to succeed, such as Social Security reform, he will be hard pressed to get it as long as huge majorities of ordinary Democrats disapprove of him and his proposals.

In the final chapter, I step back to take a wider view of the cultural, economic, and psychological contours of American politics as revealed and expressed by popular responses to George W. Bush and his policies. Here, I speculate about the extent to which political differences, especially partisan differences, have come to reflect differences in perceived, felt, and lived realities, and are therefore destined to outlast the Bush administration. I also speculate about the possible impact of Hurricane Katrina, which hit New Orleans and the Gulf Coast just as I was finishing this book, on the president's standing with the public both in the near future and during the remainder of his second term.

CHAPTER 2

❖

Primed for Partisanship

In December 1998 the House of Representatives voted to impeach President Bill Clinton for perjury and obstruction of justice in the investigation of his dalliance with White House intern Monica Lewinsky. All but four Republicans voted for at least one of the four articles of impeachment. Only five Democrats voted for any of them. In what was billed as a "conscience" vote, 98 percent of Republican consciences dictated a vote to impeach the president, while 98 percent of Democratic consciences dictated the opposite. The Senate's verdict after the impeachment trial was only slightly less polarized. Every Democrat voted for acquittal, while 91 percent of the Republicans voted for conviction on at least one article.

Although Americans on the whole opposed impeachment, popular partisan divisions on the issue were also huge, with a large majority of Republican identifiers favoring impeachment and an even larger majority of Democratic identifiers opposing it (Table 2.1). In the end, 68 percent of Republicans wanted the Senate to convict and remove Clinton, with only 30 percent favoring

TABLE 2.1

Partisanship and Support for Bill Clinton's Impeachment (Percent)

	ALL RESPONDENTS	REPUBLICANS	INDEPENDENTS	DEMOCRATS
Yes	33.1	61.9	27.6	12.8
No	63.5	34.7	65.2	84.5
Don't know	3.5	3.4	7.2	2.7
N	12,161	4,096	1,309	5,956

NOTE: The question was, "Just from the way you feel right now, do you think President Clinton's actions are serious enough to warrant his being impeached and removed from the Presidency, or not?"
SOURCE: Thirteen CBS/*New York Times* Polls taken between August 1998 and February 1999.

acquittal; among Democrats, 89 percent favored acquittal, while only 10 percent favored conviction.[1] Indeed, it was ordinary Democrats' steadfast opposition to impeachment that kept nervous congressional Democrats from abandoning the president en masse. Partisan divisions among the congressional parties' respective electoral coalitions—the voters who supported the successful Republican or Democratic candidates—were even wider, and divisions among the parties' activists were wider still.[2]

An implicit premise behind George W. Bush's 2000 campaign promise to be a "uniter, not a divider" and to "change the tone in Washington to one of civility and respect" was that partisan polarization was an inside-the-beltway phenomenon with little popular resonance. But the public's highly partisan response to Clinton's

---

[1] Gallup/CNN/*USA Today* Poll, February 12–13, 1999, reported at http://www.pollingreport.com/scandals.htm, (accessed February 15, 1999).
[2] Gary C. Jacobson, "Public Opinion and the Impeachment of Bill Clinton," *British Elections and Parties Review*, Vol. 10, ed. Philip Cowley, David Denver, Andrew Russell and Lisa Harrison (London: Frank Cass, 2000) pp. 1–31.

impeachment was no more aberrant than the party line voting on it in Congress; both reflected the extension of trends several decades in the making. The two trends are intimately entwined and are part of a larger sea change in American political life. Their origins are multiple, complex, and still in some dispute among scholars. But their consequences are clear: Anyone elected president in 2000 would have faced a Congress and public predisposed to respond in sharply partisan terms with even the gentlest provocation.

SOURCES OF PARTISAN POLARIZATION

A variety of forces contributed to partisan polarization among politicians and citizens alike during the final third of the twentieth century. These include changes in the political attitudes of citizens, changes in the way citizens sort themselves into parties based on their attitudes, and changes in the way partisan voters are sorted into House districts and states. They also include changes in the subset of citizens who become political activists, the motives of people who pursue public office, the policy issues addressed by government, and congressional rules and procedures. And they include specific events and political battles, deliberate political strategies, and the character and style of rival partisan leaders. Telling the full story would take a volume by itself.[3] A general outline and some basic evidence will be sufficient to my purpose here, which is to demarcate the polarized political context in which George W. Bush assumed his presidency.

---

[3] Fortunately, one is on the way; Barbara Sinclair, *Partisan Polarization and the Politics of the National Policy-Making Process* (Norman, Oklahoma: University of Oklahoma Press, forthcoming).

PARTISAN POLARIZATION
IN CONGRESS

Widening partisan divisions in the United States were first observed by scholars examining roll-call voting patterns in Congress, and subsequent research has abundantly confirmed and extended their initial findings.[4] By every observed measure, the distance between the congressional parties has been growing steadily since the 1970s. The widening gap appears in party loyalty on roll-call votes,[5] adjusted ADA scores,[6] and presidential support scores[7] as well as, most prominently, in Keith Poole and Howard Rosenthal's first dimension DW-Nominate scores.[8] The Poole-Rosenthal data show that the wide ideological distance

---

[4] Keith T. Poole and Howard Rosenthal, "The Polarization of American Politics," *Journal of Politics* 46 (1984):1061–79.

[5] David W. Rohde, *Parties and Leaders in the Postreform House* (Chicago: University of Chicago Press, 1991), pp. 13–16; John H. Aldrich, *Why Parties? The Origin and Transformation of Party Politics in America* (Chicago: University of Chicago Press, 1995), pp. 195–201; Barbara Sinclair, "Hostile Partners: The President, Congress, and Lawmaking in the Partisan 1990s," in Jon R. Bond and Richard Fleisher, eds., *Polarized Politics: Congress and the President in a Partisan Era* (Washington, D.C.: Congressional Quarterly Press, 2000), pp. 137–140; Jason M. Roberts and Steven S. Smith, "Procedural Contexts, Party Strategy, and Conditional Party Voting in the U.S. House of Representatives, 1971–2000," *American Journal of Political Science* 47 (2003):305–319.

[6] Tim Groseclose, Steven D. Levitt, and James M. Snyder Jr., "Comparing Interest Group Scores across Time and Chambers: Adjusted ADA Scores for the U.S. Congress," *American Political Science Review* 93 (1999):33–50.

[7] Richard Fleisher and Jon R. Bond, "Partisanship and the President's Quest for Votes on the Floor of Congress," in Bond and Fleisher, *Polarized Politics,* pp. 168–173; Gary C. Jacobson, "Partisan Polarization in Presidential Support: The Electoral Connection," *Congress and the Presidency* 30 (Spring 2003):4–8.

[8] The DW-Nominate scale is calculated from all nonunanimous roll-call votes cast across all Congresses; each member's pattern of roll-call votes locates him or her on a liberal-conservative dimension ranging from −1.0 (most liberal) to 1.0 (most conservative), allowing us to compare the distribution of positions along the dimension taken by Republicans and Democrats in different Congresses. See Keith T. Poole and Howard Rosenthal, *Congress: A Political-Economic History of Roll Call Voting* (New York: Oxford University Press, 1999), Chapter 2, and Nolan M. McCarty, Keith T. Poole, and Howard Rosenthal, *Income Redistribution and the Realignment of American Politics* (Washington, D.C.: The AEI Press, 1997). DW-Nominate is an updated version of their D-Nominate measure; I am obliged to Keith Poole for proving theses data, which may be found at http://voteview.uh.edu/dwnomin.htm (January 5, 2005).

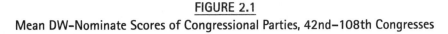

FIGURE 2.1

Mean DW-Nominate Scores of Congressional Parties, 42nd–108th Congresses

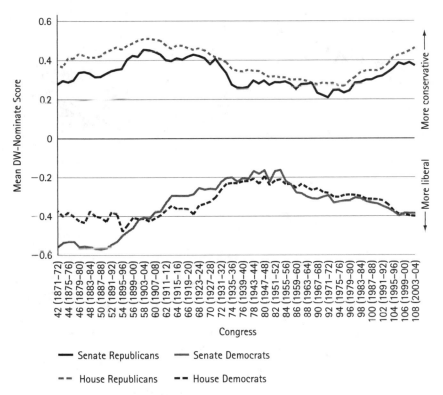

between the congressional parties observed in recent congresses is by no means unprecedented (Figures 2.1 and 2.2); the parties were even further apart in the latter half of the nineteenth century than they are now, and the recent increase in polarization followed a period in which the congressional parties were, by historical standards, unusually close to one another on the liberal-conservative

FIGURE 2.2
Party Differences in Mean DW-Nominate Scores, 42nd–108th Congresses

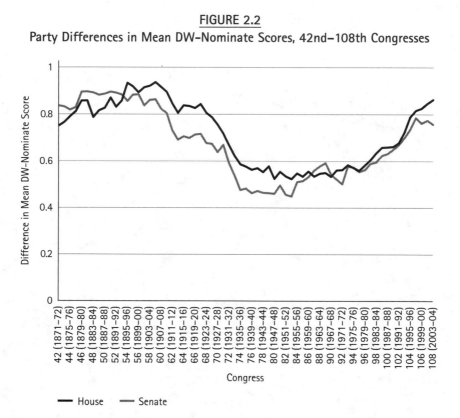

House — Senate

dimension.[9] Nonetheless, the steep increase in polarization since the Nixon administration is unprecedented, and by the time George W. Bush took office in 2001 the parties in both chambers had moved further apart than they had been at any time since before World War I. As the parties pulled apart ideologically, they also became more homogeneous internally; the standard devia-

[9] Keith T. Poole, "Changing Minds? Not in Congress!" manuscript, University of Houston, at http://voteview.uh.edu/chminds.pdf, (downloaded October 14, 2003); Sean M. Theriault, "The Case of the Vanishing Moderates: Party Polarization in the Modern Congress," manuscript, University of Texas, Austin, (2003).

tions of each party coalition's DW-Nominate scores and adjusted ADA scores have declined among both parties in both chambers since the early 1970s.[10] These changes had, by the 106th Congress, left the House and Senate with the most divergent and internally homogeneous party coalitions in living memory.

POLARIZATION AND ELECTORAL CHANGE

Initially, congressional party polarization seemed anomalous, because at the time it first began to draw scholarly attention, many journalists and not a few political scientists viewed Americans as "dealigning," growing less partisan and less ideological in their politics.[11] Indeed, as late as 2000, an astute journalist could write that "the American electorate is far less ideological than it once was and . . . far less patient with sharply partisan appeals."[12] This view of the electorate raised a pointed scholarly question. Political scientists look reflexively to the "electoral connection"[13] for explanations of basic legislative behavior; how could legislators, supposedly so acutely sensitive to their constituents' sentiments, become increasingly divided by party and ideology as the

---

[10] McCarty, Poole, and Rosenthal provide alternative measures of dispersion within the parties that display the same trends for the period under examination here; see *Income Redistribution*.

[11] Martin P. Wattenberg, *The Decline of American Political Parties* (Cambridge: Harvard University Press, 1994); Everett C. Ladd, "The 1994 Congressional Elections: The Realignment Continues," *Political Science Quarterly* 111 (Spring 1995):1–23; Everett C. Ladd, "The 1996 Election: The 'No Majority' Realignment Continues," *Political Science Quarterly* 112 (Spring 1997):1–28; Daniel M. Shea, "The Passing of Realignment and the 'Base-Less' Party System, *American Politics Quarterly* 27 (January 1999):33–57; John Kenneth White and Daniel M. Shea, *New Party Politics: From Jefferson and Hamilton to the Information Age* (Boston: St. Martin's Press, 2000), Chapter 6.

[12] Richard Berke, "A Race in Which Candidates Clung to the Center," http://www.nytimes.com/200/11/07/politics/07ELEC.html, (accessed November 10, 2000).

[13] David R. Mayhew, *Congress: The Electoral Connection* (New Haven: Yale University Press, 1974).

people who elect them became less so? The answer turned out to be that ordinary voters, like the leaders they elected, were actually growing more rather than less divided by party and ideology over these decades. Congressional partisans and their electoral constituencies were thus moving in the same, not opposite directions.

Two major trends gave the congressional parties increasingly divergent electoral coalitions. First, the partisan, ideological, and policy views of voters grew more internally consistent, more distinctive between parties, and more predictive of voting in national elections.[14] Second, electoral units into which voters were sorted became more homogeneously partisan.[15] That is, changes in the preferences, behavior, and distribution of congressional voters gave the congressional parties more internally homogenous, divergent, and polarized electoral bases.

A principal source of mass electoral change was of course the partisan realignment of the South.[16] The civil rights revolution, and particularly the Voting Rights Act of 1965, brought southern blacks into the electorate as Democrats, while moving conservative whites

---

[14] Gary C. Jacobson, "The Electoral Basis of Partisan Polarization in Congress," presented at the Annual Meeting of the American Political Science Association, Washington, D.C., August 31–September 3, 2000; Larry M. Bartels, "Partisanship and Voting Behavior, 1952–1996," *American Journal of Political Science* 44 (January 2000):35–50.

[15] Jeffrey M. Stonecash, Mark D. Brewer, and Mach D. Mariani, *Diverging Parties: Social Change, Realignment, and Party Polarization* (Boulder, Colorado: Westview Press, 2003); Gary C. Jacobson, *The Politics of Congressional Elections*, 6th ed. (New York: Longman, 2004), pp. 236–243.

[16] Earle Black and Merle Black, *Politics and Society in the South* (Cambridge, MA: Harvard University Press, 1987); Paul Frymer, "The 1994 Aftershock: Dealignment or Realignment in the South," in Philip A. Klinkner, ed., *Midterm: The Elections of 1994 in Context* (Boulder, Colorado: Westview Press, 1995), pp. 99–113; Richard Nadeau and Harold W. Stanley, "Class Polarization Among Native Southern Whites, 1952–90," *American Journal of Political Science* 37 (August 1993):900–919; M.V. Hood, III, Quentin Kidd, and Irwin L. Morris, "Of Byrd[s] and Bumpers: Using Democratic Senators to Analyze Political Change in the South, 1960–1995," *American Journal of Political Science* 43 (April 1999):465–487; Martin P. Wattenberg, "The Building of a Republican Regional Base in the South: The Elephant Crosses the Mason-Dixon Line," *Public Opinion Quarterly* 55 (1991):424–31; Charles S. Bullock III, Donna R. Hoffman, and Ronald Kieth Gaddie, "The Consolidation of the White Southern Congressional Vote," *Political Research Quarterly* 58 (June 2005):231–243.

FIGURE 2.3
The Rise of Southern Republicanism, 1952–2004

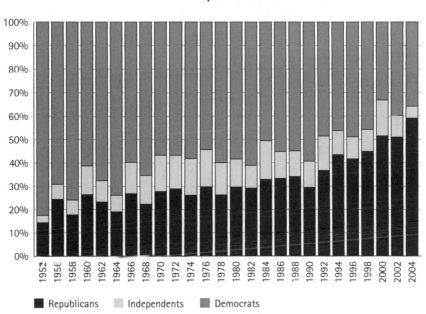

■ Republicans   ▨ Independents   ▨ Democrats

to abandon their ancestral allegiance to the Democratic party in favor of the ideologically and racially more compatible Republicans. In-migration also contributed to an increasingly Republican electorate, which gradually replaced conservative Democrats with conservative Republicans in southern House and Senate seats. Figure 2.3 displays the growth of southern Republicanism. Fifty years ago, Republicans were rare in the South; by the time George W. Bush sought the presidency, they comprised a majority.[17]

---

[17] If analysis is confined to voters, the Republican rise is even steeper; Figure 2.3 treats independents who lean toward a party as partisans. The data in Figures 2.3 through 2.9 are from The American National Election Studies (www.electionstudies.org). THE 1948–2004 ANES CUMULATIVE DATA FILE [dataset]. Stanford University and the University of Michigan [producers and distributors], 2005.

FIGURE 2.4
Party Identification of Conservatives, 1972–2004

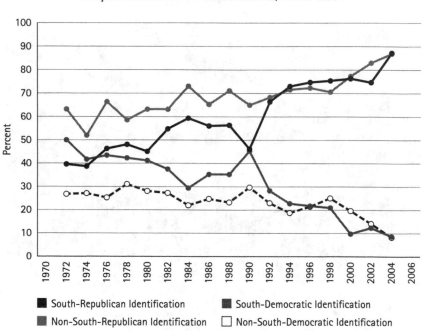

- ■ South-Republican Identification   ■ South-Democratic Identification
- ■ Non-South-Republican Identification □ Non-South-Democratic Identification

This change was primarily a result of the gradual movement of conservative whites into the Republican camp (Figure 2.4).[18] In the 1970s, white southern conservatives were about as likely to consider themselves Democrats as Republicans. By 2004, they had become overwhelmingly Republican. Conservatives whites outside the South also increasingly sorted themselves into the ideologically appropriate party, though they did not have as far to go

---

[18] Conservatives are those respondents who placed themselves at 5–7 on the NES 7-point liberal conservative scale; the liberal end of the scale is 1–3; 4 is the middle (moderate) category.

as southern conservatives. By the 1990s, regional differences between the two groups had virtually disappeared. The proportion of self-identified liberals calling themselves Democrats also grew during this period, from about 73 percent in the 1970s to about 84 percent since 1994, while the proportion identifying themselves as Republicans fell from 15 percent to 11 percent. Thus the level of consistency between party identification and ideology grew across the board—and at a time when the proportion of voters who were willing to place themselves on the liberal-conservative scale, and the proportion doing so who chose other than the center category, also grew substantially.[19]

Party loyalty among congressional voters also increased over this period,[20] so the relationship between ideology and voting became notably stronger. Figure 2.5 displays the growing proportion of self-identified liberals, and diminishing proportion of self-identified conservatives, voting for Democratic candidates for House and Senate since 1972. The shift among conservatives is particularly notable, as is the pivotal role of the 1994 election in solidifying support for Republican candidates among conservatives. In the most recent congressional elections, 80 percent of self-identified liberals voted for Democrats, while 80 percent of conservatives voted for Republicans. Among presidential voters in 2004—the election is analyzed in detail in Chapter 7—82 percent of conservatives voted for Bush, while 92 percent of the liberals voted for Kerry.

---

[19] Jacobson, "Electoral Basis of Partisan Polarization."
[20] Jacobson, *Politics of Congressional Elections*, pp. 119–120.

FIGURE 2.5

Ideology and Voting in Congressional Elections, 1972–2004

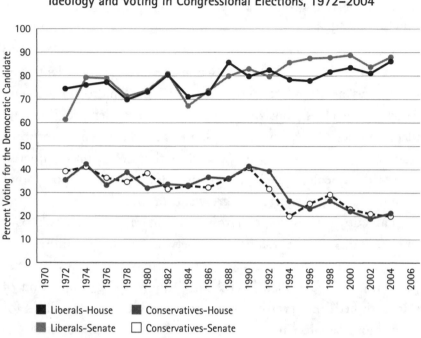

Liberals-House   Conservatives-House

Liberals-Senate   Conservatives-Senate

These changes in voting behavior gave the parties increasingly divergent electoral coalitions (Figure 2.6). The gap between the mean locations on the 7-point liberal-conservative scale of Democratic and Republican voters grew for all three types of federal elections. Although the changes may not seem large—totaling about a point for House and Senate voters on a 7-point scale—the trends for both Republican and Democratic voters are statistically significant ($p < .001$). It is also worth noting that the scale is effectively only a 5-point scale, as only 5 or 6 percent of respondents choose the extreme points; the enlarged gap thus

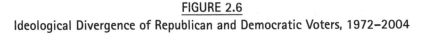

FIGURE 2.6
Ideological Divergence of Republican and Democratic Voters, 1972–2004

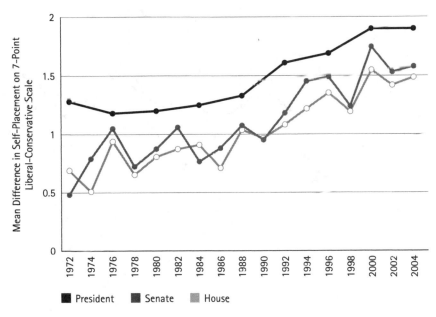

covers a larger proportion of the effective scale than appears at first glance.

The electorate's growing partisan coherence is also evident in correlations between voters' party identification and positions on several of the National Election Studies' 7-point issue scales and the abortion question, displayed in Figure 2.7.[21] On every issue—ranging from the government's economic role, to race, to women's

---

[21] I use the tau-b statistic to measure the relationship because the analysis is of ordinal variables; alternative measures of association, including the product-moment correlation, reveal precisely the same trends; all of these analyses are confined to respondents who reported voting for one of the major party candidates in the House election.

FIGURE 2.7
Correlations Between Party Identification and Issue Positions, 1972–2004

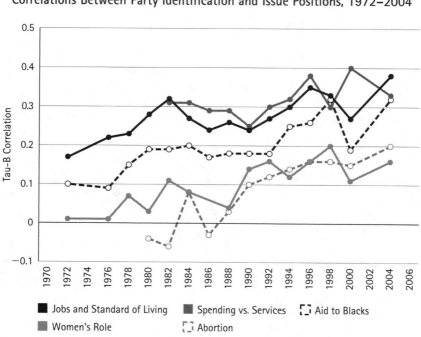

Jobs and Standard of Living   Spending vs. Services   Aid to Blacks
Women's Role   Abortion

role in society, to abortion policy—the overall trend is upward. Notice that although economic issue positions are normally most strongly related to partisanship—reflecting the venerable New Deal cleavage—the steepest increases have occurred on social issues. For example, 25 years ago, opinions on abortion were unrelated to party identification (indeed, Republicans tended to be a bit more pro-choice than Democrats); now we observe a substantial correlation. In 1980, only 29 percent of voters who thought abortion should be illegal under all circumstances identified themselves as Republicans; by 2004, 63 percent did so; the proportion of these voters calling themselves Democrats fell from 61 percent to 34 percent.[22]

National politicians and ordinary voters, then, have not moved in opposite directions since the 1970s; both have become increasingly divided along party lines by political issues and ideology. But it is clear that political leaders were the first movers: Changes in the electorate were mainly a response to shifts in political fault lines initiated or furthered by national leaders and their policy choices. The passage of civil rights legislation during the Johnson administration, for example, contributed decisively to the gradual but cumulatively radical electoral change in the South. Political leaders' responses to the 1973 Supreme Court decision in *Roe* v. *Wade* helped turn abortion into an issue that redefined the two parties, altering their popular bases and mobilizing new cohorts of activists. Battles over taxes, spending, and budget deficits initiated during the Reagan administration and continuing (with a brief respite during the second Clinton administration) to this day repeatedly pitted the parties against one another in a high-stakes standoff that crystallized and expressed fundamental political differences.

Nor is there any doubt that elite partisanship was proactive and strategic as well as resonant of national policy disputes. Although the increasingly bitter partisan struggles observed in Washington over the past 30 years reflected sincere disagreements, strategic considerations were never far from the surface, with divisive issues

---

[22] For additional evidence regarding the partisan effects of the abortion issue, see Greg D. Adams, "Abortion: Evidence of and Issue Evolution," *American Journal of Political Science* 41 (July 1997):718–73. On growing mass partisan policy differences in general, see Mark D. Brewer, "The Rise of Partisanship and the Expansion of Partisan Conflict within the American Electorate," *Political Research Quarterly* 58 (June 2005), 219–229.

and confrontational tactics selected as much to move activists and electorates as to prevail on the Hill.[23] The Republicans' devotion to slashing taxes, for instance, has always been as much an electoral ploy as an expression of ideological faith and has, since the Reagan administration, helped frame budget politics in starkly partisan terms. The action in Washington has shaped the electoral environment by redefining party images through the clash of personalities (Ronald Reagan, Tip O'Neill, Henry Hyde, Newt Gingrich, Bill Clinton, Tom DeLay, George W. Bush) as well as conflict over issues. These clashes also had a strategic component; inflaming partisan conflict was part of Newt Gingrich's successful strategy for achieving Republican control of Congress.

Evidence that these struggles inspired changes in mass attitudes and behavior lies not only in the temporal sequence—for example, realignment in the South following the Democrats' decision to champion civil rights, partisan divisions on the abortion issue surfacing first in Congress, then in the electorate [24]—but also in variations in responses to them. Their effects were calibrated by a citizen's level of political involvement and awareness; activists and strong partisans were more inclined to adopt the ideological positions staked out on economic, social, and racial issues by their national leaders than were the less politically involved; and the more attentive and informed the involved citizens were, the more their views came to mirror those of their leaders.[25] Political inde-

---

[23] John Gilmour, *Strategic Disagreement: Stalemate in American Politics* (Pittsburgh: University of Pittsburgh Press, 1995).

[24] Adams, "Abortion," pp. 720–735.

[25] Geoffrey C. Layman and Thomas M. Carsey, "Party Polarization and 'Conflict Extension' in the American Electorate," *American Journal of Political Science* 42 (October 2002):786–802; John Zaller, *The Nature and Origins of Mass Opinion* (Cambridge: Cambridge University Press, 1992), pp. 98–113; Jacobson, "Electoral Basis of Partisan Polarization," pp. 25–28.

pendents, along with nonvoters and other politically uninvolved people, participated in the polarizing trends marginally if at all.

IS POLARIZATION CONFINED
TO ACTIVISTS?

Morris P. Fiorina takes this point further, arguing that the observed partisan polarization among citizens is almost entirely confined to a narrow political class—politicians, activists, commentators, journalists, bloggers, and other political junkies—with most ordinary Americans appearing to diverge only because extremists on both sides have reduced the choices to polar opposites, excluding middle options.[26] In Fiorina's view, popular polarization—or at least the aspect of it characterized as a "culture war"—is a myth. He reads the survey evidence to show that the distribution of Americans' opinions on cultural issues such as abortion, homosexuality, and gun control has not become measurably more polarized—except among the minority of citizens most active in politics as candidates, activists, and professional observers. Both out of sincere belief and for tactical reasons (raising money, mobilizing the faithful, keeping an audience), these zealots of the left and right bring a fiercely contentious agenda and tone to national politics that is alien to the real needs and sentiments of a large majority of Americans. Fiorina also shows how shifts in policy positions taken by the parties or the emergence of a new issue dimension can polarize the electorate even if its members' opinions do not change at all. Ordinary Americans, by this argument, do not share the passion or extremism of

---

[26] Morris P. Fiorina, *Culture War? The Myth of a Polarized America* (New York: Longman, 2005).

the active stratum but are forced into what appear to be polar camps because the set of alternatives includes only polar options.

Fiorina's argument highlights the important distinction between polarization in general and *partisan* polarization. That voters have increasingly sorted themselves into parties consistent with their ideological and policy positions says nothing about how divided the public as a whole is on ideology or policy dimensions. But even with no change in the distribution of mass opinion, or even increasing signs of consensus on some formerly divisive issues,[27] if opinion cleavages fall increasingly along party lines, the political consequences can be and, as I show in subsequent chapters, have been profound.

Moreover, Fiorina's analysis implies that political leaders and operatives have been free to follow their own ideological fancies, leaving voters no choice but to line up accordingly. But as strategic vote-seekers, candidates and parties anticipate voters' potential responses to their political initiatives and so are constrained by them. The Republican "southern strategy" emerged because Republican strategists saw an opportunity to win converts among conservative white southerners hostile to civil rights legislation. Ambitious Republican candidates adopted conservative positions on social issues to attract voters alienated by the Democrats' tolerance of nontraditional life styles but indifferent at best to Republican economic policies. Democrats emphasized "choice" on abortion because they recognized its appeal to well-educated, affluent voters who might otherwise think of themselves as

---

[27] John R. Evans, "Have Americans' Attitudes Become More Polarized?—An Update," *Social Science Quarterly* 84 (2003):71–90.

Republicans. In the budgetary wars of the past two decades, Democrats have vigorously defended middle-class entitlements such as Social Security and Medicare, while Republicans have championed tax cuts because each position has a large popular constituency. In adopting positions, politicians are guided by the opportunities and constraints presented by existing configurations of public opinion on political issues. Intensified partisan conflict in Washington on such issues depended on the expectation that voters would reward or at least not punish the politicians engaging in it.

If party polarization were alienating ordinary, more moderate citizens, we would expect to observe the distance between respondents' self-described ideological locations and those they estimate for both parties and their candidates to grow over time. This has not happened. Figure 2.8 displays the gap between the self-placement of partisan voters and their placement of the parties on the 7-point liberal-conservative scale in NES surveys from 1972 through 2004. Democrats have tended to place themselves slightly to the right of their party and Republicans, slightly to the left of theirs, but the distance between partisans and their own parties is small and, more important, did not increase at all over this period; among Democrats, it has actually narrowed a bit, with the trend significant at $p < .001$. What has changed is the gap between partisans' locations and the perceived locations of the rival party, which has grown by a full point on the scale for both Republican and Democratic voters (both trends significant at $p < .001$).[28]

---

[28] The same results hold if we include nonvoters in the analysis, although the degree of change in perceived distance from the rival party is slightly smaller.

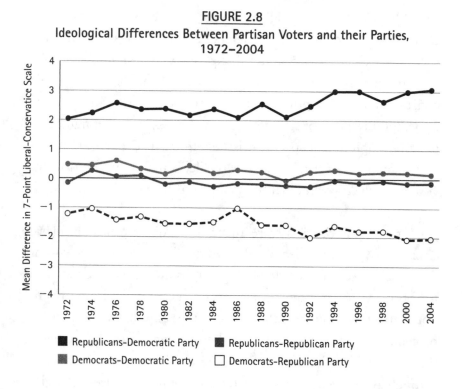

FIGURE 2.8

Ideological Differences Between Partisan Voters and their Parties, 1972–2004

Similarly, the mean distance between perceived ideological locations of partisans and their own party's House candidates has been modest all along and does not increase over time (Figure 2.9). Moreover, Republicans place themselves on average slightly to the right of their candidates, and Democrats place themselves slightly to the left of theirs. Again, the ideological gap widens only between partisan voters (especially Democrats) and the other party's candidate, although it is not as wide for candidates as for parties. Party leaders and candidates have not, by this

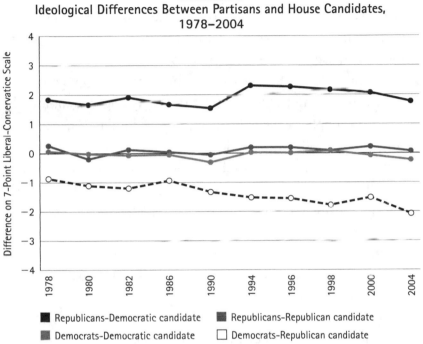

FIGURE 2.9

Ideological Differences Between Partisans and House Candidates, 1978–2004

Republicans-Democratic candidate   Republicans-Republican candidate
Democrats-Democratic candidate   Democrats-Republican candidate

evidence, drawn away from their followers, but they have come to be viewed as considerably more distant by those of the other side.

Nonetheless, Fiorina is certainly right in highlighting the crucial contribution of the activist stratum to partisan polarization over the past several decades. The most active participants in politics did display the steepest increase in partisan coherency, consistency, and loyalty; as theory predicts, they were more likely than other Americans to be aware of and respond more readily to intensified party and ideological conflict in Congress and other national institutions.[29] And there is also little doubt that activists made their own independent contribution to partisan polarization. Devotion to ideological or policy goals is one reason citizens become activists. People attracted to electoral politics by the strategically calculated appeals of campaigners end up constraining the winning candidates, shaping the party's agenda and public image, and supplying the next generation of candidates, campaign professionals, and party leaders. Thus, for example, in many parts of the country, the social conservatives who found a home in the Republican Party in the 1970s and early 1980s have become its core constituency, principal recruitment pool, and public face.

Fiorina is also surely right in pointing out that the character and style of Bill Clinton aggravated culturally-based partisan divisions. Clinton came to exemplify (not least through the calculated efforts of his opponents) everything social conservatives detested about the post-1960s trends in American culture, while the religious right's attacks on Clinton provoked a backlash among social liberals alarmed by what they saw as a fundamentalist takeover of the Republican Party.[30] But the cultural divisions that came to a head during the Clinton administration began long before 1992 and did not end when Clinton left office in 2001. In particular, the religious dimension of partisan conflict had been growing for nearly two decades before Clinton sought the presi-

---

[29] Zaller, *Mass Opinion*, pp. 100–113.
[30] Louis Bolce and Gerald De Maio, "Religious Outlook, Culture War Politics, and Antipathy Toward Christian Fundamentalists," *Public Opinion Quarterly* 63 (Spring 1999):29–61

dency and did not fade with his departure; quite the contrary, religious cleavages became a primary source of the public's highly polarized responses to George W. Bush.

RELIGION AND PARTISANSHIP

The relationship between religion and partisanship changed in several notable ways between the 1960s and 1990s. As Figure 2.10 shows, white, non-Latino Roman Catholics and evangelical

FIGURE 2.10
Religion and Partisanship, 1960–1996

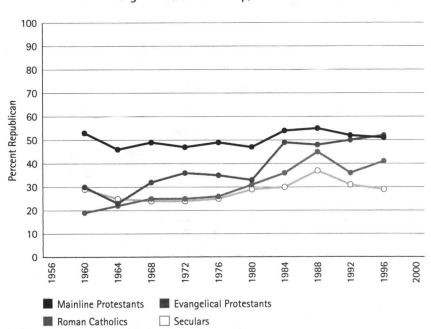

Mainline Protestants ■ Evangelical Protestants
Roman Catholics □ Seculars

Protestants became more Republican, while white mainline Protestants and seculars showed no sustained trend (neither did African Americans or Jews).[31] Note that most of the change among evangelicals occurred during the Reagan administration, well before Bill Clinton appeared on the scene. The abortion issue was of course a crucial source of these trends, but it was only the most salient of a congeries of social issues, including those involving race,[32] that contributed to partisan change. Research sensitive to distinctive currents within these broad categories suggests that trends have also varied widely depending on, among other things, the respondent's (or the respondent's denomination's) theological stance, level of involvement in religious activities and the nature of his or her religious faith.[33] The Republican Party has been most attractive to theological traditionalists, regular attendees, and, among Christians, those who consider themselves "born again," and least attractive to theological modernists or seculars, the nonobservant, and those for whom religion is not so important. The largest swing to the Republicans occurred among white evangelicals with strong religious commitments.[34] These aggregate changes are naturally related to, although by no means entirely explained by, the southern realignment, for the South is where

---

[31] David C. Leege, Kenneth D. Wald, Brian S. Krueger, and Paul D. Mueller, *The Politics of Cultural Differences* (Princeton: Princeton University Press, 2002), pp. 232–233.

[32] David O. Sears and Nicholas A. Valentino, "Race, Religion, and Sectional Conflict in Contemporary Partisanship," presented at the Annual Meeting of the American Political Science Association, San Francisco, September 1, 2001.

[33] Lyman A. Kellstedt and Corwin E. Smidt, "Doctrinal Beliefs and Political Behavior: Views of the Bible," in David C. Leege and Lyman A. Kellstedt, eds., *Rediscovering the Religious Factor in American Politics* (New York: M.E. Sharp, 1993), pp. 177–198; Kyle L. Saunders and Alan I. Abramowitz, "Ideological Realignment and Active Partisans in the American Electorate," *American Politics Research* 32 (2004):285–309.

[34] Warren E. Miller and J. Merrill Shanks, *The New American Voter* (Cambridge: Harvard University Press, 1996), 540.

evangelical Christianity and religious traditionalism are most widespread.

The multidimensional character of religious identity and behavior defies easy survey measurement, but Figure 2.11 illustrates some key patterns in the relationship that have developed between religiosity and partisanship. Lyman Kellstedt and his colleagues developed a classification of religious affiliations that

FIGURE 2.11
Religiosity and Party Identification, 1996

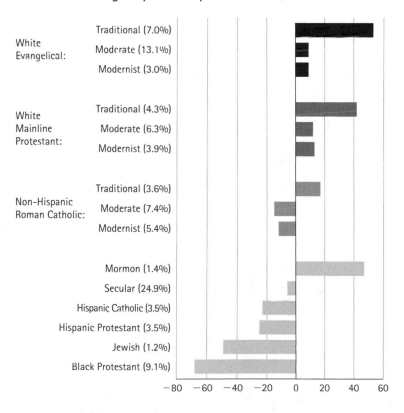

includes what they designate the *religious tradition* (the main categories in Figure 2.11) and further subdivisions within the three largest Christian traditions based on a combination of reported beliefs and behaviors.[35] Their analysis reveals that among white Christians, partisanship is more strongly related to the degree of religious traditionalism—theological orthodoxy and/or identification with sectarian movements (fundamentalist, Pentecostal, and charismatic)—than to membership in the broader groupings. Specifically Republican identification is much more prevalent among religious traditionalists of all denominations.

These developments in the confessional basis of partisanship set the stage for Bill Clinton to become the nexus of sharp, culturally-fueled partisan divisions. Reinforced by the Clinton years, the partisan cultural divide primed Americans to react in strongly partisan terms to any president whose rhetoric, positions, or behavior brought its symbols to the forefront. George W. Bush and his campaign strategists were well aware of this and, as we shall see in the next chapter, worked effectively during the 2000 campaign to cultivate strong ties to religious conservatives but with sufficient subtlety to avoid provoking a backlash from more secular moderates. Later, when the president's policies, particularly regarding Iraq, did provoke increasing hostility from Democrats and independents, Bush's support among religious conservatives remained rock-solid, contributing strongly to the record partisan gap approval of his job performance and the Iraq War (see Chapter 6).

---

[35] Lyman A. Kellstedt, John C. Green, Corwin E. Smidt, and James L. Guth, "Faith and the Vote: The Role of Religion in Political Alignments," presented at the Annual Meeting of the American Political Science Association, Atlanta, September 205, 1999.

ECONOMIC EQUALITY AND THE IDEOLOGICAL FRAGMENTATION OF THE NEWS MEDIA

Two other components of the political context inherited by the George W. Bush administration deserve mention. McCarty, Poole, and Rosenthal highlight increasing economic inequality as both a cause and consequence of increasing partisan polarization. They show that partisanship became increasingly stratified by income between 1952 and 2002, interpreting the change as a response to heightened partisan conflict in Washington over redistributive issues (taxes and social spending).[36] Again, the southern realignment contributed importantly to this change, as upscale whites moved into the Republican camp. Thus cultural cleavages have not supplanted economic cleavages, but have been added to them.[37]

In addition, the sources of information Americans rely on for political news have become increasingly fragmented, ideologically diverse, and openly biased. Mainstream news sources—the network news programs and the mainstream press—have lost audiences to tendentious radio talk shows, internet bloggers, and Fox News. Most of the innovation has come from the right side of the political spectrum, often with the intention of countering the alleged liberal bias of the mainstream media. Fanning the flames of partisan and ideological conflict is central to the business model. Not only does this development make for a more polarized public sphere—if nothing else, it makes politics *seem* more nastily contentious—but it also enables people to adopt news

---

[36] Nolan McCarty, Keith Poole, and Howard Rosenthal, *Polarized America: The Dance of Ideology and Unequal Riches* (MIT Press, forthcoming), Chapter 3.

[37] Fiorina, *Culture War?*, pp. 70–72.

sources that tend to confirm and reinforce rather than challenge their beliefs and opinions (I have more to say about the news media in Chapter 9).

CONCLUSION

George W. Bush assumed the presidency after three decades of increasing partisan and ideological polarization among political elites and ordinary voters alike. This situation did not foreordain his presidency to set new records for divisiveness; Bush's own strategies and political choices, unexpected events, his reactions to these events, and the partisan configuration of Congress were necessary factors as well. But the American polity was thoroughly primed to respond to his presidency in highly partisan terms if offered any opportunity, and the first of these arose even before he took the oath of office.

CHAPTER 3

✦

To the White House
Via Florida

Although ordinary Americans took part in the trend toward greater partisan and ideological polarization in national politics during the final decades of the twentieth century, they did not like its manifestations. Partisan squabbling in Washington has never been popular,[1] and the spectacle presented by impeachment politics in 1998 and 1999 exemplified for many people its worst aspects. In a poll taken just after the Senate had voted to acquit Bill Clinton, 78 percent said they thought the whole process had been more about politics than about the investigation of possible crimes (58 percent of Republicans as well as 91 percent of Democrats took this view), 71 percent believed the Senators voted on the basis of partisan politics rather than the facts of the case, and 81 percent said they were sick of hearing about the whole

---

[1] Alan Rosenthal, Burdett A. Loomis, John R. Hibbing and Karl T. Kurtz, *Republic on Trial: The Case for Representative Democracy* (Washington, D.C.: CQ Press, 2003), pp. 136–140.

thing.[2] Popular revulsion against the partisan fighting over impeachment and more broadly during the Clinton administration gave George W. Bush one of his central campaign themes for 2000: He was an outsider with no role or stake in the D.C. wars who could therefore bring the country together again.

As governor of Texas, Bush had worked effectively and cordially with Democrats in the legislature on an agenda aimed at reforming Texas's education, juvenile justice, tort, and welfare systems. He refrained from campaigning against Democrats who backed his initiatives, and many returned the favor, offering support or at least positive reviews of his performance in Texas when Bush sought the White House.[3] It helped that Democrats in Texas's amateur, part-time legislature were on the whole far more conservative than those he would find in Congress. Bush's record of consensus building helped make him the consensus choice among Republican leaders, particularly fellow governors, looking for a candidate who could reach beyond the party's conservative base to build a coalition broad enough to take back the White House.

"COMPASSIONATE CONSERVATISM"

Bush's stance as an outsider was also calculated to distinguish him from the hard-line Republicans in Congress who had been the party's national face since 1994. Bill Clinton and his Democratic

---

[2] CBS/*New York Times Poll*, February 12, 1999 and ABC News Poll, February 12, 1999, reported at http://pollingreport.com/scandal1.htm (accessed June 3, 2005).
[3] John C. Fortier and Norman J. Ornstein, "President Bush: Legislative Strategist," in Fred I. Greenstein, ed., *The George W. Bush Presidency: An Early Assessment* (Baltimore: Johns Hopkins University Press, 2003), pp.141–145.

allies had worked with some success to characterize Republican leaders as mean-spirited partisan ideologues, hostile or insensitive to the interests of minorities, women, and the needy. Aware of this, Bush did not spare Republicans when denouncing partisan bickering in Washington. More important, by his choice of campaign issues and themes, Bush offered himself as a different kind of Republican. The focus on education ("no child left behind"), the promise to "strengthen" Social Security and to support a prescription drug benefit, the advocacy of a "compassionate conservatism" that both acknowledged and proposed to address social ills, were all aimed at attracting moderate swing voters, not only by poaching on issue turf that Democrats claimed as their own, but by giving the party a softer, more inclusive and attractive image. The effort to make the party look inclusive verged on self-parody during the first day of the 2000 Republican national convention, which featured a parade of speeches delivered almost exclusively by women, children, and minorities expounding on themes of compassion and inclusion.[4] But its intent was clear: portraying a party and candidate that people who were not conservative white males could still feel comfortable supporting.

Congressional Republicans, eager to defeat Clinton's heir, went along with this strategy, keeping unusually quiet during the months leading up to the election and avoiding any confrontation with Clinton that might reinforce their party's negative image among moderate voters. They and the rest of the party's conservative base could also see that that Bush's new "compassionate conservatism" did not require any serious pruning of the old

---

[4] In fact, only about 10 percent of the delegates were African American, Latino, or Asian American.

Republican agenda. To economic conservatives and the corporate and business sectors, Bush promised major tax cuts, partial privatization of Social Security, deregulation of business, tort reform, and priority for resource extraction over environmental protection. For social conservatives, his platform included support for a constitutional amendment banning abortion, opposition to gay rights, gun control and affirmative action, and support for school vouchers. Bush's ability to appeal effectively to the party's two main constituencies—the business community and social conservatives of the religious right—was a major reason so much of the Republican establishment had rallied behind his nomination.

ONE OF US

The relationship George W. Bush forged before and during the campaign with religious conservatives, particularly evangelical Christians, deserves special attention, as it is central to understanding the forces that have made him such a polarizing figure. Bush had served as his father's political ambassador to religious conservatives, and their doubts about the devotion of the father to their cause did not extend to the son. More important, Evangelical Christians came to regard him, quite rightly, as one of their own. His personal story of turning at age 40 from alcohol to God with the help of evangelist Billy Graham, his naming Jesus Christ as his favorite philosopher because "He changed my heart," his unaffected references to the role of prayer and Bible reading in his life, allowed no doubt about his religious identity. Moreover, unlike Bill Clinton or Al Gore, also self-described born-again Christians, Bush shared religious conservatives' positions on social issues: opposition to abortion (Bush made exceptions for rape, incest, or protecting the life of the mother), opposition to gay rights (including gay marriage, gay adoptions, and coverage of gays by hate crimes legislation), promotion of "abstinence only" sex education, and support for tuition vouchers useable in religious schools.

Bush's identification with religious conservatives was strengthened during the campaign with the unwitting help of Sen. John McCain, his last remaining rival for the nomination. McCain had attacked Bush for speaking during the South Carolina primary campaign at Bob Jones University, a fundamentalist stronghold, without condemning the anti-Catholicism of its founder or its policy banning interracial dating. Bush won that primary handily but, after losing the Michigan primary to McCain, felt compelled to apologize and disavow any anti-Catholicism or support for racial discrimination. McCain then went on to lump Jones together with conservative Christian leaders Pat Robertson and Jerry Falwell as "agents of intolerance" akin to Al Sharpton and Louis Farrakhan, going so far as to call Falwell and Robertson "evil." McCain's intemperate outburst instantly alienated large blocs of Christian conservatives, delivering them en masse to Bush in subsequent primaries.[5]

Bush's standing among evangelical Christians as "one of us" gave him leeway to state his positions in language designed to avoid scaring off more moderate voters without running the risk that social conservatives would mistake his true beliefs. Rather than dwelling on his support for a constitutional ban on abortion,

---

[5] James W. Ceasar and Andrew E. Busch, *The Prefect Tie: The True Story of the 2000 Presidential Election* (Lanham, MD: Rowman & Littlefield, 2001), pp. 92–93.

he could talk about encouraging a "culture of life" that would eventually lead to broad public support for such a step. He could temper his opposition to gay rights by refusing to condemn gays wholesale and expressing his willingness to appoint gays to his administration. He could call for tolerance of all religions, even of atheists, without raising doubts about his own commitment to Jesus Christ as his personal savior. The leaders of the religious right, for their part, were sophisticated enough to keep a low profile during the campaign and to refrain from pushing Bush to make overly explicit commitments to their agenda. Knowing what he *was*, they worried less about what he *said*. The Bush campaign could thus pursue its strategy of presenting a more moderate, inclusive, and tolerant candidate and party without much danger of a backlash from social conservatives.

THE CAMPAIGNS

Bush's opponent, Al Gore, also presented himself as more moderate than his congressional party, although by the end of the campaign he was indulging in some old fashioned liberal corporate bashing. His selection as his running mate of Joe Lieberman, among the most socially conservative Democratic senators, signaled his centrist intentions. On social and economic issues, Gore was a "New Democrat" in the Clinton mold, supporting the death penalty and welfare reform, advocating middle-class tax cuts, and proposing a prescription drug benefit and a few other modest new social programs. He was also a supporter of "charitable choice," a sort of compassionate conservatism lite, pioneered during the Clinton administration. Indeed, across a broad range of issues, the two candidates were not very far apart; they both offered more continuity than change, not surprising in the prevailing context of peace and prosperity.[6]

Running against peace and prosperity, George W. Bush's only hope was to make Clinton's moral legacy weigh more heavily than his economic legacy in voters' minds. The Bush campaign worked endlessly to keep the Clinton-Gore connection at the forefront. As Dick Cheney said in accepting the vice presidential nomination, "Mr. Gore tries to separate himself from his leader's shadow. But somehow we will never see one without thinking of the other."[7] At least not if the Bush campaign had anything to do with it. The idea was to exploit the public's unhappiness with the moral tone as well as the partisan acrimony of the Clinton years to offset contentment with the economy and its beneficial social fallout (reduced unemployment, crime, welfare dependency and so forth). In both his acceptance speech and later regularly on the stump, Bush roused the Republican faithful with this peroration: "And so, when I put my hand on the Bible, I will swear to not only uphold the laws of our land, I will swear to uphold the honor and dignity of the office to which I have been elected, so help me God." It not only called attention to the supposed dishonor and indignity visited on the office by Bill Clinton (and by association, Al Gore), but it also served to remind listeners of Bush's fealty to God and the Bible. Bush's references to Clinton's morals were almost always this indirect; Republicans had learned

---

[6] Ibid, 36–37; Kathleen Frankovic and Monica McDermott, "Public Opinion in the 2000 Election: The Ambivalent Electorate," in Gerald M. Pomper, ed., *The Election of 2000* (New York: Chatham House, 2001), p. 84.

[7] http://www.cbsnews.com/stories/2000/08/02/politics/main221310.shtml (accessed June 14, 2005).

the hard way that frontal attacks on Clinton could backfire, doing as much damage to the attacker as to the target.

With disputes over policy issues somewhat muted, the contest (at least as portrayed by the news media) tended to center on character, ability, and personality. Gore was knowledgeable, but he was stiff and perhaps disingenuous. Republicans sought to hammer home the idea that Gore was a serial exaggerator who would say anything to win (and who thus shared Clinton's deviousness). Bush was pleasant and jovial, but inarticulate and vague; was he up to the job? Democrats portrayed him as intellectually shallow, uninformed, and dependent on family ties for whatever success he had achieved in business or politics.

To the degree that campaigns focused on the candidates' personal traits, they were not particularly polarizing, for the traits at issue did not themselves carry partisan overtones. Neither, according to various postelection analyses, were other salient aspects of the electoral environment in 2000. Gerald Pomper characterized the race as "sharply contested but reasonably civil. Attacks abounded, but they focused on real issue differences between Gore and Bush, as each contestant worried over the public's declared aversion to personal, negative campaigning."[8] In Wilson Carey McWilliams' view, "The campaign certainly didn't set off any skyrockets. Neither candidate aroused much enthusiasm, let alone suggested greatness, nor was either the object of much antipathy."[9] Kathleen Frankovic and Monica McDermott emphasized the candidate's similarities in background and agenda,

---

[8] Gerald M. Pomper, "The Presidential Election," in Pomper, *Elections of 2000*, 144.
[9] Wilson Carey McWilliams, "The Meaning of the Election," in Pomper, *Elections of 2000*, p. 179.

voters' ambivalence on many policy issues, their complacency, and their generally positive if unenthusiastic evaluations of the candidates. They conclude: "Because voters could not resolve issue conflicts in their own minds, their candidate support was muddled. The candidates had similar strengths and weaknesses, and although the choice satisfied most voters, many of them ended up on election day with qualms about their vote."[10]

THE VOTE

The 2000 presidential campaigns were, then, not calculated to emphasize partisan divisions or polarize the electorate; if anything, the opposite. And there is little evidence that the candidates and their campaigns did arouse strong partisan feelings in most voters. All the more noteworthy, then, that party line voting—self-identified Republicans voting for Bush, Democrats for Gore—matched its highest level in the 48-year history of the National Election Studies: 87 percent.[11] Party loyalty reported in the national exit poll was even higher, 89 percent, highest since the beginning of exit polling in 1976.[12] Despite campaigns designed to broaden each candidate's appeal, neither attracted many voters from the opposite party; according to the NES, Bush won 11.1 percent of Democrats, Gore, 9.4 percent of Republicans; if partisan leaners—independents who say they lean toward one of

---

[10] Frankovic and McDermott, "Ambivalent Electorate," in Pomper, *Elections of 2000*, p. 90.
[11] The party loyalty rate for 2000 was 86.5 percent, 0.1 percent below 1988 but at least 0.7 percent higher than for any other previous election.
[12] The 2000 Voter News Service election poll is from http://www.cnn.com/ELECTION/2000/epolls/US/P000.html. Results from earlier election polls are in *The Public Perspective* (December/January 1997), pp. 8–10.

the parties (and who tend to vote like weak partisans of that party)—are excluded, the defection rates become 7.7 percent and 7.6 percent, respectively.

The high level of party loyalty in 2000 reflected, in part, the absence of any detectable partisan tide that might have favored one party over the other.[13] But it also reflected the general rise in partisan coherence and consistency documented in Chapter 2; if many voters were ambivalent about their decisions—and in the exit polls, 55 percent reported having reservations about their vote—they were remarkably consistent in resolving the choice in their own party's favor. One consequence was that the vote in 2000 expressed the underlying distribution of party support with unusual accuracy, and exit poll results offered a clear snapshot of the sources of partisan division in the electorate as Bush was about to enter the White House.

Figure 3.1 displays some of the salient demographic character-istics that distinguished Bush from Gore voters. The bars on the graph show how far support for Bush fell above or below the 50 percent mark among people in each category. The percentage of the electorate comprising each category appears in parentheses. Men favored Bush, women Gore, the difference amounting to 11 percentage points. Bush won decisively among whites, while Gore took more than 90 percent of the African American vote. Hispanic voters also favored the Democrat, but by smaller mar-gins than in past exit polls, reflecting Bush's support among Lati-nos in his home state of Texas. Bush was a strong favorite in the South, while Gore was a strong favorite in the Northeast. The

---

[13] Gary C. Jacobson, "A House and Senate Divided: The Clinton Legacy and the Congressional Elec-tions of 2000," *Political Science Quarterly* 116 (Spring, 2001): 7–8.

FIGURE 3.1
Demographic Characteristics and the Presidential Vote

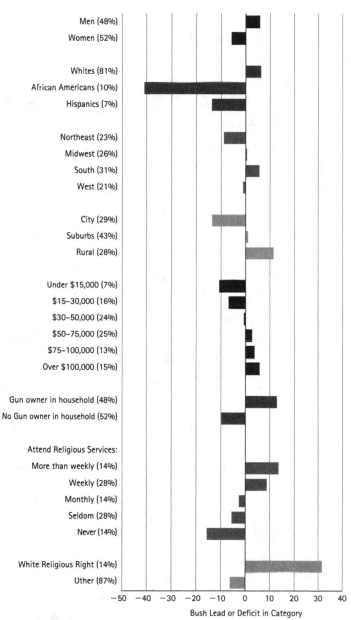

Bush Lead or Deficit in Category

Source: 2000 Voter News Service exit poll.

division in the Midwest was nearly even, as it was in the West, where Democratic majorities in the coastal states were balanced by the solidly Republican Mountain states. Urban-rural differences were even sharper than regional differences.

Support for the candidates differed by income category in the expected direction: the higher a voter's income, the more likely a vote for Bush. But notice that differences in support for the candidates based on the two noneconomic factors, gun ownership and religiosity, are even larger than differences associated with income. The difference in support for Bush and Gore between the lowest and highest income categories is 17 percentage points, while the difference between people in households with and without guns is 23 percentage points, and between the most and least religiously active voters, 29 percentage points. Bush's greatest advantage was among whites who considered themselves part of the religious right; comprising 14 percent of the electorate, they gave Bush 80 percent of their votes, Gore, only 18 percent.

The idea that noneconomic considerations were at least as potent as economic issues in sorting voters into electoral coalitions is reinforced by examining the relationship between the presidential choice and voters' positions on selected issues (Figure 3.2). Support for the candidates varied most widely according to views on abortion, with support for Bush 51 percentage points higher among people who thought abortions should always be illegal than among people who though they should always be legal. The third largest difference is associated with opinions on gun control (41 points, exceeded slightly by differences related to the tax question, 42 points). On these and other matters—school vouchers, tax cuts, prescription drug programs

FIGURE 3.2
Issue Positions and the Presidential Vote

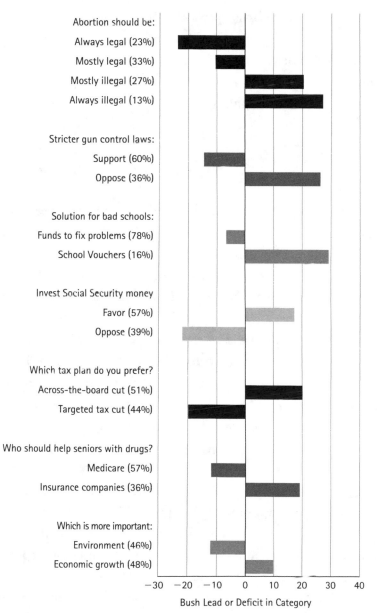

Source: Voter News Service exit poll.

for seniors, and the partial privatization of Social Security, economy growth vs. environmental protection—Bush won the support of those who favored his approach but was opposed by those who did not. Not at all surprising, of course, but a sign that Bush's agenda, should he have the opportunity to pursue it, would be a divisive one.

FLORIDA

Any illusion that the bitter partisanship of the Clinton years was a thing of the past, and any hope George W. Bush might have entertained for an inauguration that bridged the partisan divide, expired almost instantly in the election's aftermath. Gore won the popular vote by about 540,000 of the 105 million votes cast, but presidents are chosen by the Electoral College, and election night found George W. Bush with a tiny lead in Florida which, if sustained, would give him a majority of electoral votes and thus the White House. The close Florida tally triggered an automatic machine recount amid revelations of balloting irregularities sufficiently serious and widespread to leave the accuracy and legitimacy of any final count in question, probably permanently. On November 26, following the machine recount, Florida's Republican secretary of state certified Bush as the winner by a margin of 537 votes. Gore's lawyers contested the result the next day in state court, eventually persuading Florida's Supreme Court to order a recount of all ballots not included in the machine count and to include ballots from hand counts submitted after the certification deadline. Bush's lawyers appealed to the U.S. Supreme Court, which on December 4 issued an order halting the count of disputed ballots pending a hearing. On December 12, a day after that hearing, the Court, by a 5-4 majority, concluded there was not enough time for the state court to fashion a constitutionally valid process for counting disputed ballots, effectively ending the contest. Gore conceded defeat on December 13.

From election night onward, and ignoring the real uncertainties about what had occurred, partisan elites and activists rallied in lock-step to their party's presidential candidate. Both the heated rhetoric ("They're stealing it, they're stealing it, they're stealing it" is how Republican representative Charles W. Pickering, Jr. of Mississippi put it, unprompted, to a reporter[14]) and clean partisan split loudly echoed the struggle over Clinton's impeachment. And as with impeachment, partisan divisions were not confined to politicians and activists. Although ordinary voters were more bemused by than passionately involved in the postelection events in Florida, they too divided strongly along party lines in responding to questions about them. Polls assessing public opinion on the election's aftermath found immediate, sustained, and huge differences between Bush and Gore supporters (that is also to say, between Republicans and Democrats[15]) on relevant questions. Some examples appear in Table 3.1. Among Bush voters, 93 percent were satisfied with the election outcome, 92 percent thought Bush had won the election legitimately, and 95 percent approved of the Supreme Court's decision stopping

---

[14] Andrew Taylor, "First Test of Promised Comity is Late Lame-Duck Session," *Congressional Quarterly Weekly Report*, November 18, 2000, p. 2723.

[15] Polls that report responses broken down by party identification rather than presidential preference replicate the results reported in Table 3.1. For example, a Gallup Poll taken December 15–17 found 85 percent of Republicans saying that Bush won "fair and square," while 49 percent of Democrats thought he had won on a technicality, and 37 percent said he stole the election. See http://www.gallup.com/poll/release/pr001220.asp.

TABLE 3.1
Public Opinion on the Presidential Election Outcome (Percent)

	ALL	GORE VOTERS	BUSH VOTERS
1. "In general, are you satisfied or dissatisfied with the outcome of the election?"			
Satisfied	50	9	93
Dissatisfied	45	89	6
Don't know	5	2	1
2. "Would you say George W. Bush legitimately won the election, or not?"			
Legitimately won	53	11	92
Did not	40	81	3
Don't know	7	8	5

3. "As you may know, on Tuesday the United States Supreme Court ruled in George W. Bush's favor, and stopped the manual recounting of votes in Florida that had been ordered by the Florida Supreme Court. Do you approve or disapprove of the U.S. Supreme Court's ruling that stopped the manual recount?"

	ALL	GORE VOTERS	BUSH VOTERS
Approve	54	16	95
Disapprove	42	80	4
Don't know	2	4	1

4. "Do you think the Supreme Court's decision was based more on partisan politics, or more on an objective interpretation of the law?"

	ALL	GORE VOTERS	BUSH VOTERS
Partisan politics	37	65	10
Objective interpretation	54	29	84
Both (vol.)	1	1	2
Neither (vol.)	1	0	1
Don't know	7	5	3

5. "Regardless of what the current vote total is, who do you think more Florida voters intended to vote for: Al Gore or George W. Bush?"

	ALL	GORE VOTERS	BUSH VOTERS
Gore	46	83	13
Bush	34	7	59
Don't know	20	10	28

continued

TABLE 3.1 (continued)

	ALL	GORE VOTERS	BUSH VOTERS

6. "This week, by margin of 5 to 4, the United States Supreme Court reversed the Florida courts' decision and stopped hand recounts of presidential ballots in Florida. All in all, do you think the Supreme Court's decision to stop hand recounts in Florida was fair or unfair?"

	ALL	GORE VOTERS	BUSH VOTERS
Fair	51	19	88
Unfair	44	78	9
Don't know	5	3	3

SOURCES: Questions 1–5, CBS News Poll. Dec. 14–16, 2000; question 6, *Newsweek* Poll conducted by Princeton Survey Research Associates. Dec. 14–15, 2000, both reported at http://www.pollingreport.com, January 3, 2000.

the manual recount of ballots in Florida. Among Gore voters, 89 percent were dissatisfied with the outcome, 81 percent thought Bush was not the legitimate victor, and 80 percent disapproved of the Supreme Court's decision. Most Gore supporters (65 percent) thought the Court's decision was partisan, while most Bush supporters (84 percent) thought it was impartial. Gore voters were convinced that more Florida voters intended to vote for Gore than for Bush (83 percent), while most Bush voters believed the opposite (59 percent, with another 28 percent uncertain). The two sides were also sharply divided on whether the Court's decision to stop the vote count was fair.

The Florida controversy was, in fact, ideally suited to provoke polarized partisan responses of this sort. The balloting and vote count were such a mess that no one honestly knew for sure who won the most votes (or whom more of Florida's voters actually preferred). The appropriate procedure for settling the question was equally uncertain. Under such conditions, everything we have learned about the psychology of political opinion formation predicts that partisans would believe their side's leaders and arguments and reject (or ignore) those of the other side.[16] Ambiguity provides nothing to override the default option and thus gives partisan biases full sway.

Moreover, the public had good reason to view the conflict through partisan spectacles. Once the action began in Florida, the fight *was* nakedly partisan, which shifted the odds overwhelmingly in Bush's favor because his party controlled all the venues where the ultimate decision might be made. To be sure, Florida's attorney general and many local election officials were Democrats, and Democratic appointees dominated the Florida Supreme Court, where Gore won some initial skirmishes. But Florida's secretary of state was a Republican activist, and Bush could count on his brother, Republican Governor Jeb Bush, as well as Republican legislative majorities, if Florida's legislature chose the state's electors (which it threatened to do if the vote count were not completed in time to certify an official slate). Had the dispute moved to Congress for resolution, Republicans would have had the votes to award the election to Bush. And the U.S. Supreme Court had the authority to trump the Florida court, as it finally did when five Supreme Court justices, all conservative Republican appointees, preemptively terminated the recount, making certain that Bush received Florida's decisive electoral votes. Democrats were thus likely to think the process was rigged against their candidate no matter how the final decision was reached.

---

[16] Richard E. Petty and Duane T. Wegener, "Attitude Change: Multiple Roles for Persuasion Variables," in Daniel T. Gilbert, Susan T. Fiske, and Gardner Lindzey, *The Handbook of Social Psychology*, 4th ed., Vol. I (Boston: McGraw-Hill, 1998), p. 331.

The denouement in Florida had two important effects on public attitudes toward the newly elected president. First, it divided
the public along party lines over the legitimacy of his victory in a
way that persisted throughout his entire first term in the White
House (Figure 3.3). If anything, partisan differences on this question were wider in October 2004 than they had been at the beginning of Bush's first term, with more than 90 percent of Republicans
saying he was elected legitimately, and three-quarters of the
Democrats saying he was not (a slim majority of independents

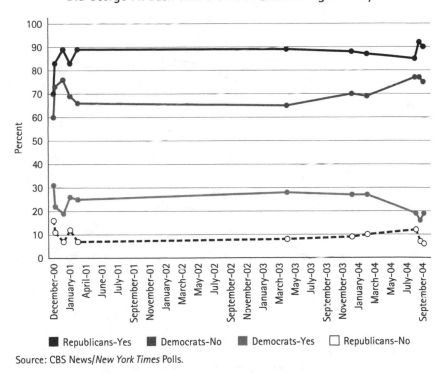

FIGURE 3.3
Did George W. Bush Win the 2000 Election Legitimately?

Source: CBS News/*New York Times* Polls.

agreed with the Republicans in most of these polls). Unfortunately, the question was not asked between March 2001 and May 2003, so we do not know if the post-9/11 rally temporarily softened Democrats' opinions on this question.

Second, it deprived Bush of any early-term "honeymoon" during which citizens who had opposed his election might have been willing to withhold judgment or give him the benefit of the doubt. As Figure 3.4 shows, Bush provoked the widest partisan differences in responses to the Gallup Poll's job approval question dur-

FIGURE 3.4
Partisanship and Approval of Newly Inaugurated Presidents

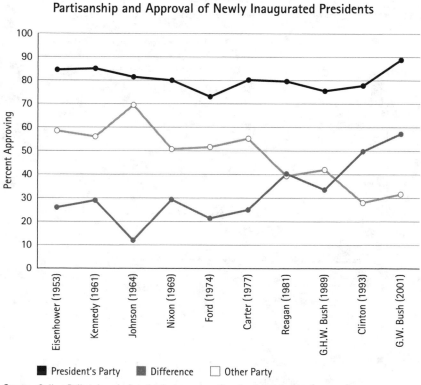

■ President's Party   ■ Difference   □ Other Party

Source: Gallup Polls taken during the first quarter of each administration (average).

ing the first quarter of an administration of any newly elected president for which we have data, surpassing the runner-up Bill Clinton by more than 7 percentage points. His rating among his own partisans was the highest ever for this period, while Democrats were only slightly more positive about him than Republicans had been about Clinton in early 1993. Observe, though, that the partisan gap had been on the rise for at least two decades, almost entirely a consequence of declining approval ratings among rival-party identifiers. The data suggest that, even before George W. Bush, the presidential honeymoon was becoming a thing of the past, again reflecting the polarizing trends discussed in Chapter 2. Still, Bush's extraordinary path to the White House no doubt made things worse for him in this regard; in the NES's postelection survey, Democratic voters interviewed during the first week after the election rated Bush at 50.4 degrees on the 100-degree feeling thermometer, during the second week, 46.0 degrees, and thereafter 39.1 degrees (with no further trend).[17]

CONCLUSION

Although George W. Bush's 2000 presidential campaign sought to shed the image of unbridled partisanship and conservative zealotry projected by the Republican Party's congressional wing, even before the postelection battle for Florida, seeds had been planted that could easily blossom into a continuation of intense partisan conflict after the election. While mostly avoiding head-on

---

[17] The difference between the first one or two weeks and the rest is significant at p < .01. Gore's ratings among Democrats increased significantly as well; there was no significant postelection trend among Republican identifiers in ratings of either candidate.

attacks on Bill Clinton, the campaign's attempt to exploit popular disgust with the moral tone of his administration to undermine Al Gore's support meant that the bitter legacy of impeachment politics was never far below the surface. The social and cultural differences that have increasingly come to distinguish Republicans and Democrats were clearly visible in the distribution of votes. And while some parts of the "compassionate conservatism" agenda could, properly packaged, attract bipartisan support, Bush's broader agenda advocated orthodox Republican economic and social policies on a range of issues that had divided the parties fundamentally since at least the Reagan administration. In particular, insofar as Bush's affinity with and obligations to the religious right guided his appointments and policies, he was certain to alienate most ordinary Democrats. Much would depend on how, once the Supreme Court had awarded him his victory, Bush intended to govern.

CHAPTER 4

❖

The First Two Years: Before and After 9/11

George W. Bush's disputed victory was part of a broader partisan stalemate in 2000. The same election left the Senate divided exactly in half, with Republicans and Democrats each holding 50 seats; vice president Dick Cheney would cast the tiebreaking vote. The Republicans held on to their slim majority in the House of Representatives, losing a net two seats but keeping control, 221–212 (the two independents also split on which party they routinely supported). With questionable legitimacy, no mandate, and the slimmest of Republican margins in the House and Senate (Republicans had actually lost seats in both chambers), more than a few postelection analysts predicted that Bush would have to govern from the center in bipartisan fashion or face almost certain failure.[1]

---

[1] See for example, Gerald M. Pomper, "The Presidential Election," p. 148; Wilson Carey McWilliams, "The Meaning of the Election," 178; and Paul S. Herrnson, "The Congressional Elections," 155; all in Gerald M. Pomper, ed., *The Election of 2000* (New York: Chatham House 2001); Gary C. Jacobson, "Congress: Elections and Stalemate," in Michael Nelson, ed., *The Elections of 2000* (Washington, D.C.: Congressional Quarterly Press, 2001), p. 206.

Some wilder flights of fancy envisioned a kind of coalition government, with Bush bringing substantial Democratic representation into his cabinet and encouraging bipartisan power-sharing in Congress.[2] Had Bush moved in this direction after his inauguration, it is most doubtful that he would have become the most polarizing president in modern history, and this book would not have been written.

Of course Bush did nothing of the sort. One reason is that congressional Republicans would have mutinied. Were it not for the Florida debacle, the big story of the 2000 election would have been that it gave the Republicans full, if tenuous, control of Congress and the White House for the first time since the first Congress of the Eisenhower administration (1953–1954). After six years of being stymied and out-maneuvered by Bill Clinton, Republicans on the Hill were scarcely in the mood for bipartisan compromises. A more important reason is that it is simply not in Bush's nature to concede ground without a fight. It would go against his conceptions of strategy and leadership as well as his conviction that his positions are the right ones. It is also unlikely that any of his closest advisors recommended caution; as Dick Cheney is reported to have said, "A notion of sort of a restrained presidency because it was such a close election, that lasted maybe 30 seconds. . . . We had an agenda, we ran on the agenda, we won the election—full speed ahead."[3]

---

[2] "What's the Mandate? The overriding message for the next President: All roads lead to the center," *Business Week Online*, November 20, 2000, reported at http://www.businessweek.com/2000/00_47/ b3708001.htm (accessed June 28, 2005).
[3] Bob Woodward, *Plan of Attack* (New York: Simon and Shuster, 2004), p. 28.

THE BUSH AGENDA

The agenda was not, as I noted in the previous chapter, one to pro-mote consensus. Polls taken in the spring of 2001 found that the early partisan split on Bush extended to most of his policies. Majori-ties of Democrats opposed and Republicans favored his proposals on taxes, energy development, Social Security, military spending, and budgeting more generally. Democrats joined Republicans in supporting only some elements of "compassionate conservatism": spending more on education, funding faith-based organizations to deliver social services, and providing a prescription drug benefit.[4]

The Bush administration's strategy for achieving legislative victories on its agenda also promised to be divisive. Bush's idea of legislative leadership, by his own and others' descriptions,[5] is to stake out a firm position right at his own ideal point ("the moment I negotiate with myself, I lose," he puts it[6]), defend it against all objections, pursue it with focus and tenacity, and com-promise only at the last minute and to the smallest extent possible to gain the victory. Backed by his unwavering commitment, the leader's "team" of strategists, aides, and congressional allies con-ducts a coordinated, disciplined, but tactically flexible campaign,

---

[4] "Bush and the Democratic Agenda," CBS News/New York Times Poll, June 14–18, 2001, at http://www.cbsnews.com/htdocs/pdf/bushbac.pdfm (accessed July 7, 2003); CBS News/New York Times Monthly Poll, March 2001; Los Angeles Times Poll #455: "Bush's Budget Speech to Congress," March 2001.

[5] Ivo H. Daalder and James M. Lindsay, American Unbound: The Bush Revolution in Foreign Policy (Washington, D.C.: The Brookings Institution, 2003), pp. 32–33; Charles O. Jones, "Capitalizing on the Perfect Tie," in Fred I. Greenstein, ed., The George W. Bush Presidency: An Early Assessment (Baltimore: Johns Hopkins University Press, 2003), pp. 176–178; Bob Woodward, Bush At War (New York: Simon and Shuster, 2002), p. 256.

[6] Quoted in Jones, "Capitalizing on a Perfect Tie," p. 181.

with everyone speaking from the same prepared script. The payoff to this approach was clear in Bush's first important legislative victory, the $1.35 trillion tax cut enacted by Congress on May 26, 2001; the administration compromised only far enough to peel off the handful of Senate Democrats needed to prevent a filibuster and got 80 percent of what it had initially proposed.[7] A legislative strategy aimed at winning all the Republicans and a few necessary Democrats made sense and could be effective, but it was also polarizing, with the degree of polarization mitigated only to the extent that policy had to be moderated to pick up the Democrats. Victories could be celebrated by ordinary Republicans but were not appreciated by ordinary Democrats; about two-thirds of Democrats opposed Bush's tax and budget proposals, while about 85 percent of Republicans supported them.[8] Bush did not invariably adopt a partisan legislative strategy; major bills dealing with education in 2001 and prescription drug benefits in 2004 were truly bipartisan—by necessity, because some conservative Republicans in Congress opposed both. But the partisan strategy was the more common on domestic legislation, and partisans in the electorate divided in response to the results accordingly.

At least as divisive as Bush's legislative agenda was his administrative agenda, which amounted to a concerted effort to undo as much of the regulatory work of the Clinton administration and its predecessors as was politically feasible. On the environmental front, it included reopening public lands set aside for protection

---

[7] John C. Fortier and Norman J. Ornstein, "President Bush: Legislative Strategist," in Fred I. Greenstein, ed., *The George W. Bush Presidency: An Early Assessment* (Baltimore: Johns Hopkins University Press, 2003), pp. 147–151.
[8] CBS News/*New York Times* Poll, March 8–12, 2001.

to commercial exploitation, weakening protection of endangered species, easing standards on air and water pollution (including those covering arsenic, mercury, selenium, and perchlorate), and rejection of the Kyoto Protocol on global warming. The administration's attitude toward the environment was typified by its proposal to open the Alaskan National Wildlife Refuge to oil exploration as part of an energy program designed behind closed doors by lobbyists from the oil and gas industries under the supervision of Vice President Cheney. Cheney's dismissive response to the criticism that the proposal ignored conservation—"conservation may be a sign of personal virtue, but it is not a sufficient basis for a sound, comprehensive energy policy"—set the tone.[9]

Not all of these initiatives succeeded, but they made it clear where the administration stood when environmental values were at stake, squarely on the side of private industry and resource development. This obviously pleased an important Republican constituency (and major source of campaign funds) and was supported by ordinary Republicans, although not always by overwhelming majorities.[10] Environmental activists were predictably outraged and soon came to regard the Bush administration as the worst ever on environmental issues. Their opinion was widely shared by ordinary Democrats, and although environmental protection was not a top priority for most, it contributed to negative views of the president.[11] The regulatory tilt toward the business

---

[9] http://www.nytimes.com/aponline/national/AP-Cheney-Energy.html (accessed April 30, 2001).
[10] In March of 2001, for example, 55 percent of Republicans said they approved of drilling for oil in ANWR, compared to 27 percent of Democrats. See CBS News/*New York Times* Poll, March 8–12, 2001.
[11] In a June 2001 poll, only 23 percent of Democrats approved of Bush's handling of the environment; see the CBS News/*New York Times* Poll, June 14–18, 2001.

sector was repeated in other domains as well, generating divisions along predictable partisan and ideological fault lines between business interests and consumer groups.

TACTICS

George W. Bush's decision to pursue his agenda full throttle despite the lack of a popular mandate and with only the narrowest margins in Congress, combined with his conception of leadership, encouraged (if any encouragement was necessary) the adoption of tactics for dealing with the public that contributed profoundly to deep partisan differences in evaluations of him and his administration. The full consequences of these tactics only become clear when we examine public views of the war in Iraq in the following two chapters, but their potential was evident from the beginning.

With some risk of caricature, the Bush administration's typical approach can be described like this: Policy proposals are designed in-house in great secrecy so that any internal disagreements are thrashed out and resolved (by Bush as final arbiter if necessary) before presenting a unified front to the outside world. The president then announces his proposal as "the right thing for the American people," and he, his staff, and Republican allies in Congress go to work turning it into policy. The public campaign takes the form of a multifaceted sales exercise; the aim is not to explain the product, but to sell it. Everyone on the team is expected to "stay on message," reiterating with little variation arguments and rhetoric carefully vetted in advance. The message depends on what Bush's strategists think will sway the public (and thereby other politicians in Washington) and may be altered as necessary as circumstances shift (for example, the tax cut was first justified by the Clinton surplus and then, when recession erased the surplus, by the need to stimulate the economy). Contrary messages and messengers are denounced (a favorite ploy is to portray opposition as motivated solely by partisanship). Probing questions from reporters are ducked or ignored if straightforward answers might undermine the message. The idea is to control not only the agenda, but also the framing, language, and definition of what count as relevant facts regarding the issue at hand.

All of this is understandable from the perspective of a president who entertains no doubts or second thoughts about the rightness of his goals and wants to achieve major changes in public policy despite a narrow political base, widespread political resistance, and general public indifference or opposition to what he wants to do. It may be difficult to imagine succeeding on any other basis. Yet in practice, this mindset and consequent emphasis on marketing bred a cavalier approach to truth: dishonesty not by lying, but by a deceptive selection of truthful but misleading statements. In pushing to get his tax cut enacted, for example, Bush repeatedly claimed that his plan would "reduce taxes for everyone who pays taxes," which was true only if you exclude Social Security and Medicare taxes (the biggest federal tax burden on millions of low-income workers). He also said it offered "the greatest help for those most in need" because "the highest percentage tax cuts got to the lowest income Americans." True, but only because the lowest income groups already paid so little; reducing a tax liability from $200 to $100 represents a large percentage cut but small substantive benefit for the taxpayer. He extolled the reduction of the top income tax bracket from 39.6 percent to 33 percent as a boon to America's 17.4 million small business owners without mentioning that only 1.4 percent of them were paying the top rate. In fact, about 72 percent of the total tax reduction would be enjoyed by the top 20 percent of taxpayers, 45 percent by the top 1 percent of taxpayers.[12] But anyone who brought this up was accused of fomenting "class warfare."

This kind of marketing is inherently polarizing. Republicans, positively disposed toward the president, will tend to accept his "facts" and arguments uncritically because of both their source and their fit with prior attitudes; people do not devote cognitive resources to picking apart statements of opinion leaders with whom they prefer to agree.[13] Unless the president's arguments are clearly false (as opposed to merely deceptive) and widely exposed in the news media as such, his supporters are under no psychological pressure to reject them; quite the contrary. In contrast, Democrats and others not inclined to follow the president's lead or accept his word will be open to (and may even seek out) analyses by critics busy parsing the rhetoric and pointing out the deceptions. And they will be ready to recognize "facts" ignored by the president that undermine his case. Insofar as their initial reflexive doubts about the policy and its promoter appear to be confirmed, these attitudes can only be strengthened. A president who pursues policy goals by deceptive rhetoric and careful selection of misleading facts may succeed in getting a Congress run by his partisans to do his bidding, but one price is the alienation of those on the

---

[12] Ben Fritz, Bryan Keefer, and Brendan Nyhan, *All the President's Spin: George W. Bush, the Media, and the Truth* (New York: Simon and Schuster), pp. 75–78.
[13] Petty and Wegener, "Attitude Change," *Handbook of Social Psychology*, pp. 344–348.

losing side who resent the manipulation and deception and regard the victory as illegitimately won. It is, then, a polarizing victory.

The Bush administration applied the same kind of salesmanship to its administrative and regulatory policies. Again, decisions were taken behind closed doors and, if likely to promote popular resistance, then carefully marketed to the public. Expert analyses and scientific findings that did not support the policy were "off message" and routinely suppressed or rewritten by political appointees to conform to the administration's line. Rejecting the Kyoto Protocol, Bush acknowledged the reality of global warming but emphasized the uncertainties about how much and how fast it would happen—accurate but misleading about the scientific consensus on the severity and immediacy of the threat—as the excuse for doing nothing beyond funding more research and encouraging voluntary action to reduce hydrocarbon admissions. The distortion of science for political ends became prevalent enough to provoke a public protest by 60 senior scientists, including 20 Nobel laureates.[14] Language was reconfigured to soften opposition. On the advice of Republican strategist Frank Luntz, the administration replaced "global warming" with the more innocuous "climate change" in addressing the topic.[15] The administration's plan to open national forests to more extensive logging became the "Healthy Forests Initiative." The Environmental Protection Agency's rollback of pollution control requirements for power plants was called the "Clear Skies Initiative."

---

[14] "Preeminent Scientists Protest Bush Administration's Misuse of Science," news release, Union of Concerned Scientists, February 18, 2004, reported at http://www.ucsusa.org/news/ press_release.cfm? newsID=381 (accessed July 5, 2005).
[15] Fritz, et al, *President's Spin*, 94.

None of this contrived naming would bother people who agreed with the substance of the administration's policies, and it may have reassured people not particularly attuned to the issue involved. But to those who cared and disagreed with the policy, the language was infuriatingly Orwellian. Again, its effect was polarizing.

In both content and form, then, the Bush administration's actions in its first eight months were not calculated to reduce partisan divisions in Washington or in the broader public, and they did not. As Figure 4.1 shows, partisan differences in evaluations of

FIGURE 4.1
Party Differences in Presidential Approval in the First Three Quarters of a New Administration

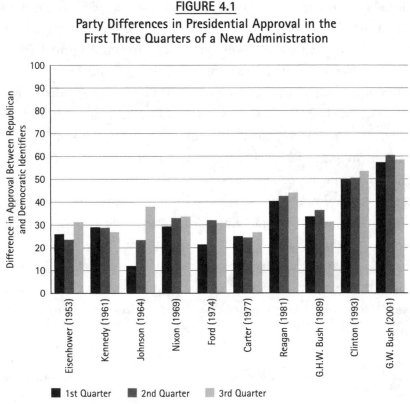

Source: Gallup Polls.

Bush were wider during each of the first three quarters of his administration (for the third quarter, before September 11) than for any previous president. The gap was an average of 7.4 percentage points wider than for the previous record holder, Bill Clinton.

Another consequence of Bush's approach was a temporary loss of the Senate. The administration's hard-line conservatism on most issues led one of the few remaining moderate Republicans, Sen. James Jeffords of Vermont, to announce on May 24, 2001, that he would henceforth serve as an independent who would vote on organizational matters with the Democrats.[16] Jeffords's defection raised a new roadblock to the administration's goals, giving Democrats a platform to resist the president and to articulate a competing agenda. By late summer the Bush administration seemed stuck in the doldrums. Then, on September 11, 2001, everything changed.

AFTER SEPTEMBER 11

The Washington community responded to the terrorist attacks of September 11, 2001 on the World Trade Center in New York and the Pentagon in Washington D.C. with a remarkable display of bipartisan unity. The day's events awakened human responses that transcended party; conservative Republican Dick Armey was observed draping a consoling arm around Maxine Waters, among the House's most liberal African-American Democrats. Republican and Democratic leaders found themselves getting acquainted in a

---

[16] Jeffords explained his decision as a direct reaction to the Bush administration's policies: "Looking ahead, I can see more and more instances when I will disagree with the President on very fundamental issues—issues of choice, the direction of the judiciary, tax and spending decisions, missile defense, energy and environment and . . . other issues large and small"; see CQ Weekly (May 26, 2001): 1243.

new way as they shared an emergency bunker while waiting out the immediate threat of further attacks.[17] President Bush received a thundering bipartisan ovation as he addressed a joint session of Congress on the crisis. In the days that followed, bipartisan consultation and cooperation flourished as Congress quickly complied with the president's requests for emergency legislation to deal with the consequences of the attack. Only a single member of Congress[18] voted against the joint resolution passed on September 14 authorizing the president "to use all necessary and appropriate force against the nations, organizations, or people that he determines planned, authorized, committed, or aided the terrorist attacks on the United States that occurred September 11, 2001" (PL 107-46). A week later, the airline relief bill (PL 107-42) passed 356-54 in the House, 96-1 in the Senate. A broad antiterrorism bill requested by the administration (PL 107-56) passed 357-66 in the House, 98-1 in the Senate during the last week of October.

The bipartisan unity displayed by Congress in its response to the president's call for action against terrorism was echoed in the public, and Americans of all political persuasions rallied around their president.[19] As documented earlier in Figure 1.1, Bush's approval ratings shot up from the 50s to the highest levels ever recorded, topping 90 percent in some September and October polls. The largest change by far occurred among Democratic identifiers (Figure 1.2). Approval of Bush among Democrats jumped

---

[17] Janet Hook, "Under the Shadow of War, Congress Declares a Truce," *Los Angeles Times*, September 22, 2001, A21.

[18] Democratic Rep. Barbara Lee of California.

[19] The "rally-round-the-flag phenomenon is discussed most thoroughly in John E. Mueller, *War, Presidents and Public Opinion* (New York: John Wiley and Sons, 1973), pp. 208–213 and Richard A. Brody, *Assessing the President: The Media, Elite Opinion, and Public Support* (Stanford: Stanford University Press, 1991), Ch. 3.

almost overnight by more than 50 percentage points, from an average of less than 30 percent in the summer before September 11 to an average of 81 percent in the month following the attacks. Support also rose among Republicans (to 98 percent in polls taken through October) but it was already so high (89 percent) that the Republican contribution to the overall rise could be only modest. Independents approximated the national figures, going from an average of 52 percent approving before September 11 to an average of 86 percent approving over the following month.

The rally was by no means confined to the president, however. Approval of Congress reached 84 percent in one October Gallup Poll, topping its previous all-time high by 27 percentage points (Figure 4.2). The proportion rating House Speaker Dennis Hastert's performance as "excellent" or "pretty good" rose from 27 percent in August to 52 percent in October; the equivalent ratings of Senate majority leader Tom Daschle went from 26 percent to 60 percent.[20] There were also sharp increases in positive responses to questions about the direction of the country, trust in government, satisfaction with the United States, even assessments of the economy.[21] A naïve observer might wonder why a spectacular failure of a government to deliver that most basic of public goods, protection from foreign attack, would inspire a dramatic surge in approval of its leaders and institutions. But of course the public's reaction reflected a radical change in the context in which

---

[20] Harris Polls, August 15–22 and October 17–22, 2001, reported at http://pollingreport.com/h-j.htm (accessed June 24, 2005).
[21] For data on evaluations of the direction of the country, see the Gallup, *Los Angeles Times*, NBC News/*Wall Street Journal*, Ipsos-Reid/*Cook Political Report*, and Fox News/Opinion Dynamics polls; for data on satisfaction with the U.S, see the Gallup polls; all are at http://www.pollingreport.com (accessed January 27, 2003); for trust in government, see *Washington Post* and CNN/*USA Today*/Gallup polls at http://www.pollingreport.com/institut.htm.

FIGURE 4.2
Approval of Congress's Performance 2001–2002

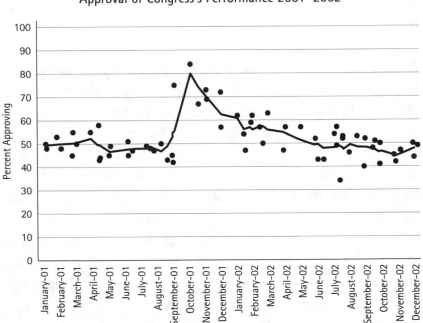

Source: ABC News/*Washington Post*, CBS News/*New York Times*, *Los Angeles Times*, NBC News/*Wall Street Journal*, and Gallup polls, at http://www.pollingreport.com/job.htm (accessed March 22, 2005).

people responded to such survey questions. The president was now to be evaluated as the defender of the nation against shadowy foreign enemies rather than as a partisan figure of dubious legitimacy. Congress stood for once as the institutional embodiment of American democracy rather than as the playground of self-serving politicians addicted to petty partisan bickering. For a time, politicians and government institutions enjoyed the kind of broad public support normally reserved for such national symbols as the flag and the Constitution. With Americans just coming to grips with the countless ways their society was vulnerable and, by way of illustration, spooked by deadly anthrax spores mailed to news organizations and political leaders, this was not the moment to point fingers or to doubt their institutions and leaders.

The moment did not last, of course, and by the summer of 2002, the effects of the rally had all but disappeared—except for approval of the president, which remained on average above 70 percent into July and above 60 percent through the end of the year. Indeed, Bush's ratings remained above 60 percent for 16 months, the longest streak at this level for any president since Roosevelt during World War II. The terrorist attacks had completely redefined the priorities and purpose of his presidency; Bush was now first and foremost a war president, and in that capacity, he drew overwhelming bipartisan support for his initial responses to the attacks. The public was nearly unanimous in backing the president's decision to use military force to go after Osama bin Laden and his al Qaeda forces in Afghanistan when its Taliban government refused to hand them over (Figure 4.3). With nearly 90 percent of the public favoring military action against the terrorists, anything less might have actually cost him public support; the administration's main concern while preparing to fight in Afghanistan was to avoid the perception that it was reacting too slowly or with insufficient force.[22]

Adopting the role of war president and taking decisive steps to retaliate against the attackers and their Taliban protectors, Bush began earning the high marks for his handling of the war on terrorism that have buoyed his overall approval levels ever since. Initially, the shift in national focus to terrorism helped to insulate

---

[22] Woodward, *Bush at War*, pp. 150, 175, 207, 278.

FIGURE 4.3
Popular Support for the War in Afghanistan

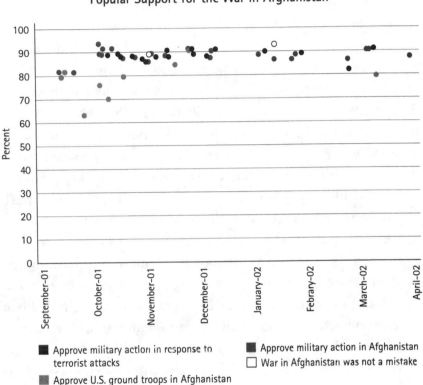

Sources: ABC News/*Washington Post,* CBS News/*New York Times,* Gallup, Pew Center for the People and Press, Harris, Fox News, and *Newsweek* polls.

him from the full force of economic discontent that followed the dot.com crash and brief recession early in his term. Although the president sought to blame the terrorist attacks for the weak recovery, he could not escape generally negative views of his economic performance. But despite less than stellar grades on the economy, his leadership in the war on terrorism kept his overall ratings high. Normally, a president's overall job performance rating does not differ by much from his rating on handling specific policy

FIGURE 4.4
Approval of George W. Bush's Performance by Policy Domain, 2001–2005

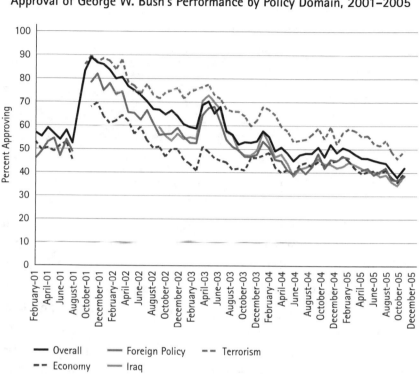

Sources: Gallup Polls, available at http://www.gallup.com, CBS News/New York Times, available at http://www.cbsnews.com/selections/opinion/polls/main500160.shtml, ABC News/Washington Post Polls, available at http://www.washingtonpost.com/wpsrv/politics/polls/polls.htm, and Los Angeles Times Polls, available at http://www.latimes.com/news/custom/timespoll; Time poll, available at http://www.srbi.com/TimePoll3531-Political-Final_Report-2005-05--13--5:30pm.pdf.

domains, and economic perceptions help determine levels of presidential approval.[23] As Figure 4.4 indicates, this was the case with Bush before but not after September 11. Prior to the attacks, his overall rating was on average only 6 percentage points higher than his rating on the economy; for the year afterward, it averaged

---

[23] Brody, *Assessing the President*, Ch. 6.

18 points higher. The initial rally in approval of Bush's handling of the economy after September 11 had totally dissipated by the end of 2002, but his overall ratings continued to be held up by the very high ratings he received on terrorism.

Approval of Bush's performance on terrorism also muted partisan differences on his overall performance. As we saw in Figures 1.5 and 1.6, partisans were much more sharply divided on Bush's handling of the economy than on his handling of terrorism during the year following September 11. On average, only 34 percent of Democratic identifiers approved of his handling of the economy during this period, while 69 percent approved of his handling of terrorism, helping to raise his overall rating among Democrats to an average of 58 percent. The difference between approval ratings of Republicans and Democrats was only 26 points on terrorism, compared to 45 points on the economy. High marks on terrorism— 79 percent approving—also helped prop up independents' approval ratings of Bush, which averaged 72 overall but only 51 percent on the economy. In year one of the war on terrorism, then, Bush did succeed in uniting the country behind his leadership in that mission.

Bush's strong bipartisan approval for his handling of terrorism did not, however, spill over into unrelated domestic matters. The administration's positions on energy development, taxes, abortion, prescription drug benefits, and Social Security did not become more popular after September 11; partisan divisions in the public on these issues remained as wide as ever.[24] Bush tried to use the unity generated by the war on terrorism to drum up bipar-

---

[24] Compare the responses to issue questions in the CBS News/*New York Times* polls conducted between February 2001 and January 2003.

tisan support for his economic stimulus proposal, renaming it the "economic security plan": "It's time to take the spirit of unity that has been prevalent when it comes to fighting the war and bring it to Washington, D.C. The terrorists not only attacked our freedom, but they also attacked our economy. And we need to respond in unison. We ought not to revert to the old ways that used to dominate Washington, D.C. The old ways is [sic]: What's more important, my country or my political party?"[25] But the attempt to delegitimize partisan opposition to the administration's economic policies fell flat; congressional Democrats felt no more pressure from their constituents to support the president's pre-September 11 domestic agenda after the attacks than they had before.

2002 ELECTION

The political fallout from September 11 and its aftermath dramatically improved the Republicans' electoral prospects for 2002. Despite the steady decline from its lofty peak, Bush' approval level remained at an impressive 63 percent on election day.[26] While not as high as Bill Clinton's rating in November 1998 (66 percent), it tied Ronald Reagan's 1986 rating for the second highest in any postwar midterm election. Bush's high public approval, like that of Clinton and Reagan before him,[27] clearly helped his party's congressional candidates. Indeed, it helped in

---

[25] Speech January 5, 2002 in Ontario, California, quoted in Fritz et al., *President's Spin*, p. 113.
[26] This was his rating in the final Gallup Poll taken prior to the election—the measure used in standard referendum models of midterm elections—and also the average of the thirteen polls take during the month leading up to the election.
[27] Democrats picked up five House seats in 1998; Reagan's Republicans lost only five seats in 1986, the best performance at the midterm for any Republican administration before 2002.

just the way that standard aggregate models of midterm congressional elections would predict.[28]

The crisis benefited Republicans in ways that went well beyond its contribution to the president's popularity. Bush's meteoric rise in public esteem shielded his administration from the consequences of financial scandals, epitomized by the collapse of Enron, involving Bush's political cronies and campaign contributors.[29] It is easy to imagine how Democrats would have exploited the president's vulnerability on the issue had his status as commander in chief in the war on terrorism not put partisan criticism beyond the pale at the very time the scandals surfaced. The war on terrorism also helped deflect blame from the administration and its congressional allies for the return of budget deficits. The extraordinary expense of dealing with the physical and economic damage inflicted by the September 11 attacks and of tightening homeland security against future threats was unavoidable. Wars, after all, are always fought on borrowed money.

In addition, Bush's popularity scared off high quality Democrat challengers. His uncommonly high approval ratings during the period when potential candidates had to make decisions about running evidently convinced politically experienced and ambitious Democrats that 2002 was not their year. As a result,

---

[28] For a discussion of such models, see Gary C. Jacobson, *The Politics of Congressional Elections*, 5th edition (New York: Longman, 2001), pp. 143–145 and 158; for an application to 2002, see Gary C. Jacobson, "Terror, Terrain, and Turnout: Explaining the 2002 Midterm Election," *Political Science Quarterly* 118 (Spring 2003): 1–22, footnote 6.

[29] Enron, once the nation's seventh largest company, was a Houston-based energy conglomerate that collapsed into bankruptcy in late 2001 after the exposure of accounting schemes that had inflated its earnings by more than $1 billion. Enron's stockholders collectively lost billions of dollars, and thousands of former Enron employees had their pension savings wiped out. The head of Enron, Kenneth Lay, was a long-term supporter of fellow Texan George W. Bush and one of his leading campaign contributors. By one count Enron and its executives had contributed a total of $736,800 to Bush's various campaigns since 1993; see http://www.opensecrets.org/alerts/v6/enron_bush.asp.

Democrats fielded their weakest cohort of House challengers (in terms of prior success in winning elective public office) of any postwar election except the 1990 midterm.[30]

September 11 also shifted the political focus from domestic issues to national defense and foreign policy, moving the debates from Democratic turf to Republican turf. In pre-election polls, most respondents thought the Democrats would do a better job dealing with health care, education, Social Security, prescription drug benefits, taxes, abortion, unemployment, the environment, and corporate corruption. Most thought Republicans would do the better job of dealing with terrorism, the possibility of war with Iraq, the situation in the Middle East, and foreign affairs generally.[31] Republicans enjoyed the advantage because voters put terrorism and the prospect of war at the top of the list of concerns. Without September 11, the election would have hinged on domestic issues, and the talk of invading Iraq, if any, would have seemed like "wagging the dog," a transparent ploy to deflect attention from the economy.[32] Instead, the Democrats' inept handling of legislation establishing a Department of Homeland Security (delaying passage until after the election in a dispute over personnel policy involving unionized government workers) gave Republicans an issue that played to their strength and that they exploited effectively in several close Senate races.

---

[30] Only 10.8 percent of Republican incumbents were opposed in 2002 by Democrats who had ever held elective public office—Figure 1.9 standard deviations below the postwar mean of 24.9 percent. The postwar low was 10.1 percent in 1990.
[31] Jeffrey M. Jones, "Republicans Trail in Congressional Race Despite Advantage on Issues," Gallup News Service, September 26, 2002, reported at http://www.gallup.com/poll/releases/ pr020926.asp?Version=p, Lydia Said, "National Issues May Play Bigger-Than-Usual Role in Congressional Elections," Gallup News Service, October 31, 2002, at http://www.gallup.com/poll/releases/pr021031.asp?Version=p.
[32] "Wag the Dog" is a 1997 film comedy in which a president's media advisor fakes a war in order to distract attention from the president's involvement in a sex scandal.

Bush's accusation that Senate opponents of his preferred version of the Homeland Security Department were "more interested in special interests in Washington and not interested in the security of the American people" provoked an outraged response and demand for an apology from Senate majority leader Tom Daschle, to which Republicans responded by accusing *Daschle* of being divisive.[33] With no apologies, the Republicans used the issue in Senate campaigns, most notoriously in Saxbe Chambliss's successful Senate challenge of Georgia Democrat Max Cleland, who had lost both legs and an arm in Vietnam. The Chambliss campaign featured a television ad that followed footage of Osama bin Laden and Saddam Hussein with an unflattering shot of Cleland and a voiceover claiming that he had "voted against the president's vital homeland security efforts." The ad, and Cleland's defeat, infuriated his Democratic colleagues in Washington and was arguably the single largest contributor to the post-September 11 revival of partisan acrimony on the Hill.

Bush's popularity, along with successful Republican gerrymanders in Michigan, Pennsylvania, Ohio, and Florida, helped Republicans pick up a net six House seats. They also gained a net two Senate seats, one essentially by a tragic accident.[34] Aside from reapportionment, what kept the election from duplicating the 2000 stalemate was turnout. Republicans did a better job of mobilizing their core supporters. Bush's near-universal approval among Republicans, his energetic fundraising and fren-

---

[33] "Gephardt Joins the Fray," reported at http://www.cbsnews.com/stories/2002/09/25/politics/main523246.shtml (accessed June 27, 2005).
[34] Sen. Paul Wellstone of Minnesota died in a plane crash with his wife and daughters 11 days before the election; Republican Norm Coleman defeated his hastily chosen replacement, former Sen. Walter Mondale, after Democrats' use of a memorial service as a partisan pep rally generated a public backlash.

zied last-minute campaigning in competitive states, combined with effective Republican grass roots drives to get out the vote, put Republicans over the top.[35] The election was a major victory for the president, as Republicans avoided the midterm losses usually suffered by the president's party. But it was won by mobilizing the base rather than broadening the party's appeal to independents and Democrats. The electorate was as polarized along party lines as it had been in 2000; the upsurge in national unity provoked by the war on terrorism had not brought Americans together on the issues that put them into opposite party camps prior to September 11.[36]

GOD'S INSTRUMENT

Religious conservatives were a key target of Republican mobilization efforts; by one estimate, their share of the electorate went from 14 percent in 2000 to 18 percent in 2002, foreshadowing even larger increases in 2004 (see Chapter 7).[37] Even before September 11, Bush had continued to display his religious commitments, for example, by letting it be known that he kneels in prayer every morning and studies the Bible daily and by opening cabinet meetings with a prayer.[38] He had also filled his cabinet with the faithful, most prominently Attorney General John

[35] Mary Clare Jalonick, "Senate Changes Hands Again," *CQ Weekly* (November 9, 2002): 2907–2909; Rebecca Adams, "Georgia Republicans Energized By 'Friend to Friend' Campaign, *CQ Weekly* (November 9, 2002): 2892–2893.
[36] Jacobson, "2002 Midterm Elections," pp. 3–12.
[37] Daron R. Shaw, "Door-to-Door With the GOP," *Hoover Digest* (Fall 2004), reported at http://www.hooverdigest.org/044/shaw.html (accessed June 27, 2005).
[38] Judy Keen, "White House staffers gather for Bible study," *USA Today*, reported at http://www.usatoday.com/ news/washington/2002-10-13-bible-usat_x.htm (accessed June 27, 2005).

Ashcroft, a devout Pentecostal, nominated many judges who were pro-life Catholics and evangelicals, and pursued a variety of policies pleasing to religious conservatives. These included banning federal funding for stem-cell research except for "existing lines" (of which there were far fewer available than the administration initially claimed), signing a ban on late-term abortion, and pursuing his faith-based initiatives. Bush did not always go as far as urged by their leaders—some want to ban all stem-cell research, for example—but on the whole this part of his base had plenty of reason to be satisfied.[39]

The tectonic shift in national politics generated by September 11 raised Bush's connection to conservative Christians to an entirely new level. Bush deliberately adopted Christian dualism's language of good and evil to refer to his new mission, most famously in his State of the Union address four months after the attacks designating Iraq, Iran, and North Korea as an "axis of evil."[40] Although he stopped referring to the war on terrorism as a "crusade" after the term triggered a counterproductive backlash among Muslims, he left the sense that it was just that. An unnamed Bush family member is reported to have said, "George sees this as a religious war. He doesn't have a p.c. view of this war. His view of this is that they are trying to kill the Christians. And we the Christians will strike back with more force and more ferocity than they will ever know."[41]

---

[39] James L. Guth, "George W. Bush and Religious Politics," in Steven Shier, ed., *High Risk and Big Ambition: The Presidency of George W. Bush* (Pittsburgh: University of Pittsburg Press, 2004), pp. 129–134.
[40] http://www.whitehouse.gov/news/releases/2002/01/20020129-11.html (accessed July 5, 2005).
[41] Quoted in Peter Schweizer and Rochelle Schweizer, *The Bushes: Portrait of a Dynasty* (New York: Doubleday, 2004), p. 517.

Many conservative Christians, on their side, came to see Bush as God's chosen instrument in the battle between good and evil. Ralph Reed, one-time leader of the Christian Coalition and later a Republican official, told a reporter, "I've heard a lot of 'God knew something we didn't.' In the evangelical mind, the notion of an omniscient God is central to their theology. He had a knowledge nobody else had: He knew George Bush and the ability to lead in this compelling way."[42] Bush himself denied that he ever said he believed God had chosen him to lead the war on terrorism: "I think God sustains us, but I don't think I was chosen. I was chosen by the American people."[43] Yet others close to him have said otherwise. "I think, in his frame, this is what God has asked him to do."[44] And given his religious beliefs, it would be difficult to think otherwise. As he told a meeting of religious leaders in February 2002, "Events aren't moved by blind change and chance. Behind all of life and all of history there's a dedication and purpose, set by the hand of a just and faithful God."[45]

For people who believed Bush was God's chosen instrument to lead a global war pitting good against evil, it became a religious duty to give him unwavering, unquestioning support. In the five ABC News/*Washington Post* polls taken during the year following September 11 that asked if respondents considered themselves born-again or Evangelical Christians, Bush's approval rating

---

[42] Dana Milbank, "Religious Right Finds It's Center in the Oval Office," *Washington Post*, December 24, 2001, A2.
[43] Quoted in Howard Fineman and Martha Brant, "This is Our Life Now," *Newsweek* (December 3, 2001): 29.
[44] Unidentified "close friend" reported in Frank Bruni, "For President: A Mission and a Role in History," *New York Times*, September 22, 2001, A1.
[45] Quoted in Daalder and Lindsay, *American Unbound*, p. 89.

among white Republicans who did so (about 38 percent of all Republicans in these surveys) ranged from 98 to 100 percent. This was not so important in sustaining adequate public backing for the war in Afghanistan, which was nearly unanimous. But, as we shall see in the next two chapters, it became very important in sustaining support for the president and his venture in Iraq, especially after its original justifications, that Saddam Hussein possessed weapons of mass destruction and was in league with al Qaeda, became untenable.

CHAPTER 5

❖

Going to War in Iraq

Well before September 11, the George W. Bush administration had been contemplating military action to take out Iraqi dictator Saddam Hussein and his regime. Savagely brutal to his own people, Saddam was also believed to be intent on acquiring weapons of mass destruction (WMD) in defiance of the United Nations and agreements made after the Gulf War in 1991. His past record of using chemical weapons and invading neighboring countries marked him as a continuing menace and had made "regime change" in Iraq a goal of U.S. policy even before Bush entered the White House. As the United States's arch-enemy in the Middle East, Saddam immediately became a prime suspect, second only to al Qaeda's Osama bin Laden, as sponsor of the terrorist attacks on New York and Washington D.C. Some members of Bush's national security team, notably deputy secretary of defense Paul Wolfowitz, argued for making Saddam's regime the first target in the war against terrorism but did not persuade the president. "I believe Iraq was involved," Bush reportedly told a meeting of his National Security Council on September 17, "but I'm not going to strike them now. I don't have the evidence at this point."[1]

The public shared the president's opinion of Saddam Hussein and was likewise ready to assume the worst. In a poll taken on September 13, 34 percent of respondents thought it "very likely" and another 44 percent thought it "somewhat likely" that Saddam was "personally involved in Tuesday's terrorist attacks" (the comparable figures for bin Laden were 78 percent and 14 percent, respectively).[2] It is not surprising, then, that Americans generally backed military action against Iraq; in polls taken between September 2001 and March 2002, an average of 73 percent said they supported or approved of such a step (Figure 5.1).[3] Support for attacking Iraq was also largely bipartisan at this time (Figure 5.2). Large majorities of all political persuasions—on average, 80 percent of Republicans, 69 percent of Democrats, and 68 percent of independents—favored the action.

As noted in Chapter 4, however, popular support for going after bin Laden in Afghanistan was even higher, reflecting the greater certainty of his involvement in the attacks. Bush also opted to focus on Afghanistan first, partly because the case for bin Laden's involvement was far easier to make, and partly because military action could be initiated sooner, with wider international

---

[1] Bob Woodward, *Bush at War* (New York: Simon and Schuster, 2002), p. 99.
[2] *Time*/CNN Poll, Sept. 13, 2001, reported at http://pollingreport.com/terror9.htm (accessed July 6, 2005).
[3] In a total of 23 polls taken by ten major media polling organizations, an average of 73.3 (standard deviation, 3.5 percent) approved of or supported military action in Iraq during this period; see Philip Everts and Pierangelo Isernia, "Trends: The War in Iraq," *Public Opinion Quarterly* 69 (Summer 2005): 291–294; and http://pollingreport.com/iraq.htm (accessed July 6, 2005).

FIGURE 5.1
Support for War in Iraq Before It Began

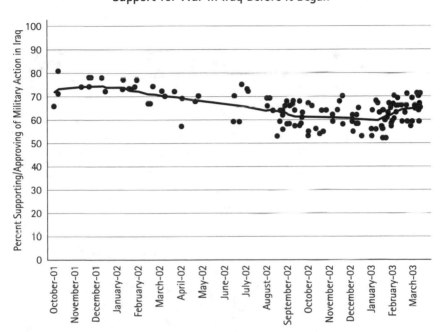

Sources: 128 ABC News/*Washington Post*, CBS News/*New York Times*, Gallup, Fox News, NBC News/*Wall Street Journal*, Pew Center for the People and the Press, *Los Angeles Times*, Harris, Quinnipaic College, and *Time*/CNN polls.

backing, and with better prospects for quick results.[4] But as early as November 21, 2001, the president told his secretary of defense, Donald Rumsfeld, to begin drafting a new war plan for Iraq. On April 7, 2002, Bush told a British television interviewer, "I made up my mind that Saddam needs to go," and in June of that year, Bush formally announced he would order preemptive strikes against countries he considered serious threats to the United States.[5]

---

[4] Woodward, *Bush at War*, pp. 49, 99.
[5] Ibid, 131–133; Bob Woodward, *Plan of Attack* (New York: Simon and Schuster, 2004), pp. 2, 119, 330.

FIGURE 5.2
Support for Military Action in Iraq Before the War, by Party

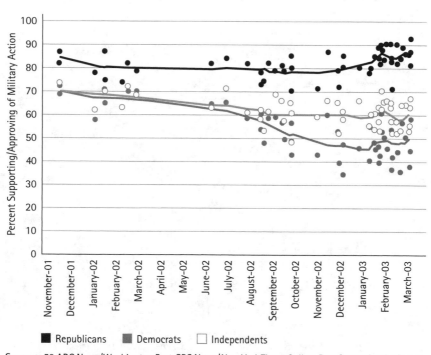

◼ Republicans   ◼ Democrats   ☐ Independents

Sources: 52 ABC News/*Washington Post*, CBS News/*New York Times*, Gallup, Pew Center for the People and the Press, *Los Angeles Times*, Quinnipiac College, and *Time*/CNN polls.

Exactly when Bush made the final decision to invade Iraq remains in dispute. The administration's position is that the decision was not taken until after secretary of state Colin Powell's speech to the United Nations on February 5, 2003, only weeks before the March 20 invasion. But other accounts, including Bob Wood-ward's *Plan of Attack*, leave a powerful impression that Bush had decided almost immediately after September 11 to use military force to effect regime change in Iraq if that is what it took to do it.[6] In any case, there is little question that the president believed strongly that removing Saddam and his regime was both important to American national security and morally justified by the regime's treatment of Iraq's people and neighbors. The question was how to justify initiating a preemptive (more accurately, preventive) war to Congress, the American public, and, if possible, the international community.

In May 2003, Wolfowitz told an interviewer that there were four main reasons for invading Iraq: Saddam's pursuit of WMD, his support for terrorism, the possibility that he might supply WMD to terrorists, and his brutality to his own people. But "the truth is that for reasons that have a lot to do with the U.S. government bureaucracy we settled on the one issue that everyone could agree on which was weapons of mass destruction as the core reason."[7] This became the centerpiece of the White House's characteristically carefully planned, tightly run campaign to persuade Americans that their security required military action to overthrow Saddam's regime. The campaign was coordinated by a high-level task force assembled by Andrew Card, the White House chief of staff, which included Karl Rove, the president's chief political advisor, Karen Hughes, Mary Matalin, and James Wilkinson, communications specialists, Condoleezza Rice, national security advisor, and I. Lewis Libby, Cheney's chief

---

[6] A *Time* article reported Bush responding to a question on Iraq from one of three senators attending a March 2002 meeting with national security advisor Condoleezza Rice with "Fuck Saddam, we're taking him out"; see http://www.time.com/time/archive/preview/0,10987,1101030331-435907,00.html. The public believed he had made up his mind well before February 2003; in a Gallup Poll taken November 22–24, 2002, 58 percent believed he had already decided to invade, 38 percent thought he had not; see http://www.pollingreport.com/iraq4.htm, accessed March 31, 2003.

[7] Interview with Sam Tannenhaus, May 9, 2003, at http://www.defenselink.mil/transcripts/2003/tr20030509-depsecdef0223.html (accessed July 7, 2005).

of staff. The White House Iraq Group, as it was named, super-
vised a "strategic communications" staff charged with formulat-
ing and articulating the case for war. Its first fruits appeared in
September, 2002, because, as Card put it, "From a marketing
point of view, you don't introduce new products in August."[8]

THE CASE FOR WAR

The administration's marketing strategy became clear immediately
and was not subtle: not only was Saddam hiding chemical and
biological weapons, but he was pursuing nuclear weapons and, if
successful, would use them to attack or blackmail the United
States and its allies. On September 8, Rice said in an interview on
CNN that "there will always be some uncertainty on how quickly
he can acquire nuclear weapons, but we don't want the smoking
gun to be a mushroom cloud."[9] Bush invoked the mushroom
cloud again on October 7, as did General Tommy Franks, head of
the U.S. Central Command, on November 12. Bush and Cheney
also raised the specter of "nuclear blackmail" and the danger of
Saddam giving nuclear weapons to terrorists.[10] The evidence that
Iraq had an active program to produce nuclear weapons was in
fact exceedingly thin, discounted by many intelligence experts,
and, according to postwar investigations, unreliable. But the
nuclear threat put the onus on Democrats or others in Washington

---

[8] Barton Gellman and Walter Pincus, "Depiction of Threat Outgrew Supporting Evidence," *Washington Post*, August 10, 2003, A01.
[9] Ibid.
[10] Ben Fritz, Bryan Keefer, and Brendan Nyhan, *All the President's Spin: George W. Bush, the Media, and the Truth* (New York: Simon and Schuster), pp. 154–155.

skeptical about the need to invade Iraq to explain why the United States should take the risk of letting Saddam Hussein remain in power when the worst-case scenario was so horrific.

Bush and his spokespersons were even more adamant in claiming that that, as the president put it in a Rose Garden address on September 26, "the Iraqi regime possesses biological and chemical weapons [and] is building the facilities necessary to make more biological and chemical weapons."[11] Cheney was equally unequivocal: "Simply stated, there is no doubt that Saddam now has weapons of mass destruction [and] there is no doubt that he is amassing them to use against our friends, against our allies, and against us."[12] This theme was repeated and elaborated until the war began; in his March 17, 2003 speech giving Saddam 48 hours to leave Iraq, Bush reiterated that "Intelligence gathered by this and other governments leaves no doubt that the Iraq regime continues to possess and conceal some of the most lethal weapons ever devised."[13]

SADDAM AND 9/11

The administration also wanted to tie Saddam to the terrorist attacks of September 11 or at least to al Qaeda more generally. The problem, as Bush had noted from the beginning, was the lack

---

[11] Dana Priest and Walter Pincus, "Bush Certainty On Iraq Arms Went Beyond Analysts' Views," *Washington Post*, June 7, 2003, A01.
[12] Ibid.
[13] http://www.whitehouse.gov/news/releases/2003/03/20030317-7.html. There was, in fact considerable doubt about the intelligence itself; see Douglas Jehl, "Report Warned Bush Team About Intelligence Doubts," *New York Times*, November 6, 2005, p. 6; and Bob Drogin and John Goetz, "Germans: U.S. Warned of Bad Data," *Los Angeles Times*, November 20, 2005, p. 1. On the case for war more generally, see James P. Pfiffner, "Did President Bush Mislead the Country in His Arguments for Going to War in Iraq?," *Presidential Studies Quarterly* 24 (March, 2004): 25–46.

of evidence. And although the administration mobilized U.S. intelligence agencies to look for connections—Donald Rumsfeld, Secretary of Defense, reportedly asked the CIA on ten separate occasions for evidence linking Saddam to September 11—nothing tangible could be found.[14] Cheney and some of his staff claimed the link was a meeting in April 2001 between the Mohammed Atta, the hijackers' leader, and an Iraqi agent in Prague, but the evidence that the meeting took place was weak and was eventually discredited in the *9/11 Commission Report*.[15] On somewhat more solid ground was the claim, articulated by Secretary of State Colin Powell in his February 5, 2003, speech to the United Nations asking its approval for removing Hussein, that al Qaeda allies, notably Abu Massad Al-Zakawi, were active in Iraq, suggesting a "potentially much more sinister nexus between Iraq and the al-Qaida terrorist network."[16] The problem here was that the sinister activities Powell described—mainly training al Qaeda recruits in use of poisons—went on in a Kurdish area of Iraq not under Saddam's control, although Al-Zakawi—a terrorist but not a member of al Qaeda—had been in Baghdad for medical treatment.

The thinness of the evidence for Saddam's complicity in September 11 and plotting with al Qaeda did not stop the president and his team from repeatedly linking Saddam rhetorically with the terrorist attacks. For example, in an address to the nation on October 7, 2002, he put it this way: "Some citizens wonder, 'after 11 years of living with this [Saddam Hussein] problem, why

---

[14] Daniel Eisenberg, "We're Taking Him Out," *Time*, May 13, 2002, at http://archives.cnn.com/2002/ALLPOLITICS/05/06/time.out/ (accessed July 7, 2005).

[15] Official U.S. Government version, pp. 228–229.

[16] Remarks to the United Nations Security Council, at http://www.globalsecurity.org/wmd/library/news/iraq/2003/iraq-030205-powell-un-17300pf.htm (accessed July 7, 2005).

do we need to confront it now?' And there's a reason. We have experienced the horror of September the 11th. We have seen that those who hate America are willing to crash airplanes into buildings full of innocent people. Our enemies would be no less willing, in fact, they would be eager, to use biological or chemical, or a nuclear weapon." In the same speech, he reminded Americans that "after September the 11th, Saddam Hussein's regime gleefully celebrated the terrorist attacks on America."[17] Rice, asked if there was any hard evidence linking the Iraqi government to September 11 and al Qaeda, replied: "There is certainly evidence al Qaeda people have been in Iraq. There is certainly evidence that Saddam Hussein cavorts with terrorists," and then added, "I think if you asked, do we know that he had a role in 9/11, no we do not know that he had a role in 9/11. But I think that this is the test that sets a bar that is far too high."[18] House speaker Dennis Hastert was even less equivocal: "There is no doubt that Iraq supports and harbors those terrorists who wish harm to the United States. Is there a direct connection between Iraq and al Qaeda? The president thinks so."[19] Rumsfeld told a Chamber of Commerce luncheon audience in September 2002 that the case for links between al Qaeda and Saddam's government was "bulletproof."[20]

Although, like Rice, Bush and others speaking for the administration admitted when questioned directly that there was no

[17] "President Bush Outlines Iraqi Threat," White House press release, October 7, 2002, at http://www.whitehouse.gov/news/releases/2002/10/20021007-8.htm, (accessed July 7, 2005.)
[18] Interview with Condoleezza Rice conducted by Wolf Blitzer, CNN Late Edition, September 8, 2002 at http://www.mtholyoke.edu/acad/intrel/bush/wolf.htm (accessed July 7, 2005).
[19] Gebe Martinez, "Concerns Linger for Lawmakers Following Difficult Vote for War," CQ Weekly (October 12, 2002): 2673.
[20] Eric Schimtt, "Rumsfeld Says U.S. Has 'Bulletproof' Evidence of Iraq's Links to Al Qaeda," New York Times, September 28, 2002, A1.

hard evidence that Saddam had a hand in September 11, they nonetheless conveyed to the public impression that they believed it was true. In a poll taken in December 2003, just before Saddam's capture, 57 percent of respondents said they thought the Bush administration believed Saddam was involved in September 11, while only 25 percent thought the administration believed he was not. [21] Perhaps more revealing, of respondents asked in a January 2003 survey to estimate "how many of the September 11 terrorists were Iraqi citizens" and given a range of options, 21 percent chose "most," 23 percent, "some," 6 percent, "one," and only 17 percent got it right: "none."[22] Prior suspicions and all the rhetoric associating Iraq with al Qaeda evidently left half the public with the false impression that Iraqis had been in on the hijackings.

It is unclear whether Bush and his senior officials continued to believe Saddam was complicit in September 11 as, despite their best efforts, U.S. intelligence agencies continued to come up short in their search for a connection. Rumsfeld's maxim that "the absence of evidence is not evidence of absence"[23] was (and remains) available to anyone who wanted to believe in Saddam's involvement.[24] There is little doubt, however, that Bush and his advisors were certain that Iraq was hiding WMD, as were most outside experts, American and foreign. Saddam's history of producing and using such weapons, his government's evasive deal-

[21] CBS News/*New York Times* Poll, December 12–15, 2003.

[22] The remaining 33 percent did not know; see the Knight Ridder poll, January 3–6, 2003, at http://www.pollingreport.com/Iraq4.htm (accessed March 31, 2003). Although there is some uncertainty about the identities of some of the hijackers, 15 were evidently from Saudi Arabia, two from the United Arab Emirates, one from Lebanon and one, the leader Mohammed Atta, from Egypt.

[23] "Rumsfeld Says Iraqis Growing More Confident About Country's Future," Defense Department Report, August 5, 2003, at http://www.globalsecurity.org/wmd/library/news/iraq/2003/08/iraq-030805-usia03.htm (accessed July 8, 2005).

[24] Woodward, *Plan of Attack*, pp. 290–292.

ings with UN weapons inspectors, the biological and chemical weapons material Iraq possessed prior to the Gulf War in 1991 still not accounted for, and plenty of other circumstantial if inconclusive evidence made it easy to believe that hidden WMD must exist. When Bush reacted to the case for WMD presented by the CIA at a December 21, 2002, meeting with "this is the best we've got?" George Tenet, director of the agency, reassured him: "Don't worry, it's a slam dunk."[25] If there were skeptics, at home or abroad, they would be confounded when Iraq fell and the U.S. forces exposed Saddam's hidden caches.[26] More to the point, Bush and his advisors were far more worried about failing to do enough than about doing too much in defending the nation from further terrorist assaults. The worst-case scenarios used to bring the public and Congress on board, however unlikely, were certainly frightening enough to make leaders less risk-acceptant than Bush willing to initiate a war.

THE PUBLIC'S RESPONSE

The Bush Administration's campaign to drum up public support for a preventive war against Iraq ultimately succeeded, but to a greater extent with Republicans than with Democrats and independents, and Americans on the whole displayed a stubborn reluctance to go to war without the support of the United Nations or traditional allies. The chief justification for invading Iraq, that

---

[25] Ibid., p. 249.
[26] As Bush told Woodward in an interview in Crawford, Texas on August 20, 2002, "Confident action that will yield positive results provides kind of a slipstream into which reluctant nations and leaders can get behind and show themselves that there has been—you know, something positive has happened toward peace." Woodward, *Bush at War*, p. 341.

FIGURE 5.3
The Public's Beliefs in Justifications for the Iraq War Before it Began

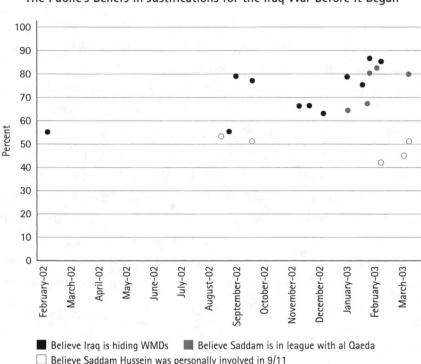

■ Believe Iraq is hiding WMDs　　■ Believe Saddam is in league with al Qaeda
☐ Believe Saddam Hussein was personally involved in 9/11

Sources: ABC News/*Washington Post*, CBS News/*New York Times*, Gallup, Fox News, Knight-Ridder, and CNN/*Time* polls.

Saddam was hiding WMD, was accepted by a majority of Americans from the beginning, and acceptance rose during the months leading up to the invasion to greater than 80 percent (Figures 5.3). Partisan differences on this question were relatively small, on the order of 15 percentage points, and did not grow over the period leading up to the war. Beliefs about Hussein's personal involvement in September 11 remained essentially unchanged, with about half the public believing he was involved (again, partisan differences were small, fewer than 10 percentage points). However, the belief Saddam was in league with al Qaeda was much more widespread, exceeding 80 percent in February and March. An even larger share of respondents—86 to 88 percent— thought Saddam was "involved in supporting terrorist groups that have plans to attack the United States."[27] About three quarters of the public believed that if Iraq acquired nuclear weapons, Saddam would use them against the U.S.[28] or his neighbors.[29] Four of five Americans accepted the general proposition that Iraq posed a threat to the United States.[30]

That most Americans believed that Hussein was hiding WMD, conniving with al Qaeda terrorists, and threatening the United States did not, however, necessarily mean that they believed the administration had made a convincing case for preventive war. Asked in six ABC News/*Washington Post* polls taken between September 12, 2002, and February 1, 2003, "Do you think Bush has presented enough evidence showing why the United States should use military force to remove Saddam Hussein from power, or would you like him to present more evidence," an average of only 41 percent thought he had presented enough evidence, while 57 percent wanted to see more.[31] Later, in February and March 2003, when the question did not include the option of seeing more

---

[27] CNN/*USA Today*/Gallup Poll, August 5–8, 2002 and March 14–15, 2003, at http://www.polling report.com/iraq2.htm (accessed March 31, 2003).
[28] Fox News/Opinion Dynamics Poll, January 14–15, 2003 and CNN/*USA Today*/Gallup Poll, September 13–16, 2003 at ibid.
[29] *Newsweek* Poll, March 13–14, 2003, at ibid.
[30] In four ABC News/*Washington Post* polls taken in September and December 2002 and January and March 2003, the share of the public expressing this belief was 79 percent, 81 percent, 81 percent, and 79 percent, respectively. See http://www.pollingreport.com/Iraa3.htm, 4 (accessed March 31, 2003).
[31] ABC News/*Washington Post* polls, September 12–14, 2002, December 12–15, 2002, January 16–20, 2003, January 27, 2003, January 28, 2003, and January 30–February 1, 2003, at ibid. The distribution of responses showed no trend over these months.

evidence, a larger proportion said that the administration had produced enough evidence, but it still amounted to a modest majority, an average of 54 percent in eight surveys.[32] Partisan differences on these questions were substantial. In the first set, an average of 59 percent of Republicans thought the evidence was sufficient, compared to only 28 percent of Democrats; in the second, the comparable figures were 77 percent and 37 percent.

Agreement with the premises of the war also did not mean that Americans gave Bush an automatic green light to invade Iraq. Although the administration claimed it already had full authority to act,[33] large majorities—including majorities of Republicans—wanted the president to get Congress's approval first.[34] If the president and Congress disagreed on going to war, large majorities also wanted Congress rather than the president to have the last word.[35] The public also wanted the Administration to get the backing of America's traditional allies and the United Nations before taking action. As Figure 5.4 shows, support for attacking Iraq was much higher if the United States was joined by allies and the UN; with only one or two major allies (the eventual case), support barely passed 50 percent on the eve of the war. Most did not want the United States to go it alone if that were the only option,

---

[32] CBS News/*New York Times* Polls February 5–6, 2003, February 10–12, 2003, March 4–5, 2003, March 7–9, 2003, March 15–16, 2003; ABC News/*Washington Post* polls, January 30–February 1, 2003, February 5, 2003, February 6–9, 2003, at ibid. A slightly higher proportion—56 and 57 percent, respectively, in February and March Gallup polls—said they thought the Bush administration had "made a convincing case about the need for the U.S. to take military action against Iraq." See ibid.

[33] Miles A. Pomper, "Senate Democrats in Disarray After Gephardt's Deal on Iraq," *CQ Weekly* (October 5, 2002): 2606.

[34] In the four CBS News/*New York Times* polls taken between August 6 and October 10, 2002, an average of 69 percent of respondents wanted Bush to get congressional authorization first, including 57 percent of Republicans and 75 percent of Democrats.

[35] It was Congress over Bush, 59–37 and 61–34 in the ABC News polls of August 7–11 and August 29, 2002; see http://www.pollingreport.com/iraq5.htm (accessed March 31, 2003).

FIGURE 5.4
Would you Support or Oppose U.S. Military Action [Against Iraq] in this Circumstance?

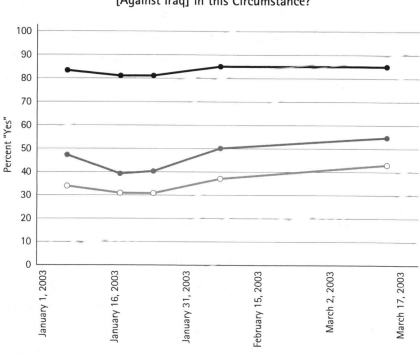

■ The United States joined together with its major allies to attack Iraq, with the full support of the United Nations Security Council

■ The United States and one or two of its major allies attacked Iraq, without the support of the United Nations

☐ The United States acted alone in attacking Iraq, without the support of the United Nations

Source: *Newsweek* polls, at http://www.pollingreport.com/iraq2.htm, p. 11–12 (accessed March 31, 2003).

although support for unilateral action rose just before the onset of the war. In nineteen surveys taken between February 2002 and March 2003 (using a variety of question wordings), the option of invading Iraq without UN support was backed on average by only 33 percent of respondents and never received majority support; a majority (averaging 55 percent) always preferred invading only with UN approval, with the remainder not wanting to invade at all. These averages did not change much as the war approached; in the eight polls taken in February and March 2003, an average of 36 percent supported action without UN approval and 58 percent, only with it.[36]

BRINGING CONGRESS ON BOARD

With public opinion this clear cut, it was politically infeasible to ignore Congress and the UN in steering the course toward war no matter what the administration believed about the president's existing authority to act. Bush had relatively little difficulty winning congressional support for a resolution giving him wide latitude in deciding whether or when to invade Iraq, which he requested in a prime-time speech on October 7, 2002. Although many Democrats were reluctant to give the president such broad authority, the resolution passed the House on October 10 by 296-133, with substantial Democratic support (81-126; among Republicans, the vote was 215-6). The Senate vote the next day was 77-23, with a majority of Democrats (29-21) and all but one of the 49 Republicans backing it.[37] Some Democrats justified sup-

---

[36] Everts and Isernia, "Trends: The War in Iraq," p. 302.
[37] Gebe Martinez, "Concerns Linger for Lawmakers Following Difficult Vote for War," CQ *Weekly* (October 12, 2002): 2671.

porting the resolution as a way of putting pressure on the UN to act more forcefully on renewing demands for weapons inspections in Iraq, with the ultimate goal of avoiding war.[38] Others feared political attacks questioning their devotion to national security in the upcoming midterm election, less than a month away. (Many congressional Democrats suspected the preelection timing of the request for authority was not accidental, and their partisans evidently agreed, with 56 percent of Democrats but only 12 percent of Republicans believing that Bush was "deliberately using the talk of war in Iraq to distract attention from other issues in this year's congressional elections.")[39] But it was the memory of September 11 and the specter of mushroom clouds that produced greater Democratic support for the resolution than Bush's father had gotten for the Gulf War in 1991. In light of the dire threat depicted by the administration and genuine uncertainties about Saddam's weapons, associations, and intentions, prudence lay in not opposing the war. If it turned out to be unjustified, unnecessary, or disastrous in some way, Bush would get the primary blame. But if Democrats opposed the war and Saddam's complicity in September 11 and WMD were confirmed, or if the Iraqi people welcomed Americans as liberators and democracy blossomed from the ashes of Saddam's sadistic regime, Democrats could face a political reckoning. Worse, if they succeeded in hindering the president's plans and another terrorist attack occurred

---

[38] Miles A. Pomper, "Senate Democrats in Disarray After Gephardt's Deal on Iraq," CQ Weekly (October 5, 2002): 2606.

[39] Newsweek Poll, September 26–27, 2002, at http://www.pollingreport.com/iraq4.htm (accessed March 31, 2003).

on American soil, no matter what its provenance, they could wind up scapegoats.

Bush had a much tougher time getting U.S. allies and the UN on board and largely failed, although the effort helped to increase public support for the action that was eventually taken by his "coalition of the willing." Speaking at the UN on September 12, 2002, the president told the organization to enforce its resolutions against Iraq or else the United States would do so by itself; however, he also asked for further "necessary resolutions" from the UN Security Council authorizing action if Saddam refused full compliance. On November 8, the Security Council unanimously passed a resolution imposing tough new arms inspections on Iraq and threatening "serious consequences" if Saddam resisted, but the resolution did not include the automatic authority for war on any Iraqi failure to comply that the administration had wanted; a second resolution would be necessary to get the UN's approval to use force. Saddam backed down, and on November 18, UN weapons inspectors returned to Iraq for the first time since 1998. Their searches turned up no solid evidence of WMD, and Iraq denied having any, but there was enough missing information and uncooperative behavior to convince administration hawks that Saddam was continuing his cynical games of deception.

In his State of the Union address on January 28, 2003, the president announced that he was prepared to invade Iraq even without a UN mandate. Nonetheless, Secretary of State Colin Powell was dispatched to the UN to make the case for war based on U.S. intelligence, which he did in a 76 minute speech on February 5. Powell was the administration's most popular figure—he enjoyed approval ratings at the time of around 75 percent and

favorability ratings of around 85 percent, both figures substantially higher than the president's[40]—and he was known to be less
eager for war than Rumsfeld, Cheney, and other administration
hawks, so his presentation had an impact on American public
opinion, if not on the Security Council. This may have been its
principal objective: not only to have the administration's most
credible voice articulate the most persuasive case it could muster
for war, but also to show it had made every effort to get the UN's
approval and help before taking the unpopular step of going to
war without it.

POPULAR SUPPORT FOR A DISCRETIONARY WAR

A majority of Americans had supported military action to take
out Saddam Hussein ever since September 11, but by margins that
had been trending downward until early February 2003, after
which the Bush administration's campaign succeeded in boosting
support for the war by about 5 percentage points (Figure 5.1). In
polls taken in the final week before the war began, an average of
about two-thirds of respondents backed going to war. But as
Figure 5.2 indicates, partisan differences in support for war in
Iraq grew over time, especially after September 2002, when the
administration began its concerted effort to make the case for taking action. Large majorities of Republicans backed war all along;
their support rose another 10 percentage points or so after the

---

[40] See his ratings for the period September 2002–February 2003 in various polls reported at
http://pollingreport.com/P-Z.htm (accessed July 14, 2005).

first of the year and stood at close to 90 percent just before the war began. Support for war declined among Democrats after September and typically remained below 50 percent until just before the onset of fighting. Even then, as late as March 16, 64 percent of Democrats (compared to 30 percent of Republicans) said the United States should "wait and give the United Nations and weapons inspectors more time" rather than "take military action against Iraq fairly soon."[41] The proportion of Republicans who thought that "Iraq presents such a clear and present danger to American interests that the United States needs to act now, even without support of its allies" grew from 34 percent in August–October 2002 polls to 58 percent in February 2003 polls, while the proportion of Democrats taking this view scarcely budged, moving from 20 percent to 22 percent.[42] In March, 62 percent of Republicans answered a parallel question in which "United Nations" substituted for "allies" by saying the United States should act rather than wait for UN approval, compared to only 22 percent of Democrats.[43] On all of these questions, independents were on average much closer to Democrats than to Republicans.[44] Clearly, even when they believed that regime change in Iraq was imperative, most Democrats and independents remained reluctant to resort to force and opposed to unilateral action on the part of the United States. People whose prior attitudes did not incline them to trust Bush or his advisors seemed to be look-

---

[41] CBS News/*New York Times* Poll, March 15–16, 2003 at http://www.pollingreport.com/iraq2.htm (accessed March 31, 2003).
[42] CBS News/*New York Times* Poll, March 4–5, 2003, August 6–7, 2002, September 2–5, 2002, October 3–5, 2002, February 10–12, 2003, and February 24–25, 2003, at ibid.
[43] CBS News/*New York Times* Poll, March 4–5, 2003, at ibid.
[44] The distribution of responses among independents' typically falls about one-third of the distance from the Democrats' to the Republicans' distributions on these questions.

FIGURE 5.5

Beliefs about WMD and Saddam Hussein's Involvement in 9/11 and Approval of Military Action to Remove Saddam Hussein from Power (September 2002)

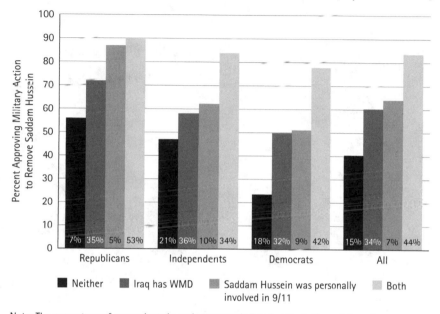

Note: The percentage of respondents in each category is listed at the bottom of the column.
Source: ABC News/*Washington Post* Poll, September 23–26, 2002.

ing to America's European allies and the UN weapons inspectors to provide independent confirmation of the administration's rationale for an invasion of Iraq before giving it their complete backing.

Such as it was, support for military action among Democrats and, to a lesser extent, independents, depended crucially on beliefs that Iraq possessed WMD and that Saddam Hussein had been personally involved in the terrorist attacks of September 11. Figures 5.5 and 5.6, based on polls taken at the beginning and end

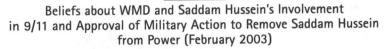

FIGURE 5.6

Beliefs about WMD and Saddam Hussein's Involvement
in 9/11 and Approval of Military Action to Remove Saddam Hussein
from Power (February 2003)

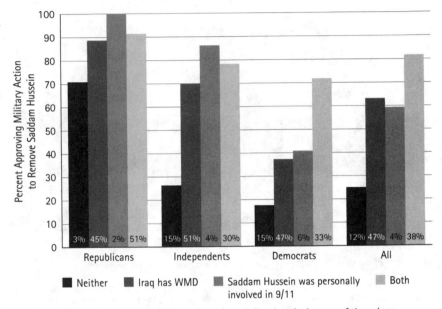

Note: The percentage of respondents in each category is listed at the bottom of the column.
Source: CBS News/*New York Times* Poll, February 10–12, 2003.

of the administration's campaign to mobilize support for attacking Iraq, illustrate this point. In September 2002, people who believed Saddam's regime was guilty on both counts were much more supportive of war than those who believed it was guilty on neither, but with effects far more pronounced for Democrats than for Republicans. Those believing in only one of the charges fell in between. By February 2003, Republicans had come to support military action by huge majorities regardless of which charges they believed; moreover, 97 percent accepted at least one of the grounds for going to war, and more than half accepted both. Substantial majorities of independents who accepted either one or both (about 85 percent of independents in this poll) also supported military action. Among Democrats, only the third who believed both charges favored going to war (slightly more than 70 percent of this group did so); support for war among those who believed only one of the charges was around 40 percent, and among the minority who believed neither, it was below 20 percent.

On the eve of the Iraq War, then, partisan divisions on its wisdom and necessity were substantial, on the order of 35 to 40 percentage points. As we shall see in the next chapter, this partisan gap was much wider than it had been for other military actions involving the United States since the Second World War. In part, the gap reflected the prior polarized evaluations of Bush himself; support for war was of course highly correlated with presidential approval.[45] But it also reflected the fact that, more than any of the other comparable U.S. military actions, the Iraq War was discretionary and preventive. The Iraqi regime had not attacked the United States or any of its allies, nor was it currently engaged in a civil war against a faction backed by the United States. Although the war's proximate provocation was the terrorist attacks of September 11, and the administration's mobilization campaign included insinuations of Saddam's involvement, the war's public justification was not retaliation but prevention, leaving both the need for war and the urgency of taking action

---

[45] The direction of causality is of course hopelessly ambiguous, but across partisan categories in the February 2003 poll used for Figure 5.5, support for the war was 36–49 points higher among those who approved of Bush's performance, and approval of Bush's performance was 33–50 points higher among respondents who supported going to war.

open to question. The UN Security Council and major European allies, including France and Germany, were not convinced, so it is not surprising that Americans not predisposed by partisanship to follow George W. Bush's lead would also be inclined to doubt that war was necessary or, if it was, could not be put off while diplomacy was given more time.

The evidence justifying the war was underwhelming even for some of the president's staunchest supporters in Congress. After a meeting on February 5 in which Bush and Rice briefed 20 key members of Congress on war plans, Senator John Warner (Rep-Va.), chair of the Senate Armed Service Committee, reportedly told a senior aide to Rice, "You got to do this and I'll support you, make no mistake. But I sure hope you find weapons of mass destruction because if you don't you may have a big problem."[46] Not least, it could be added, with those segments of the American public whose support for the war depended on belief in its premises.

---

[46] Woodward, *Plan of Attack*, p. 309.

CHAPTER 6

Illusion, Disillusion, and Faith in the President after "Mission Accomplished"

The Iraq War began with the launch of Operation Iraqi Freedom on March 20, 2003. The initial military phase of the war was a swift and stunning success; the British took Basra on April 7, Baghdad fell to American forces April 9, the Kurds took control of Kirkuk on April 11. The most fearsome consequences of invading Iraq envisioned before the war—burning oil fields, chemical or biological weapons used against U.S. forces, Iraqi attacks on Israel, uprisings in other middle eastern countries, terrorist operations in the U.S. homeland, bloody house-to-house combat in major Iraqi cities, thousands of U.S. casualties, mass destruction of Iraqi cities, widespread civilian deaths, millions of

refugees—did not materialize.[1] The sense of relief among political
leaders and ordinary Americans alike was palpable. Pictures of
celebrating Iraqis and the exposure of mass graves of Saddam's
victims and the torture chambers where they had suffered underlined the point that, no matter what else it may have accomplished, the war had at least deposed a sadistic tyrant. Bush
celebrated the victory on May 1 by landing on the aircraft carrier
Abraham Lincoln in full flight regalia to greet sailors returning
from the Middle East. A huge sign reading "Mission Accomplished" served as the backdrop for his nationally televised speech
from the carrier's deck in which he declared that "major combat
operations in Iraq have ended. In the Battle of Iraq, the United
States and our allies have prevailed."[2]

The battle may have been won but the war was not over.
Although the worst fears had not been realized, unanticipated
troubles appeared immediately with the complete collapse of law
and order, widespread and destructive looting, incidents of summary vengeance, and the beginnings of an insurgency that only
intensified over the following months. Prewar testimony by
administration officials that Iraqi oil revenues would pay for the
war or that other nations would pitch in a major way[3] turned out
to be wildly optimistic, as did low-ball estimates of the war's
drain on the U.S. Treasury. Extensive corruption as well as lack of

---

[1] The public had shared many of these fears; in a *Newsweek* Poll taken March 13–14, 2003, 76 percent
thought "Iraq would retaliate by using biological or chemical weapons against the United States";
73 percent, against Israel; 82 percent thought war "would inspire terrorist attacks against American citizens"; and 69 percent thought "it would cause serious problems for the U.S throughout the Arab
world"; see http://www.pollingreport.com/Iraq2.htm (accessed March 31, 2003).
[2] Text of speech displayed at http://www.cbsnews.com/stories/2003/05/01/iraq/main551946.shtml
(accessed July 15, 2005).
[3] Warren Vieth, "War with Iraq: Iraq Debts Could Add Up to Trouble," *Los Angeles Times*, April 4,
2003, A1.

security hampered reconstruction; the trashed and looted infra-structure made life difficult for ordinary Iraqis, souring many toward both their American liberators and the new Iraqi govern-ment being constructed under their sponsorship. More than two years after the main fighting had stopped, Iraqi oil production had yet to return to prewar levels, power and gas shortages continued to plague the country, and the Iraqi people were still beset by high levels of both criminal and political violence.

Amid these difficulties, the Bush administration faced an esca-lating embarrassment: the search for Iraq's caches of WMD and evidence of Saddam's links to terrorists targeting the United States continued to come up empty handed. Any dreams Bush and his advisors may have entertained of a "told you so" reckoning with leaders of France, Germany, and other countries who had blocked UN support for the war melted away; that (diplomatically, implicit) satisfaction belonged to those who had argued that the UN had Saddam contained, and it gave them an excuse to stint on help in dealing with the war's expensive aftermath.

It was many months before the administration publicly con-ceded that prewar intelligence on Iraq's WMD had been faulty. In an interview with journalist Bob Woodward on December 10, 2003, the president acknowledge that WMD had not been found, but only on the condition that Woodward not publish that infor-mation until his book came out months later.[4] On January 28, 2004, David Kay, former head of the U.S. weapons inspection team in Iraq, told the Senate Intelligence Committee that no WMD had been found and that prewar intelligence had been

---

[4] Bob Woodward, *Plan of Attack* (New York: Simon and Schuster, 2004), p. 423.

"almost all wrong."[5] But he continued to regard Iraq as a threat because it retained the know-how and intent to produce biological and chemical weapons once UN sanctions were lifted. Bowing to strong political pressure after Kay's testimony, Bush reluctantly appointed a commission to look into the intelligence failures, admitting in a television interview on the subject in February that WMD caches had yet to be found. The commission was to report in March 2005, five months after the 2004 presidential election.[6] On March 2, 2004, the UN weapons inspection teams reported that Iraq had possessed no WMD of any significance after 1994. The CIA's Iraq Survey Group's leader, Charles Duelfer, told the Senate Armed Services Committee on October 4, 2004, that they had found no evidence that Iraq had produced WMD since 1991, when UN sanctions had been imposed.[7] In January 2005 the U.S. military forces officially abandoned the search for WMD without having found any. Thus the main *casus belli* was discredited, but gradually enough to allow the administration plenty of time to recast its prewar arguments and revise its public case for the war.

REVISING THE CASE FOR WAR

Revise it they did. Talk shifted from Saddam's WMD to his WMD *program*. In an April 25, 2003, interview, for example, Bush declared, "I think there's going to be skepticism until people find out there was, in fact, a weapons of mass destruction program."

---

[5] Ibid., p. 434.
[6] "Meet the Press with Tim Russert," February 7, 2004, reported at http://www.msnbc.msn.com/id/4179618 (accessed July 19, 2005).
[7] Testimony based on "Comprehensive Report of the Special Advisor to the DCI on Iraq's WMD," September 30, 2004 at http://www.cia.gov/cia/reports/iraq_wmd_2004 (accessed July 20, 2005).

He later added, "We know he had a weapons of mass destruction program."[8] On May 6, responding to a question about evidence of a biological weapons lab, Bush repeated the phrase "weapons program" 14 times. On June 9, when asked if U.S. credibility was on the line regarding WMD in Iraq, he replied, "I'm not exactly sure what that means. Iraq had a weapons program. Intelligence throughout the decade showed they had a weapons program. I am absolutely convinced that with time we'll find out they did have a weapons program."[9] On June 10, the president's press secretary, Ari Fleisher, said that "when the president talked about weapons programs, he includes weapons of mass destruction in that," and confirmed that he meant that Bush used the terms interchangeably.[10] In December when Diane Sawyer of ABC News asked Bush about the distinction between, "stated as a hard fact, that there were weapons of mass destruction" and "the possibility that [Saddam] could move to acquire the weapons still," Bush replied, "What's the difference?"[11]

At one point the president even claimed that biological weapons had been found, telling a Polish television interviewer, "We found the weapons of mass destruction. We found biological laboratories."[12] The evidence was the discovery of a pair of trailers that could have been used to make biological weapons, although there was no indication they had been used for that purpose and they had other legitimate uses. Several other administration

---

[8] *Dateline NBC* , NBC, April 25, 2003, quoted in Ben Fritz, Bryan Keefer, and Brendan Nyhan, *All the President's Spin* (New York: Simon and Schuster, 2004), p. 192.
[9] "President Discusses Middle East, Iraq and the Dollar in Cabinet Meeting," White House news release, June 9, 2003, quoted in ibid.
[10] White House press briefing, June 10, 2003, quoted in ibid., p. 196.
[11] *Primetime Live*, ABC, December 16, 2003, quoted in ibid., p. 197.
[12] Interview of president by TPV, Poland, May 29, 2003, quoted in ibid., p. 194.

voices, including Vice President Cheney, made the same claim—even after U.S. intelligence officials had publicly backed away from it.[13]

Postwar investigations also found little evidence of a meaningful al Qaeda connection. A few contacts between Iraqi officials and members of al Qaeda were documented, but investigators found no sign of any sustained or high-level cooperation and no evidence of Iraqi involvement on September 11. This did not stop the administration from continuing to imply a connection. In his address from the deck of the *Abraham Lincoln*, Bush declared, "The liberation of Iraq is a crucial advance in the campaign against terror. We've removed an ally of al Qaeda, and cut off a source of terrorist funding."[14] Asked by Tim Russert on Meet the Press in September 2003, if Cheney was surprised that a large majority of Americans believed Saddam was involved in 9/11, he replied, "No. I think it's not surprising that people make the connection." Asked further, "But is there a connection?" Cheney left it open: "We don't know."[15] Cheney also continued to refer to the unconfirmed prewar allegation of a meeting between the lead hijacker Mohammed Atta and an Iraqi intelligence official in Prague before the September 11 attacks as evidence of Saddam's complicity.

While conceding only slowly and with considerable backsliding that the case for war had been built on faulty intelligence, the administration was happy to highlight the one justification Paul Wolfowitz had listed (see Chapter 5) for forcing Saddam Hussein from office that was unassailable: Saddam's brutality to his own

---

[13] Fritz, Keefer, and Nyhan, *President's Spin*, p. 194.
[14] Text of speech displayed at http://www.cbsnews.com/stories/2003/05/01/iraq/main551946.shtml (accessed July 15, 2005).
[15] *Meet the Press*, NBC, September 14, 2003, quoted in Fritz, Keefer, and Nyhan, *President's Spin*, p. 211.

people. His regime's torture and murder of Iraqis on a grand scale was confirmed after the war, and few Iraqis appeared to be unhappy about his removal. As Bush put it at a press conference in April 2004, "I want to know why we haven't found a weapon yet. But I still know Saddam Hussein was a threat, and the world is better off without Saddam Hussein. . . . I know the Iraqi people don't believe that [they] . . . would be better off with Saddam Hussein in power."[16] Critics who said that the war was a mistake were open to the accusation that they wanted to see Saddam back in power. Even if the war's premises were mistaken, weren't its consequences worth it? Later, this approach broadened to emphasize the rationale that the war had set in motion a movement toward freedom and democracy across the Middle East; as Bush declared in his 2005 State of the Union address, "The victory of freedom in Iraq will . . . inspire democratic reformers from Damascus to Tehran, bring more hope and progress to a troubled region, and thereby lift a terrible threat from the lives of our children and grandchildren."[17]

The administration also argued for Saddam's guilt by geography. Condoleezza Rice, interviewed on July 30, 2003, noted that Saddam "was sitting astride one of the most volatile regions in the world, a region out of which the ideologies of hatred had come that led people to slam airplanes into buildings in New York and Washington."[18] Cheney said in September that "if we're successful in Iraq . . . we will have struck a major blow right at the heart

---

[16] Presidential press conference, April 13, 2004, at http://www.whitehouse.gov/news/releases/2004/04/20040413-20.html (accessed July 20, 2005).
[17] "State of the Union Address," February 2, 2005, at http://www.whitehouse.gov/news/releases/2005/02/20050202-11.html (accessed July 25, 2005).
[18] Interview with Gwen Ifil, *NewsHour with Jim Lehrer*, PBS, July 30, 2003, quoted in Fritz, Keefer, and Nyhan, *President's Spin*, pp. 212–213.

of the base, if you will, the geographic base of the terrorists who have had us under assault now for many years, but most especially on 9/11."[19]

The geographical argument tied into what became the primary justification for the war and for continuing U.S. involvement, that Iraq was a central front in the war in terrorism. As Bush put it in a nationally televised speech on September 7, 2003, "Two years ago, I told Congress and the country that the war on terror would be a lengthy war, a different kind of war, fought on many fronts in many places. Iraq is now the central front."[20] The corollary, offered in many variations over the ensuing years, was that the U.S. was fighting terrorists in Iraq so it would not have to fight them at home.[21] These claims became the main point of contention between Bush and his challenger, John Kerry, in the 2004 campaign and will be analyzed as such in Chapter 7.

Like the original, the revised case for war was persuasive—to Republicans. It was far less successful among Democrats and independents, and partisan divisions on the Iraq War became far wider than for any previous U.S. military action for which we have opinion survey data. Ultimately, partisan reactions to the war, its premises as articulated by the administration, and its consequences, form the single most important explanation of why George W. Bush became the most divisive and polarizing president in the more than 50 years presidential approval has been surveyed.

---

[19] *Meet the Press*, NBC, September 14, 2003, quoted in ibid., p. 213.

[20] "President Addresses the Nation," White House press release, September 7, 2003, at http://www.whitehouse.gov/news/releases/2003/09/20030907-1.html (accessed July 20, 2005).

[21] For example, addressing the nation from Fort Bragg on June 28, 2005, Bush put it this way: "We fight today because terrorists want to attack our country and kill our citizens, and Iraq is where they are making their stand," at http://www.whitehouse.gov/news/releases/2005/06/20050628-7.html (accessed October 10, 2005).

THE IRAQ RALLY

As noted in Chapter 1, the onset of war in Iraq inspired a substantial rally in President Bush's overall job approval ratings (Figures 1.1 and 1.2) and in evaluations of his handling of the situation in Iraq (Figure 1.7). The rally was joined by partisans across the board but was naturally smaller among Republicans than among other citizens because their ratings of the president were already so high. The war was also the subject of its own rally, visible in Figure 6.1. Assessing support for the war is complicated by the diversity of questions pollsters use to measure it;

FIGURE 6.1
Popular Support for War in Iraq (All Question Wordings)

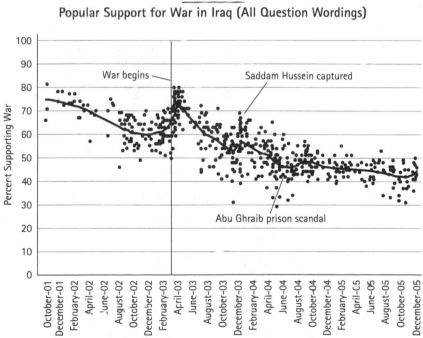

Source: See footnote 22.

different questions elicit different levels of support, and the frequency with which each is asked has changed with evolving circumstances (a list of these questions may be found in Appendix A). Figure 6.1 displays the most general picture by including data from multiple variants of 11 different questions, with a smoothing line summarizing the noisy trend.[22] As discussed in Chapter 5, support for invading Iraq was high right after September 11, when most Americans suspected Saddam Hussein was at least partly responsible. It declined as the focus turned to Osama bin Laden and Afghanistan, revived late in the administration's campaign to portray Iraq as a threat requiring immediate action, rose sharply after the onset of hostilities, and peaked in April just before the president's "Mission Accomplished" moment on the carrier.

The same trends appear when we examine separately those questions asked frequently enough for temporal comparisons (Figure 6.2). Notice that support for the war is highest when respondents are asked if the U.S. had done the "right thing" in taking military action in Iraq or if the U.S. had made a mistake going to war.[23] It is as much as 20 points lower (sometimes in the same survey) when people are asked if the results of the war were worth the cost in American lives; the falloff is smaller, however, if removing Saddam is specifically mentioned as the result.

---

[22] These data are from national polls sampling all adults or registered or likely voters conducted by the CBS News/New York Times, ABC News/Washington Post, NBC News/Wall Street Journal, Los Angeles Times, Gallup, Pew Center for the People and Press, Newsweek, CNN/Time, Fox News, Quinnipiac College, National Annenberg Election Study, Knowledge Networks, and Democracy Corps polls reported at http://www.pollinreport.com or at the polling outfit's website. The various question wordings are shown in the Appendix.

[23] These questions typically read, "Do you think the United States did the right thing in taking military action against Iraq, or should the U.S. have stayed out?" and "In view of the developments since we first sent our troops to Iraq, do you think the United States made a mistake in sending troops to Iraq, or not?"

FIGURE 6.2
Popular Support for War in Iraq (Various Question Wordings)

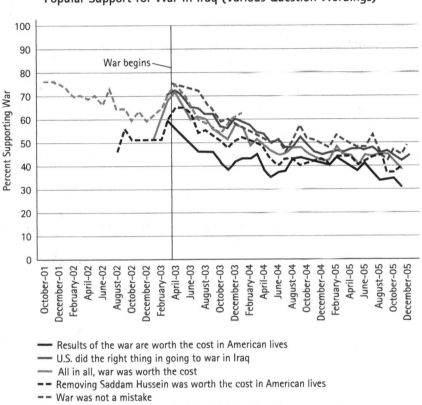

- ⎯ Results of the war are worth the cost in American lives
- ⎯ U.S. did the right thing in going to war in Iraq
- ⎯ All in all, war was worth the cost
- -- Removing Saddam Hussein was worth the cost in American lives
- -- War was not a mistake
- -- Approve of military action to remove Saddam Hussein

Although the levels differ, the trends in responses to these questions are generally parallel and consistent with the overall picture in Figure 6.1.

Expressed levels of support for the war depend not only on how the question is worded, but also on the context in which it is asked. One reason for the observed rally in support for the war once it began was the change in what the question then meant to some respondents. The average level of support expressed in response to comparable sets of questions asked in March 2003 (from 25 surveys in all) rose from 65 percent before the 20th to 74 percent after.[24] But the results of an ABC News/*Washington Post* survey taken just after the war started suggest that at least some of the increase reflected patriotic support for U.S. troops rather than approval of the war itself. Table 6.1 presents the evidence. About 20 percent of respondents who said they supported "having gone to war" also said they supported the troops but not

TABLE 6.1
Support for the War and Support for U.S. Troops in Iraq, March 20, 2003 (Percentages)

	REPUBLICANS	INDEPENDENTS	DEMOCRATS	ALL
"As you may know, the United States went to war with Iraq last night. Do you support or oppose the United States having gone to war?"				
Support having gone to war	90.4	73.1	51.2	72.6
Oppose having gone to war	8.2	23.7	46.8	25.2
"Would you say you support the troops and you support the Bush Administration's policy on Iraq, or would you say you support the troops, but you oppose the Bush Administration's policy on Iraq?"				
Support both troops and policy	79.3	52.0	38.5	56.3
Support troops but oppose policy	9.8	20.5	12.1	14.6

SOURCE: ABC News/*Washington Post* Poll, March 2003, ICPSR version. Horsham, PA: Taylor Nelson Sofres intersearch [producer], 2003. Ann Arbor, MI: Inter-university Consortium for Political and Social Research [distributor], 2003.

[24] These questions ask if respondents "support" or "approve of" military action in some format.

the administration's policy on Iraq. This response was more common among independent (28 percent) and Democratic (24 percent) than among Republican (11 percent) war supporters.

THE WIDENING PARTISAN
DIVIDE ON IRAQ

Unfortunately, this follow-up question was not repeated in later surveys, but it is likely that support for the war policy itself grew during March and April with the military successes of U.S. forces on the ground, the remarkably low American casualties,[25] and televised images of joyful Iraqis toppling Saddam's statue. Thereafter, however, the continuing chaos, insurgency, and loss of American and allied lives began to sap support for the war, particularly among Democrats and independents. Figure 6.3 displays the data and Lowess-smoothed trends in support for the Iraq War, disaggregated by party. The gap between Republicans and Democrats narrowed slightly in the first month of the war then grew steadily wider for the following 18 months. Figure 6.4 shows that the partisan gap widened regardless of how the war support question was posed. It reaches an average of about 63 percentage points in the last quarter of 2004 before narrowing a bit to an average of about 58 percent during 2005. A *Los Angeles Times* Poll question asking whether Bush had made the right decision to go to war, in light of the CIA's report that Saddam had no WMD and no active program to produce them, generated the

---

[25] American military deaths in Iraq in March and April 2003 numbered 139; there were also 33 British fatalities; the number of wounded is listed as 542. See http://icasualties.org/oif/ (accessed July 19, 2005).

FIGURE 6.3
Party Identification and Support for the Iraq War (All Question Wordings)

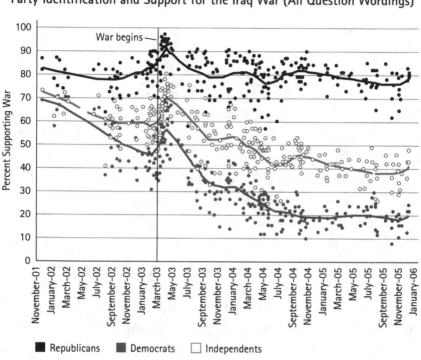

Republicans   Democrats   Independents

widest divergence of any survey, with 90 percent of Republicans but only 10 percent of Democrats answering "yes."[26]

These data stand in striking contrast to comparable data from previous wars. Figures 6.5 to 6.9 display the partisan differences in support for U.S. involvement in five earlier conflicts using the same scale as Figure 6.4. In none is the gap anywhere near as large as it is for the Iraq War. Ironically, it is lowest in the most controversial of these engagements, Vietnam, averaging only 5 percentage

---

[26] *Los Angeles Times Poll Alert*, Study #510, October 25, 2004.

FIGURE 6.4
Partisan Differences in Support for the Iraq War

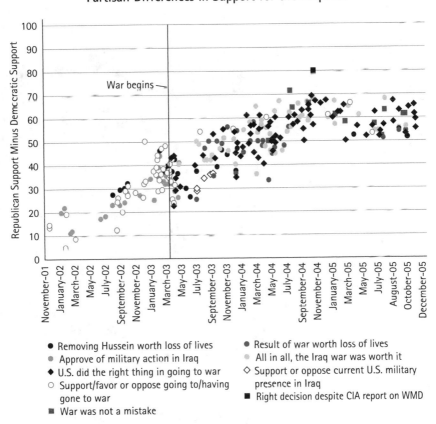

- ● Removing Hussein worth loss of lives
- ● Approve of military action in Iraq
- ◆ U.S. did the right thing in going to war
- ○ Support/favor or oppose going to/having gone to war
- ■ War was not a mistake

- ● Result of war worth loss of lives
- ● All in all, the Iraq war was worth it
- ◇ Support or oppose current U.S. military presence in Iraq
- ■ Right decision despite CIA report on WMD

points. The Vietnam War certainly divided Americans, but the division was within rather than between the parties, and support for the war declined at about the same pace for partisans in all categories. Party differences on Korea, Kosovo, and Afghanistan were of a similar magnitude, averaging 11–12 points, although the absolute levels of public support differed widely between these conflicts; for example, the action in Afghanistan was supported by

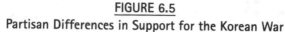

FIGURE 6.5
Partisan Differences in Support for the Korean War

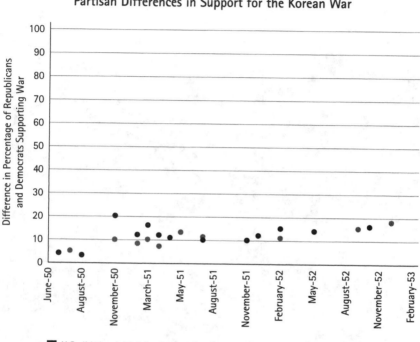

■ U.S. did the right thing by entering Korean War
■ U.S. did not make a mistake in defending South Korea

Sources: John E. Mueller, *War, Presidents, and Public Opinion* (New York: John Wiley & Sons, 1973), p. 270, and the 1952 NES Survey.

an average of 96 percent of Republicans and 84 percent of Democrats, much higher numbers than for any other conflict.[27]

Bush's father's Gulf War produced the widest partisan gap in this set. Still, the party difference averages only 20 points and never exceeds 31 points (and this observation, from a question about whether the respondent approves of sending troops to

---

[27] Partisan differences in support for military actions in Lebanon and Grenada in 1983 during the first Reagan administration averaged about 14 points, and differences on military action in Somalia in 1992–1993 during the first Bush and Clinton administrations average about 5 points, in the selection of CBS News/*New York Times* and ABC News/*Washington Post* polls I checked for these events.

FIGURE 6.6
Partisan Differences in Support for the Vietnam War

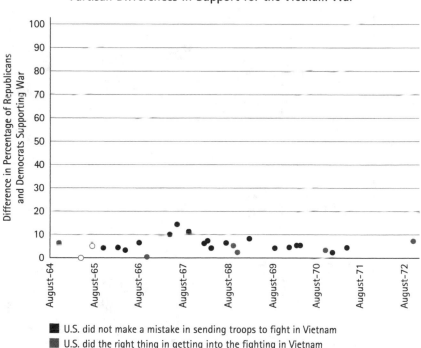

U.S. did not make a mistake in sending troops to fight in Vietnam
U.S. did the right thing in getting into the fighting in Vietnam
U.S. should have become involved in Southeast Asia

Sources: John E. Mueller, *War, Presidents, and Public Opinion* (New York: John Wiley & Sons, 1973), p. 271, and the 1964–1972 NES Surveys.

defend Saudi Arabia, appears anomalously large). Ole Holsti, comparing these to earlier war support data, notes "rather substantial partisan differences,"[28] but they seem in retrospect quite modest compared to the partisan differences on Iraq. As we would expect, the party of the president determines whether support for military action is higher among Republicans or Democrats; in only 5 of the 167 observations displayed in these five charts do

[28] Ole R. Holsti, *Public Opinion and American Foreign Policy*, revised edition (Ann Arbor: University of Michigan Press, 2004), p. 174.

FIGURE 6.7
Partisan Differences in Support for the Persian Gulf War

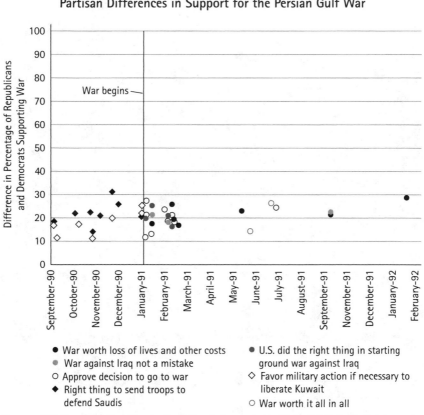

● War worth loss of lives and other costs   ● U.S. did the right thing in starting
● War against Iraq not a mistake   ground war against Iraq
○ Approve decision to go to war   ◇ Favor military action if necessary to
◆ Right thing to send troops to   liberate Kuwait
    defend Saudis   ○ War worth it all in all

Sources: CBS News/*New York Times* polls; Gallup Polls reported in Ole R. Holsti, *Public Opinion and American Foreign Policy*, Revised Edition (Ann Arbor: University of Michigan Press, 2004), p. 173, and ABC News/*Washington Post* polls.

opposing party identifiers support the action at higher levels than the president's party.[29]

For reasons discussed in Chapter 5, partisan divisions on the Iraq War were already substantial before it began. These narrowed in the early weeks of the war but soon widened again when

---

[29] This occurs in 3 of the 28 observations for Vietnam and in 2 of the 50 observations for Kosovo.

FIGURE 6.8
Partisan Differences in Support for Military Action in Kosovo

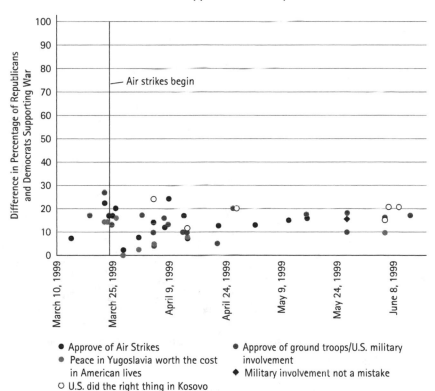

- Approve of Air Strikes
- Peace in Yugoslavia worth the cost in American lives
- U.S. did the right thing in Kosovo
- Approve of ground troops/U.S. military involvement
- Military involvement not a mistake

Sources: CBS News/*New York Times*, Harris, Gallup, NBC News/*Wall Street Journal*, *Newsweek*, CNN/*Time*, ABC News/*Washington Post*, and Pew Center for the People and Press polls.

the war's principal premises could not be confirmed and partisans responded to that emerging story quite differently. Most Republicans either refused to recognize that neither WMD nor a 9/11 connection could be substantiated or accepted the substitute justifications offered by the administration after the fact, whereas Democrats, with no inclination to miss the message or adopt new reasons for support, grew increasingly opposed to the war—and increasingly disaffected with President Bush.

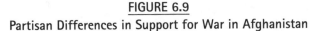

FIGURE 6.9
Partisan Differences in Support for War in Afghanistan

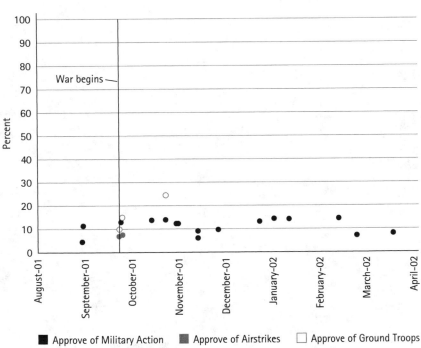

■ Approve of Military Action   ■ Approve of Airstrikes   □ Approve of Ground Troops

Sources: CBS News/*New York Times*, ABC News/*Washington Post*, *Los Angeles Times*, and Gallup Polls.

BELIEF IN THE WAR'S PREMISES

Before the war, a large majority of Americans regardless of party believed Saddam was hiding WMD, and about half thought he was personally involved in 9/11. After the war, as time passed and the search for WMD and an al Qaeda connection continued to turn up nothing of substance, these beliefs became less common, but neither rapidly or completely (Figure 6.10). Right after the war, about a third of the public thought WMD had actually been found; a year later, nearly 20 percent still clung to this misconcep-

FIGURE 6.10
Belief that Saddam Hussein was Personally Involved in 9/11 and Iraq had WMD

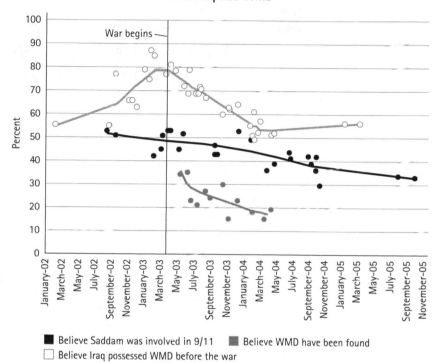

■ Believe Saddam was involved in 9/11   ■ Believe WMD have been found
□ Believe Iraq possessed WMD before the war

Sources: ABC News/*Washington Post*, CBS News/*New York Times*, Gallup, Harris, PIPA/Knowledge Networks, *Newsweek*, Fox News, and CNN polls.

tion. The proportion who believed Iraq possessed WMD (even if they had not been found) also declined, but more than a year after the war a majority held this view and continued to do so through March 2005 despite all the official reports to the contrary. The belief that Saddam had a hand in September 11 also declined, but not very steeply; more than 30 months after Baghdad had fallen, about a third of the public still thought he had been involved.

The data suggest that the main reason public opinion did not respond more sharply to postwar revelations is that they did surprisingly little to shake the faith of Republicans in Bush's original case for the war, even after the administration had officially abandoned it. Among Republicans, belief in Saddam's WMD peaked at 95 percent just before the war and has not fallen below 69 percent since; it actually increased a bit in the first quarter of 2005, averaging 81 percent and leaving a partisan gap on this question of about 46 points (Figure 6.11). In February 2003, 79 percent of Democrats had thought Saddam possessed WMD;

FIGURE 6.11
Does (Did) Iraq Possess WMD?

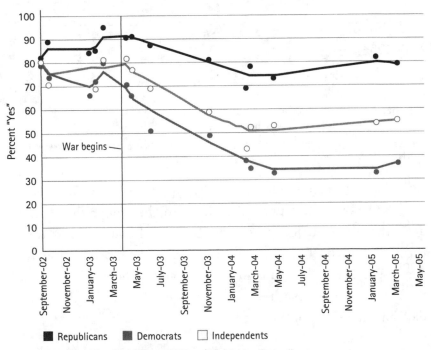

Sources: CBS News/*New York Times*, ABC News/*Washington Post* polls.

FIGURE 6.12
Was Saddam Hussein Personally Involved in 9/11?

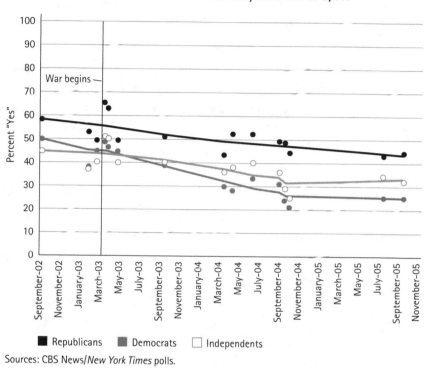

Republicans   Democrats   Independents

Sources: CBS News/*New York Times* polls.

within about 15 months, that figure had fallen to 33 percent. Belief in Saddam's involvement in 9/11 also declined less steeply among Republicans than among Democrats or independents (Figure 6.12). From a peak right after Baghdad fell in April 2003 through October 2005, it dropped from 65 to 44 percent among Republicans, from 51 to 32 percent among independents, and from 49 percent to 25 percent among Democrats in these surveys.

Rather more surprising than these partisan differences is the extent to which even Democrats continued to believe the allegations long after well-publicized official reports had found no evidence to support them and the president and his administration had ostensibly disavowed them. Evidently, Saddam's evil reputation continued to predispose Americans to think the worst and to ignore or forget exculpatory information. A March 2005 ABC News/ *Washington Post* Poll documented its staying power; a majority of Americans continued to believe that solid evidence has been found proving that Iraq had directly supported al Qaeda (21 percent) or at least to suspect such a connection (39 percent).[30] One important source of these continuing misperceptions is no doubt the Bush administration's continued use of artfully insinuating rhetoric. On March 19, 2005, the second anniversary of the U.S. invasion, the president put it this way: "We knew of Saddam Hussein's record of aggression and support for terror. We knew of his long history of pursuing, even using, weapons of mass destruction, and we know that September 11 requires our country to think differently."[31] With rhetoric like this—lumping together in two sentences Saddam Hussein, September 11, terror, and WMD—no wonder most Americans thought the administration was still advancing claims unsubstantiated by its own investigations despite having officially abandoned them.[32]

The simplest interpretation of the patterns of belief in the two major justifications for the war is that Americans of all political persuasions tended to have strong prior beliefs about Saddam Hussein that led them to assume his complicity in September 11 and possession of illicit WMD, while Republicans also had a strong prior faith in the president and thus in his administration's version of Iraqi realities. Both sets of priors have kept subsequent revela-

---

[30] ABC News/*Washington Post* Poll, March 10–13, 2005, analyzed by author.
[31] Richard Boudreaux, "Insurgent Attacks Continue 2 Years After the U.S. Invasion," *Los Angeles Times*, March 20, 2005, A4.
[32] For evidence on this point, see Table 7.2 in Chapter 7.

tions from fully undermining beliefs in the war's original rationales, with their compound effect among Republicans explaining
why the president's partisans have been especially slow to
acknowledge new, discordant information.

Republicans also were more likely to believe that the Iraq War
was justified even if WMD were never found, and this view
became more predominant after the war. In a survey taken on the
day the war started, 31 percent of Republicans thought the war
"was justified only if the U.S. finds conclusive evidence that Iraq
has weapons of mass destruction," while 63 percent said it was
justified even if conclusive evidence of WMD was not found. Ten
days later the proportion of Republicans expressing the first view
had dropped to 11 percent while the proportion expressing the
second had risen to 83 percent, a pattern that was repeated in surveys taken in December 2003 and February 2004. Among Democrats, the proportion saying the war was justified even without
conclusive evidence of WMD stood at 46 percent on March 20,
rose to 56 percent ten days later, but by February of 2004 had
dropped to 35 percent; the proportion of Democrats saying the
war was unjustified with or without WMD rose from 9 percent to
25 percent over the same period.[33] Asked in January 2005,
whether the war "will have been worth the loss of American lives
and other costs" if WMD are never found, 69 percent of Republicans said it still would be worth it, compared to 42 percent of
independents and just 16 percent of Democrats.[34]

---

[33] ABC News/*Washington Post* polls, March 20, April 3, and December 18–21, 2003, and February
10–11, 2004, analyzed by author. Among independents, the proportion saying WMD were not necessary to justify the war went from 50 percent on March 20, 2003, to 63 percent in April 2003 before
declining to 58 percent in February 2004; the proportion saying the war was not justified regardless
went from 6 percent to 19 percent.
[34] CBS News/*New York Times* Poll, January 14–18, 2005, at http://www.cbsnews.com/htdocs/CBSNews_
polls/bush_back.pdf (accessed February 10, 2005).

FIGURE 6.13

Beliefs About WMD and Saddam's Involvement in 9/11 and Belief that Invading Iraq was the Right Thing to Do (April 2004)

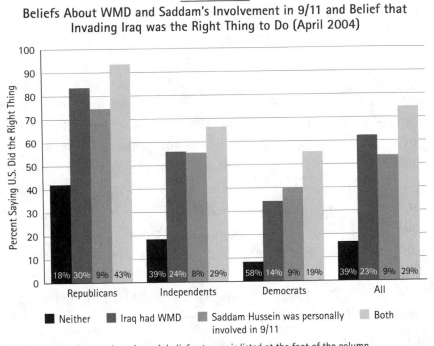

Note: Percent of respondents in each belief category is listed at the foot of the column.
Source: CBS News/*New York Times* Poll, April 23–27, 2004.

Belief in the primary rationales for the Iraq War had a potent effect on ex-post as well as ex-ante support for the venture. Figure 6.13 replicates Figures 5.4 and 5.5 from the previous chapter, except that support for the war is measured by whether the respondent believes the "the United States did the right thing in taking military action against Iraq."[35] A comparison of Figures 5.5 and 6.13 is instructive. The proportion of Republicans who still accepted as factual at least one of the war's primary justifications declined

---

[35] In Tables 5.4 and 5.5, the question was, "do you approve or disapprove of the United States taking military action against Iraq to try to remove Saddam Hussein from power?"

between February 2003 and April 2004, but by only 15 percentage points, from 97 percent to 82 percent. The decline was much larger among Democrats (down 43 points, from 85 percent to 42 percent), with independents falling in between (down 24 points, from 85 percent to 61). This is important, because support for the war is much higher among respondents who believed either premise than among those who believed neither. Note, however, that partisan differences in thinking the war was the right thing to do remain substantial even controlling for belief in the war's premises.

A naïve reading of these results would be that popular support for the war depended largely on misinformation and would have collapsed had the public absorbed the reports of U.S. investigators who had conceded that, despite their best efforts, they had found no convincing evidence of WMD or complicity of Saddam Hussein in September 11. But by itself, the widespread resistance to this information suggests that, for many Americans, particularly Republicans, support for the war came first and the specifics of the factual case for it were of decidedly secondary importance. If forced to recognize that the war's original premises were faulty, they would be willing, as loyal followers of President Bush, to accept the others he proffered. Thus, for example, most Republicans continued to accept the Bush administration's contention that Iraq posed a threat that could not be contained but required immediate action (Figure 6.14); the proportion taking this view exceeded 80 percent just after the war began and never fell below 60 percent thereafter. Forty-six percent of Democrats shared this opinion at the onset of the war but by October 2004, just 12 percent continued to do so; belief in the need for immediate action also lost ground among independents, falling from over 50 percent to below 30 percent.

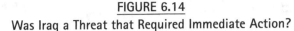

FIGURE 6.14
Was Iraq a Threat that Required Immediate Action?

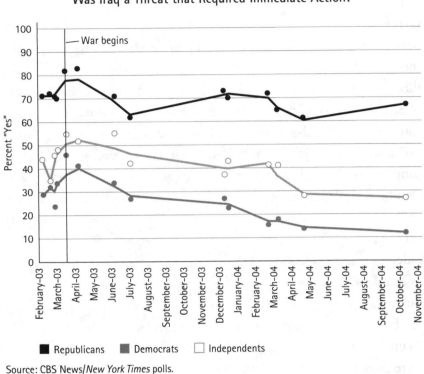

Source: CBS News/*New York Times* polls.

Opinions on this question are of course strongly related to support for the war; among respondents in the six most recent surveys used to create Figure 6.14 who agreed with the administration's position, 97 percent of Republicans, 94 percent of independents, and 88 percent of Democrats said the United States did the right thing in invading Iraq; among respondents who thought the threat could have been contained or that Iraq was not a threat at all, the respective figures were 53 percent, 34 percent, and 20 percent.

Finally, Republicans were also more receptive than other citizens to the idea that the invasion had done Iraqis a welcomed humanitarian service, and unfolding events in Iraq did little to change that perception. On six occasions between April 2003 and June 2004 the CBS News/*New York Times* poll asked respondents if they thought most Iraqis felt "grateful to the United States for getting rid of Saddam Hussein" or "resentful of the United States for being in Iraq right now." In April 2003, the balance of "grateful" to "resentful" responses among Republicans was 63 percent to 18 percent; in June 2004, the balance was 61 percent to 27 percent. The views of Democrats, in contrast, shifted substantially over time; their ratio of "grateful" to "resentful" responses fell from 48:34 in the first survey in the series to 25:59 percent in the last (the shift among independents was from 49:27 to 39:42).[36] In June 2005, 92 percent of Republicans but only 57 percent of Democrats said they thought the Iraqis were better off because of the war.[37]

In sum, revelations that its main premises were faulty did little to undermine Republicans' support for the Iraq War because they were less likely than other Americans to get the message, less likely to withdraw support if they did, and more willing to adopt alternative rationales emphasized after the fact by the Bush administration. Among independents and Democrats, however, support for the war depended heavily on its original justifications and thus fell as these became increasingly untenable. As a consequence, on virtually every question concerning the premises, necessity, wisdom, and effect of going to war in Iraq, partisan differences grew very large.

---

[36] CBS News/*New York Times* polls, April 26–27, 2003, and June 23–27, 2004.
[37] ABC News/*Washington Post* poll, June 23–26, 2005.

THE PRESIDENT'S CREDIBILITY

Public reactions to the war and its aftermath amplified partisan differences in assessments of George W. Bush. The administration's campaign justifying the war, before and after Iraq was invaded, put Bush's credibility on the line. Republicans' faith was barely shaken, while the proportion of Democrats who thought the president was "honest and trustworthy" fell from 54 percent in July 2002 to less than 30 percent in polls taken in 2004 and to only 22 percent in November 2005 (Figure 6.15). Only a small

FIGURE 6.15
Is George W. Bush Honest and Trustworthy?

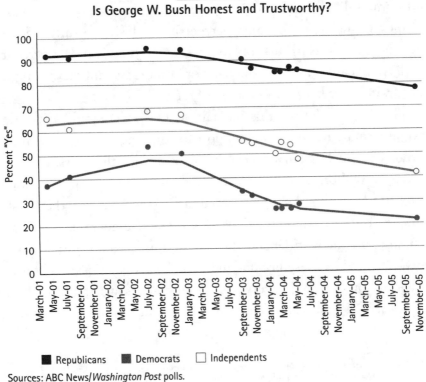

Republicans   Democrats   Independents

Sources: ABC News/*Washington Post* polls.

minority of Republicans believed that the administration intentionally exaggerated the evidence that Iraq possessed WMD, and that minority did not grow over time (Table 6.2). Among Democrats, 68 percent had reached the opposite conclusion by August 2003, and by June 2005, 81 percent had done so. Few Republicans believed that the Bush administration had intentionally misled the public in making the case for invading Iraq; very large majorities continued to think that the administration had actually believed its own alarums, although the data show some erosion, from 88 percent taking this position in July 2004, to 80 percent in November 2005. In contrast, the share of Democratic identifiers who believed the administration had intentionally misled the public grew from 69 percent to 81 percent over this period.

Opinions on administration's sincerity in arguing for military action in Iraq are, not surprisingly, strongly related to evaluations of Bush's overall performance as president. For example, among the Democrats in the June 26, 2005, poll who thought they had been intentionally misled, 6 percent approved and 93 percent disapproved of Bush's performance; among the Republicans who thought the administration told what it believed to be true, 98 percent approved, 1 percent disapproved. Among the minority of trusting Democrats, 41 percent approved, 51 percent disapproved; among the minority of distrusting Republicans, 28 percent approved, 72 percent disapproved. The presidential evaluations of 87 percent of independents (and likewise of all respondents) were consistent with their views on whether the administration had been deliberately deceptive. The Republicans' nearly unwavering belief in the Bush administration's good faith in making its case for war, and the widespread sentiment among Democrats that they had

TABLE 6.2
The Bush Administration's Honesty in Making the Case for the War in Iraq (Percent)

	REPUBLICANS	DEMOCRATS	INDEPENDENTS	ALL
I. Before the war began, do you think the George W. Bush administration did or did not intentionally exaggerate its evidence that Iraq had weapons of mass destruction?				
August 7–11, 2003				
Yes, did exaggerate	27	68	54	50
No, did not exaggerate	69	27	43	46
February 10–11, 2004				
Yes, did exaggerate	24	78	55	54
No, did not exaggerate	73	17	40	42
March 4–7, 2004				
Yes, did exaggerate	30	76	56	55
No, did not exaggerate	66	23	42	43
June 26, 2005				
Yes, did exaggerate	23	81	60	52
No, did not exaggerate	76	18	38	41
II. Do you think the Bush administration intentionally mislead the American public about possible links between Iraq and the Al Qaeda terrorist group, or do you think the administration told the American public what it believed to be true about this?				
June 17–20, 2004				
Intentionally misled the American public	14	71	55	48
Told what it believed to be true	83	27	44	40
III. In making its case for war with Iraq, do you think the George W. Bush administration told the American public what it believed to be true, or intentionally misled the American public?				
July 22–25, 2004				
Intentionally misled the American public	11	69	44	42

continued

TABLE 6.2 *(continued)*				
	REPUBLICANS	DEMOCRATS	INDEPENDENTS	ALL
Told what it believed to be true	88	28	52	55
August 26–29, 2004				
Intentionally misled the American public	9	69	43	40
Told what it believed to be true	86	30	55	57
March 10–13, 2005				
Intentionally misled the American public	13	66	45	43
Told what it believed to be true	86	32	53	55
June 26, 2005				
Intentionally misled the American public	23	76	54	52
Told what it believed to be true	77	25	46	47

SOURCE: ABC News/*Washington Post* polls.

been duped, thus contributed directly to the record partisan differences in assessments of the President Bush.

THE RELIGIOUS FACTOR

The campaign to generate support for the Iraq War, both before and after the invasion, followed the Bush administration's archetypal script (see Chapter 4). Once Bush had determined that "regime change" in Iraq was the "right thing for the American people," he and his associates undertook a coordinated effort to assert claims about the danger Saddam posed that were gauged to win the widest possible public backing for a preemptive strike. Uncertainties about the factual grounds for these claims were discounted, suppressed, or ignored.[38] Doubts raised by intelligence analysts were never allowed to dilute the campaign's message. Facts were deployed selectively and sometimes misleadingly; rhetoric made connections when evidence did not. When neither WMD nor an Iraqi alliance with al Qaeda could be documented, the administration revised its rationale without acknowledging the change (attacking critics who pointed out the revision as "revisionists"[39]—irony is not part of the Bush administration mindset) or admitting any second thoughts.[40] It's not surprising that in response to these developments, public support for the war and the president who initiated it would diminish. The puzzle is why it did not diminish more than it did. After all, had Bush proposed to spend hundreds of billions of dollars and sacrifice the lives of more than 2,100 American troops (and many times that number of Iraqi civilians) to replace Saddam's regime with the shaky democratic experiment under way amid near-chaotic conditions more than two-and-a-half years later, it is hard to imagine that more than a tiny minority of the public or Congress would have come on board. Yet the tenacious loyalty of most Republicans staved off the political debacle threatened by unfolding events in Iraq, and the most tenacious of all were white conservative Christians.

---

[38] James P. Pfiffner, "Did President Bush Mislead the Country in His Arguments for Going to War in Iraq?," *Presidential Studies Quarterly* 24 (March 2004): 25–46.
[39] Condoleezza Rice, for example, made this specific allegation on *Face the Nation* in June 2003; see Fritz, Keefer, and Nyhan, *President's Spin*, p. 217.
[40] The effort to discredit former ambassador Joseph Wilson, a critic of the administration's use of evidence regarding Iraq's alleged pursuit of nuclear material in Niger led to the exposure of Wilson's wife as a CIA agent and a lengthy and still unresolved investigation into who in the administration may have leaked this information.

National surveys conducted for news media do not ask the extensive array of questions designed to produce the detailed typologies of religious identity and beliefs developed by scholars of religion and politics (see Chapter 2), but with some regularity they have asked respondents whether they consider themselves born-again or Evangelical Christians. Surveys also sometimes inquire about frequency of attendance at religious services and about self-described degrees of religiosity. Viewing these admittedly imperfect data, it is striking how powerfully religious identities have shaped people's responses to Bush and his Iraq policies, particularly after the original case for the war unraveled. Table 6.3 revisits some of the questions examined earlier in this chapter but breaks down responses by whether or not respondents are white, born-again and/or Evangelical Christians. The entries are averages across the polls listed in the table's footnotes, all of which were conducted in August 2003 or later.

Observe, first, that white, born-again/Evangelical Christians were more likely to continue to accept the original grounds for war: Iraq had WMD and that Saddam Hussein was complicit in September 11. They were also much more likely to think that Bush did not exaggerate the evidence that Iraq possessed WMD and did not mislead the public in making the case for war. Their retrospective support for the war was also significantly higher. Although the effects of religious identity on these opinions are in many instances larger for Democrats and independents than for Republicans, the aggregate impact within these groups is limited because on average in these surveys only about 13 percent of Democrats and 17 percent of independents were white born-again/

TABLE 6.3
Religious Identity and Opinions on the Iraq War (Percent)

	REPUBLICANS	INDEPENDENTS	DEMOCRATS	ALL
Believe Iraq possessed WMDs[1]				
White, born-again/ Evangelical Christians	81.5	57.2	31.5	65.3
Others	63.4	45.2	36.3	45.0
Believe Saddam Hussein was involved in September 11[2]				
White, born-again/ Evangelical Christians	57.9	51.3	42.6	53.3
Others	49.3	35.6	32.6	38.5
Believe Bush did not exaggerate evidence of WMDs[3]				
White, born-again/ Evangelical Christians	75.8	53.7	33.2	60.2
Others	66.4	37.8	20.2	37.3
Believe Bush did not intentionally mislead the public in making the case for war [4]				
White, born-again/ Evangelical Christians	89.7	69.0	37.8	71.5
Others	78.8	47.3	26.7	47.0
Believe U.S. did the right thing going to war in Iraq[5]				
White, born-again/ Evangelical Christians	88.3	66.6	38.9	71.0
Others	78.4	51.0	29.3	49.9
Believe Iraq War was worth the cost[6]				
White, born-again/ Evangelical Christians	72.4	45.5	25.5	54.3
Others	63.2	34.0	16.1	34.6

[1] CBS News/*New York Times* polls, February 12–15 and April 23–27, 2004.

[2] CBS News/*New York Times* polls, September 28–October 1, 2003, March 30–April 1, April 23–27, June 23–27, and September 12–16, 2004.

[3] ABC News/*Washington Post* polls, August 7–11, 2003, March 4–7, 2004 and June 26, 2005.

[4] ABC News/*Washington Post* polls, August 26–29, 2004, March 10–13 and June 26, 2005.

[5] CBS News/*New York Times* polls, December 14–16 and 21–22, 2003; February 12–15, March 10–14, March 30–April 1, April 23–27, May 20–23, June 23–27, August 15–18, and September 12–16, 2004.

[6] CBS News/*New York Times* polls, September 28–October 1, December 14–16 and 21–22, 2003; January 12–15, March 10–14, March 30–April 1, April 23–27, May 20–23, and June 23–27, 2004.

Evangelical Christians. In contrast 34 percent of Republicans were in this category, and they offered by far the highest average levels of support for the war and faith in the president's sincerity about its rationales. They are also the most steadfast and, uniquely among subgroups, showed virtually no fall-off in support for the war or the president over time. This is evident in Figures 6.16 to 6.18, which display the annual averages in support for the war, approval of Bush's handling of Iraq, and approval of his overall job performance, broken down by party and religious identity (the number of polls used to compute these averages are in parentheses). The opinions of white born-again/Evangelical Christian Republicans have so

FIGURE 6.16
Party, Religious Identity, and Support for the Iraq War

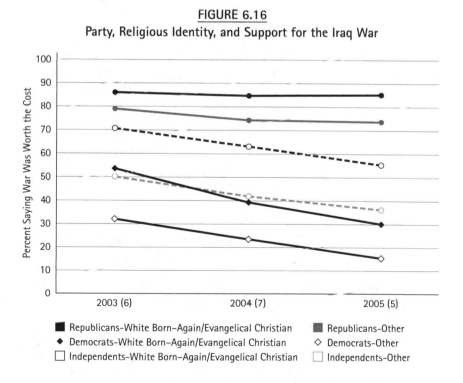

■ Republicans-White Born–Again/Evangelical Christian   ■ Republicans-Other
♦ Democrats-White Born–Again/Evangelical Christian   ◇ Democrats-Other
☐ Independents-White Born–Again/Evangelical Christian   ☐ Independents-Other

FIGURE 6.17
Party, Religious Identity, and Approval of George W. Bush's Handling of Iraq

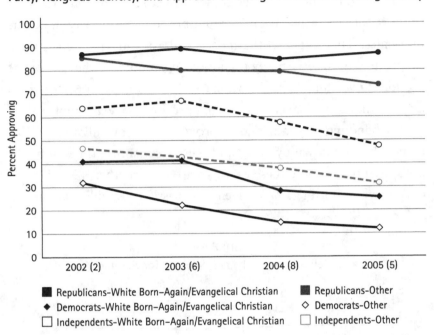

Republicans-White Born–Again/Evangelical Christian   Republicans-Other
Democrats-White Born–Again/Evangelical Christian   Democrats-Other
Independents-White Born–Again/Evangelical Christian   Independents-Other

far been nearly impervious to postwar events and revelations; they remain close to unanimous in approving Bush's performance as president. Even in the November 2005 ABC News/*Washington Post* poll that found Bush at his lowest point to that date, support from this segment of his constituency was only a few points below the averages for 2005 in these three charts.

The combination of imperturbable conservative Christian Republicans and increasingly disaffected Democrats who were not white, born-again Christians clearly contributed to increasing partisan differences on the president and the war. By 2005, the opinions

FIGURE 6.18
Partisanship, Religious Identity, and Presidential Approval

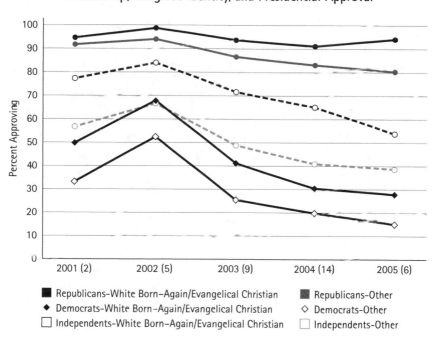

- ■ Republicans-White Born-Again/Evangelical Christian
- ■ Republicans-Other
- ◆ Democrats-White Born-Again/Evangelical Christian
- ◇ Democrats-Other
- □ Independents-White Born-Again/Evangelical Christian
- □ Independents-Other

expressed by these two polar groups (together comprising about 40 percent of the public) differed by averages of 71 percentage points on whether the war was worth the cost, 75 points on Bush's handling of the war, and 79 points on his overall performance.

MULTIVARIATE ANALYSES

Because party, ideology, and religiosity are interrelated and also linked to other demographic variables, multivariate analysis is useful to clarify their relationship with opinions on the president and the war. Table 6.4 reports regression estimates[41] of the effects of party identification, ideology, religious attendance, identity as a born-again Christian, education, sex, and race on belief in Bush's candor about the case for war and in Saddam Hussein's alleged WMD, complicity in 9/11, and connections with al Qaeda.[42] The data are from CBS News/*New York Times* polls taken in April and June of 2004.[43] Partisanship and ideology strongly influenced acceptance of claims that were central to the case for war and assessments of Bush's candor in making that case, as we would expect. But the equations indicate that, controlling party and ideology, the respondent's religious identity and behavior also affected these beliefs; more frequent religious service attendees and white born-again Christians were significantly more likely to think Bush was candid about the case for war and to accept his rationales for it. African Americans were more skeptical about Bush's candor but not necessarily about circumstances used to justify the war. Education and gender were unrelated to opinions of Bush's candor, but skepticism about the case for war increased with education, and men were less likely than women to be persuaded by it.

The dependent variables in these equations are of course intimately related. If belief about Bush's candor is added to the other

---

[41] The dependent variables are all trichotomous, so regression is not the most appropriate mode of analysis; I replicated all of the equations using ordered logit which is appropriate, and got the same substantive results. I report the regression results here because the coefficients have a more intuitive interpretation.
[42] Beliefs about Bush's candor are measured by the question, "In his statements about the war in Iraq, do you think George W. Bush is telling the entire truth, is mostly telling the truth but hiding something, or mostly lying?" The coding was: mostly telling the truth = 1, hiding something = 0, mostly lying = −1. The other three dependent variables are scored 1 if respondent believed Saddam had WMD, was complicit in 9/11 or had ties to al Qaeda, 0 if uncertain, −1 if the respondent did not believe these things. Party identification is 1 if Republican, 0 if independent, −1 if Democrat; ideology is 1 if conservative, 0 if moderate, −1 if liberal. Education is 1 if high school or less, 2 if some college, 3 if college graduate, 4 if postgraduate degree. Religious attendance is 1 if weekly or nearly weekly, 0 if occasionally, −1 if never. White, born-again Christian, African American and male are all 1 if respondent is in the category, 0 otherwise.
[43] The first and third equations combine data from the April 23–27, 2004, and the June 23–27, 2004, polls; the second includes only the April data, the fourth only the June data.

TABLE 6.4
Sources of Beliefs about George Bush's Candor and the Case for War in Iraq

	BUSH'S CANDOR	IRAQ HAD WMD	SADDAM WAS INVOLVED IN 9/11	SADDAM WORKED WITH AL QAEDA
Party identification	.266***	.310***	.198***	.271***
	(.018)	(.040)	(.028)	(.038)
Ideology	.125***	.197***	.115***	.208*
	(.019)	(.044)	(.031)	(.041)
Religious attendance	.106***	.127**	.093**	.038
	(.019)	(.044)	(.031)	(.042)
White, Born-Again Christian	.114**	.106	.104†	.233**
	(.035)	(.077)	(.055)	(.077)
Education	−.012	−.123***	−.174***	−.098***
	(.013)	(.029)	(.020)	(.028)
Male	.022	−.180**	−.277***	−.094
	(.026)	(.058)	(.041)	(.056)
African American	−.212***	−.126	.125†	.181†
	(.044)	(.098)	(.068)	(.093)
Constant	−.009	.388***	.298***	.206**
	(.034)	(.074)	(.053)	(.074)
Adjusted R^2	.27	.18	.12	.14
Number of cases	1808	926	1864	938

NOTE: Standard errors are in parentheses;†$p < .10$, *$p < .05$, **$p < .01$, ***$p < .001$, one-tailed test.

equations, it is the single strongest predictor of acceptance of the war's premises, and when these beliefs in turn are added to the first equation, they are strong independent predictors of faith in Bush's candor.

The effect of these variables on support for the war is shown in Table 6.5. Regardless of how the war support question is worded, the results are consistent, and they are reiterated when a war support index (created by summing the three responses and dividing by three to make the scales comparable) becomes the dependent variable. Beliefs about Bush's candor had the largest impact of any variable, but beliefs about WMD and Saddam's involvement in 9/11 also had large and independent effects on war support.[44] So did party identification and ideology. Religious identity and behavior, in contrast, were unrelated to war support once these other variables were controlled, indicating that the effects of religiosity on support for the war were registered indirectly, through faith in Bush and trust in his case for going to war. Men were substantially more likely than women to back the war, a familiar result[45]; African Americans were less likely to support it, but only at the generous $p < .10$ level of significance. Education affected only responses to the question of whether the war was worth the cost.[46]

CONCLUSION

The decision to invade Iraq was without question the most important of George W. Bush's presidency, and people's reactions to the venture powerfully shaped—as they were shaped by—their

---

[44] Responses to the al Qaeda question have a similar effect under these controls, but they are not included here because the question was never asked in a survey that also included both the WMD and 9/11 questions.

[45] Cf. John E. Mueller, War, Presidents, and Public Opinion (New York: John Wiley and Sons, 1972), pp. 146–147; John Mueller, Policy and Opinion in the Gulf War (Chicago: University of Chicago Press, 1994), pp. 42–43.

[46] I also tested for the effects of marital status and age in all of these equations and, finding none, have omitted these variables from the analysis.

TABLE 6.5
Effects of Beliefs about George Bush's Candor and his Case for the War on Support for the War in Iraq

	WORTH THE COST	RIGHT THING	NOT A MISTAKE	SUPPORT INDEX
Bush's Candor	.314***	.306***	.353***	.325***
	(.048)	(.046)	(.049)	(.040)
Iraq had WMD	.199***	.243***	.125***	.189***
	(.032)	(.031)	(.033)	(.026)
Saddam involved in 9/11	.074*	.208***	.170***	.151***
	(.031)	(.030)	(.032)	(.025)
Party identification	.232***	.211***	.279***	.241***
	(.038)	(.037)	(.039)	(.032)
Ideology	.114**	.145***	.107**	.122***
	(.040)	(.039)	(.041)	(.033)
Religious attendance	.047	.036	.034	.040
	(.039)	(.037)	(.040)	(.032)
White, Born-Again Christian	.033	−.059	−.007	−.011
	(.068)	(.066)	(.070)	(.056)
Education	.068**	.006	-.012	.020
	(.026)	(.025)	(.027)	(.022)
Male	.148**	.140**	.173**	.154***
	(.052)	(.051)	(.054)	(.043)
African American	−.109	−.153†	−.157†	−.140†
	(.088)	(.085)	(.090)	(.073)
Constant	−.457***	−.034	−.055	−.182***
	(.067)	(.065)	(.069)	(.056)
Adjusted R^2	.34	.42	.36	.46
Number of cases	902	902	902	902

NOTE: Standard errors are in parentheses; †p < .10, *p < .05, **p < .01, ***p < .001, one-tailed test.

assessments of the president and his administration. The war divided the public along party lines far more than any other U.S. military engagement undertaken since World War II, widening partisan differences in evaluations of Bush. Republicans, especially the conservative Christian faction, remained overwhelmingly supportive of the president and the war; Democrats and, to a lesser extent, independents, became increasingly disenchanted with both. The result when Bush sought reelection in 2004 was the most partisan presidential contest in the past half-century, which is the topic of the next chapter.

CHAPTER 7

The 2004 Election: Mobilized Bases, Reinforced Divisions

President George W. Bush's triumphal airborne visit to the *Abraham Lincoln*, with the "Mission Accomplished" banner as backdrop, was immediately tagged "the mother of all photo ops" and widely acknowledged (not least by dispirited Democrats) as a superbly crafted beginning to Bush's campaign for reelection. The rally inspired by the swift military success gave Bush an advantage of about 15 percentage points over a generic Democratic opponent in polls taken from late March through May 2003, and he did even better matched against named Democrats.[1] The gravest decision of his administration,

---

[1] In 14 relevant generic polls reported for the period, Bush's advantage ranged from 10 to 28 points, with an average of 15.2 and a standard deviation of 4.5. See http://www.pollingreport.com/wh04gen6.htm (accessed August 2, 2005).

Bush's order to invade Iraq, had carried political as well as military risks; as Colin Powell warned the president, *"this will become the first term."*[2] In the spring of 2003 it looked like Bush's risk-taking would be richly rewarded come November 2004. A year later, with U.S. soldiers still dying, the violent insurgency showing no signs of fading, lawlessness continuing to plague ordinary Iraqis, and no evidence of WMD or operational Iraqi links to al Qaeda, the war threatened to become an electoral liability instead of an asset. The "Mission Accomplished" banner became an embarrassment, and administration spokesmen claimed for months that the carrier crew had been responsible before finally admitting that the idea and the sign had come from the White House.[3]

As we saw in Chapter 6, public reactions to the war became increasingly determined by party identification, with Republicans remaining overwhelmingly supportive and Democrats and, to a lesser extent, independents, growing disenchanted with the venture. Partisan differences on the war intensified partisan differences in opinions on the president, setting the stage for the most partisan national election in at least 50 years. The election itself, in turn, magnified party differences on the war and the president as the campaigns focused public attention on the both; it is no coincidence that in all of the relevant figures in earlier chapters, partisan differences peaked around election day.[4]

---

[2] Bob Woodward, *Plan of Attack* (New York: Simon and Schuster, 2004), p. 150; emphasis in the original.
[3] David Paul Kuhn, "'Mission Accomplished' Revisited," CBS News, April 30, 2004, at http://www.cbsnews.com/stories/2004/04/30/politics/main614998.shtml (accessed August 8, 2005).
[4] See, for example, Figures 1.2, 1.5, 1.6, 1.7, 1.8, 6.3, and 6.4.

THE DEMOCRATIC NOMINATION

The growing disenchantment with the war and the president among Democrats strongly influenced the course of events leading to the nomination of Senator John Kerry to challenge Bush in the general election. Ordinary Democrats became increasingly eager to defeat Bush, and as signs that this might actually be possible grew more encouraging, the desire to nominate the Democrat with the best chance of winning also grew.

The initial beneficiary of Democrats' anger with Bush and his war was Vermont governor Howard Dean. In contrast to the other top-tier contenders, Dean, like Bush in 2000, was a Washington outsider who had no track record in national politics and could freely attack the president and his policies without the taint of having cooperated with him in the past. Among his rivals, senators Joseph Lieberman, John Edwards, John Kerry, and Representative Richard Gephardt had all voted to authorize the Iraq War; only Senator Bob Graham had voted against the authorizing resolution, and he did so because, he said, "It was too limited, too weak, and too timid."[5] Thus Dean was able to separate himself from the pack by vigorously criticizing Bush and the war in a way that resonated among grass-roots Democrats, especially the activists most likely to take part in nomination politics. Dean's pioneering internet fundraising effort not only raked more than $40 million for his campaign, it also

---

[5] Michael Barone and Richard E. Cohen, eds., *The Almanac of American Politics 2004* (Washington, D.C.: National Journal, 2003), p. 386. Second-tier Democratic candidates Dennis Kucinich, Carole Mosely Braun, and Al Sharpton also attacked Bush and his war, but none of them was regarded as viable.

exposed the breadth and depth of opposition to the president among politically active Democrats.

Dean's rise in 2003 from obscurity to a lead in the Democratic horse-race polls (Figure 7.1) served as an object lesson to his rivals, who began cranking up their own rhetorical assaults on the administration. Once Dean began to lose his comparative advantage on this dimension, his liabilities drew more attention. Democrats sought not only a candidate who would go after Bush, but also

FIGURE 7.1
Democrats' Preference for Democratic Presidential Candidates

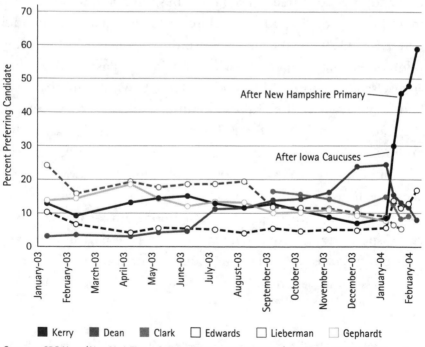

Sources: CBS News/*New York Times*, Gallup, *Newsweek*, ABC News/*Washington Post*, NBC News/
Wall Street Journal, Fox News, Pew Center for the People and Press, IPSOS, Quinnipiac University,
and Harris Polls reported at pollingreport.com during 2003 and 2004.

one who could actually beat him. Dean's inexperience and brashness made him a comparatively risky choice, and his antiwar rhetoric[6] reminded some veteran Democrats of George McGovern's disastrous candidacy in 1972. Many Democrats seemed to recognize that, with terrorism a top public concern, no candidate could defeat Bush who was not credible on issues of national security and homeland defense. Perhaps more to the point, no Democrat could win without surviving Bush campaign's inevitable charge (regardless of who was nominated) that he would not be tough enough in dealing with America's terrorist enemies. Hence we see the boomlet for General Wesley Clark, a former NATO commander, immediately after he announced his candidacy on September 17 (Figure 7.1). The boomlet faded as Clark's inexperience in electoral politics took its toll, leaving the mantle of military toughness to John Kerry, a decorated Vietnam veteran.

Kerry's astonishing comeback in the polls after his campaign for the nomination had been on the verge of collapse stands as the most eloquent testimony to Democrats' eagerness to defeat Bush. Kerry's support among Democrats was in single digits in most polls conducted during the three months preceding the Iowa caucuses; some surveys had even taken him off the list of candidates they asked about. But Kerry made an all-out effort in Iowa and managed to come out on top in the January 19 caucuses by mobilizing veterans and firefighters and sharpening his attacks on Bush while Dean and Gephardt were busy flailing one

---

[6] For example, his arguably accurate but ill-timed statement that "the capture of Saddam has not made America safer" while the United States was celebrating the event; see Associated Press, "Dean: America Not Safer After Saddam's Capture," December 16, 2003, at http://www.foxnews.com/story/0,2933, 105789,00.html (accessed August 3, 2005).

another.[7] Both his military record and long experience in national politics helped Kerry persuade Iowa's activists that he was their best bet for November. According to a survey of caucus attendees, he attracted the most support from those for whom the most important quality was "right experience" or "can beat Bush."[8] The primal scream Dean unloosed during his televised Iowa concession speech reinforced doubts about his electability, moving many Democrats into Kerry's camp and ending Dean's hopes of winning the nomination.

Kerry's victory in Iowa had a dramatic impact on Democrats across the nation, more than tripling his support virtually overnight and contributing to his victory in New Hampshire eight days later, which in turn inspired another sharp rise in the share of Democrats backing his nomination (Figure 7.1).[9] Most ordinary Democrats were apparently ready to rally behind whichever of the contenders was best positioned to defeat Bush; their problem was figuring out who it was. Thus they responded en masse when the Iowa Democrats sent a clear coordinating signal: "It's Kerry."[10] People knew little more about Kerry after New Hampshire than they had before Iowa—other than that he had won in both states. Yet that was enough: In the three *Newsweek* polls taken before the Iowa caucuses, an average of 52 percent of Democrats viewed Kerry favorably, 16 percent

[7] Barry C. Burden, "The Nominations: Technology, Money, and Transferable Momentum," in Michael Nelson, ed., *The Elections of 2004* (Washington, D.C.: Congressional Quarterly Press, 2005), p. 29.

[8] Dean did best among those for whom the most important quality was "takes strong stands," Edwards, best among those for whom it was "cares about people." See "Entrance Polls: Iowa," at http://www.cnn.com/ELECTION/2004/primaries/pages/epolls/IA/index.html (accessed August 2, 2005).

[9] These were substantially larger increases than usually follow victories in Iowa and New Hampshire; for a fuller discussion of this phenomenon, see Samuel L. Popkin, *The Reasoning Voter* (Chicago: University of Chicago Press, 1991), pp. 117–129.

[10] This is not a message they could have gotten from polls; on average in the preprimary horse-race comparisons, Kerry matched up no better against Bush than did his major rivals. See http://www.pollingreport.com/wh04gen.htm (accessed February 3, 2004).

unfavorably, and 32 percent didn't know enough to say; after the New Hampshire primary, the figures were 82 percent favorable, 7 percent unfavorable, and 11 percent unable to say.[11] In subsequent primaries, Kerry remained the overwhelming choice among Democrats for whom the most important candidate attribute was, "He can defeat George W. Bush."[12]

The Democrats' backing of Kerry was, then, more about Bush than about Kerry and remained so throughout the campaign. An election involving a sitting president is always largely a referendum on his performance, but Bush's centrality to the vote decision in 2004 was unique. As Figure 7.2 shows, a majority of Kerry supporters reported throughout the year that their vote would be more against Bush than for Kerry. This is unusual. Early in 1992, for example, 60 percent of Bill Clinton's supporters said that their vote would be more against George H.W. Bush than for Clinton, but by October only 36 percent gave this response. Early in 1996, 68 percent of Dole supporters said they were mainly anti-Clinton but only half were so by the end of the campaign. The proportion of Bush supporters who said their vote would be more for Bush than against Kerry—averaging about 80 percent and changing little over the course of the campaign—was also considerably higher than the equivalent percentage for previous presidents (Clinton, 66 percent, and Bush senior, 60 percent).[13]

---

[11] Polls reported at http://pollingreport.com/k.htm (accessed August 5, 2005).

[12] Gary Langer, with Dalia Sussman, Cheryl Arnedt, and Maureen Michaels, "Electability Helps John Kerry, But Without Southern Comfort," ABC Exit Poll News Analysis, February 2, 2004, at http://abcnews.go.com/images/pdf/JrTuesdayAnalysis.pdf (accessed August 4, 2005); Gary Langer, Dave Morris, and Dalia Sussman, "The Electability Train Runs South," ABC Exit Poll News Analysis, March 11, 2004, at http://abcnews.go.com/images/pdf/VA-TNExitPollAnalysis.pdf (accessed August 4, 2005); "How Kerry Won, and the National Impact," Gallup Poll Analysis, January 28, 2004, at http://www.gallup.com/poll/releases/pr040128.asp?Version=p (accessed January 30, 2004).

[13] Pew Center for the People & the Press, Survey Report, October 31, 2004, pp. 10–11, at http://people-press.org/reports/display.php3?ReportID=232 (accessed August 4, 2005).

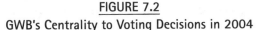

FIGURE 7.2
GWB's Centrality to Voting Decisions in 2004

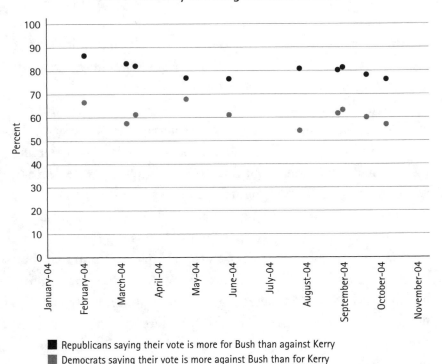

■ Republicans saying their vote is more for Bush than against Kerry
■ Democrats saying their vote is more against Bush than for Kerry

Source: Pew Research Center for the People and the Press Survey Report, October 31, 2004, at
http://peoplepress.org/reports/display.php3?ReportID=232, (accessed August 4, 2005).

AN AVALANCHE OF MONEY

Kerry's momentum after New Hampshire carried him to a quick
victory in the quest for the nomination; he clinched on March 9,
the same day as Bush, who had faced no primary opposition at
all. Kerry also began to run ahead of Bush in some horse-race
polls. The tight race and high stakes in a sharply polarized context
attracted an avalanche of campaign money for both campaigns.
Both Bush and Kerry had rejected public money for the primary

campaign and so were permitted to raise and spend unlimited sums until after the conventions. Their efforts and, more to the point, the political passions they were able to tap, attracted an astonishing amount of campaign money, mostly from individual donors. Between them, the Bush and Kerry campaigns raised $847 million, nearly twice as much as was raised by the Gore and Bush campaigns in 2000 ($426 million) and nearly three times as much as the Clinton and Dole campaigns raised in 1996 ($288 million).[14] Independent expenditures, made mostly by national party organizations, amounted to another $245 million, and separate campaigns by so-called 527 groups (named after the section in the tax code applying to them) spent another $424 million, most of it on the presidential races.[15] Bush's prodigious fundraising prior to 2004—his campaign had nearly $100 million on hand as the election year began[16]—had been expected to give him a huge financial advantage over his Democratic opponent, but Democrats eager to defeat Bush filled Kerry's coffers and, with the additional help of 527 groups, his campaign enjoyed rough financial parity with the president's, an altogether remarkable achievement.

THE WAR IN THE CAMPAIGNS

Although by no means the only issues, Bush's response to 9/11 in general and his invasion of Iraq in particular were inevitably a

---

[14] "2004 Presidential Campaign Financial Activity Summarized," Federal Election Commission news release, February 3, 2005.
[15] Steve Weissman and Ruth Hassan, "BCRA and the 527 Groups," in Michael Malbin, ed., *The Election After Reform: Money, Politics and the Bipartisan Campaign Reform Act* (Lanham, MD: Rowman and Littlefield, forthcoming 2006).
[16] "George W. Bush-Campaign Finances," at http://www.gwu.edu/~action/2004/bush/bushfin.html (accessed August 5, 2005).

major focus of the 2004 presidential campaigns. The pivotal disagreement between Bush and Kerry concerned whether the war in Iraq was central to the war on terrorism or a distraction from it. Bush insisted that, regardless of mistaken assumptions about Saddam's WMD or complicity in 9/11, the war in Iraq was central to the war on terrorism, whereas Kerry argued that the Iraq invasion had unwisely taken resources from the pursuit of Osama bin Laden and other al Qaeda terrorists who, unlike Iraq, had actually attacked the United States. In the first televised debate between the two, for example, Kerry asserted that "Iraq is not . . . the center of the war on terror. The center is Afghanistan" and criticized Bush's decision to divert forces from there to Iraq. When Bush reiterated that "Iraq is a central part of the war on terror," Kerry came back with "Iraq was not even close to the center of the war on terror before the president invaded it."[17]

These opposed views were increasingly echoed by partisans in the general public as the campaigns progressed (Figure 7.3). From the war's beginning onward, large majorities of Republicans continued to accept Bush's argument that the Iraq War was a major part of the war on terrorism, and only a small and shrinking minority thought it was separate from the war on terrorism.[18] Democrats increasingly took the latter position, and by the end of the campaign, more than 70 percent of them were doing so. Thus the gap between partisans on this issue widened steadily, reaching about 60 points in the final quarter of 2004. Both candidates,

---

[17] "Transcript: First Presidential Debate," September 30, 2004, at http://www.washingtonpost.com/wp-srv/politics/debatereferee/debate_0930.html#c (accessed August 5, 2005).
[18] The third alternative was to consider the Iraq War a "minor" part of the war on terrorism; this option was taken by an average of 17 percent of Republicans, 14 percent of Democrats, and 18 percent of independents in these polls.

then, spoke persuasively to (or for) their own supporters on this issue but made no headway with those on the other side. Independents tended to move with Democrats on this question, going from an average of 49 percent "major part" and 34 percent "separate" in polls taken in the spring of 2003 to an average of 51 percent "separate" and 32 percent "major part" in polls taken close to the election. But among independents, this shift was completed by April 2004, before the campaigns had a chance to register. When, after a hiatus of many months, this question was asked again in the summer of 2005, partisan positions had changed little from where they had been at the end of the campaign, even though by then the United States was indeed battling a new cohort of terrorists in Iraq.

There is, of course, no mystery about why Bush would want Americans to believe that Iraq was the central front in the war on terror despite the lack of evidence that it had anything to do with the attacks of 9/11. Not only did the argument offer a justification for a decision whose consequences were growing ever more problematic, but it subordinated a domain in which Bush's approval was declining—his handling of Iraq—to the domain where his approval was highest—his handling of the war on terror (recall Figure 4.4). Surveys consistently found majorities believing that Bush would be better than Kerry in dealing with the terrorist threat, and to the degree that he could focus the electorate's attention on terrorism rather than Iraq or convince people that the Iraq War and the war on terrorism were one and the same, he stood to benefit. The issue was an awkward one for Kerry; while arguing that America had been misled into a war that was unwise and unnecessary, he also had to say what he would do about it now that

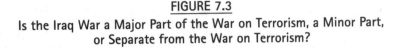

FIGURE 7.3
Is the Iraq War a Major Part of the War on Terrorism, a Minor Part, or Separate from the War on Terrorism?

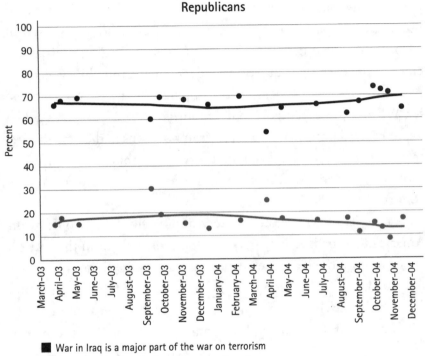

Republicans

■ War in Iraq is a major part of the war on terrorism
■ War in Iraq is separate from the war on terrorism

Colin Powell's Pottery Barn analogy ("You break it, you own it."[19]) had become all too apt. The consequences of abandoning Iraq before order had been restored and Iraqis had established some viable form of self-government were potentially disastrous now that the notion of Iraq as a center of anti-American Islamic terrorism had become a self-created reality. For all his criticism of the

---

[19] Woodward, *Plan of Attack*, p. 150.

FIGURE 7.3 *(continued)*

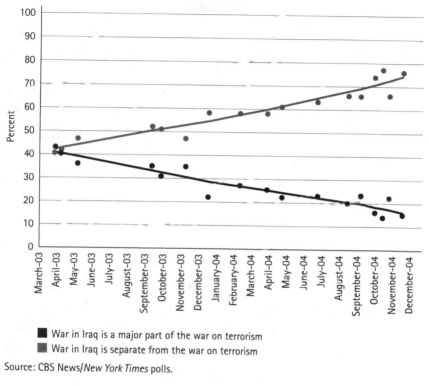

Democrats

■ War in Iraq is a major part of the war on terrorism
■ War in Iraq is separate from the war on terrorism

Source: CBS News/*New York Times* polls.

decision to invade Iraq, Kerry's ideas about what to do there now were hard to distinguish from the president's.

OPINION LEADERSHIP

The partisan reactions to the question of whether the Iraq War was central to or a distraction from the war on terrorism illustrate a feature of the relationship between public opinion and questions of war and peace that is heightened during presidential elections as the competing campaigns increase public awareness, articulate partisan cues, and accentuate partisan divisions: opinion leadership. Students of public opinion have long argued that, regarding most public issues, and especially issues pertaining to foreign affairs, a large majority of ordinary citizens are usually inattentive, uninformed, and thus largely dependent on cues from opinion leaders in deciding how to respond to survey questions. On matters of war and peace, national political elites are supposed to be the predominate cue-givers. Public responses depend on the interactive effects of predispositions and political awareness. The more politically aware an individual, the more likely he or she is to get the message; the more consistent the message is with an individual's predispositions, the more likely it is to be accepted. This creates a distinction between "mainstream" and "polarization" effects, which have predictably different observable consequences. When a unified political elite sends a consistent message, then the more politically aware people are, the more likely they are to receive and accept the message (mainstream effect). When political leaders are divided by party (or ideology) on an issue, then greater the level of awareness, the more polarized the responses as individuals follow the messenger they are predisposed to heed (polarization effect).[20]

Although my emphasis in this book has been on polarization, reactions to events during the Bush administration registered in the 2004 American National Election Study offer illustrations of both kinds of effects. Military action in Afghanistan received strong bipartisan support in Congress and among political leaders

[20] John R. Zaller, *The Nature and Origins of Mass Opinion* (Cambridge, UK: Cambridge University Press, 1992), Chapter 6.

more generally. No important figure criticized the decision to use U.S. forces to pursue al Qaeda and drive its Taliban allies from power during the presidential campaign. Elite communications about the action thus generated "mainstream" effects, as Figure 7.4 demonstrates. The more politically aware the respondent,[21] the more likely he or she was to believe that the war in Afghanistan was worth the cost. Support for the action increases with awareness

FIGURE 7.4
Political Awareness and Support for Military Action in Afghanistan

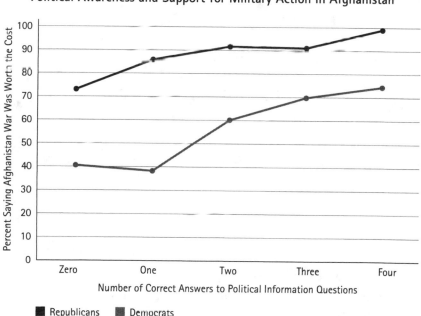

Note: Respondents were asked to identify Dick Cheney, Tony Blair, Dennis Hastert, and William Rehnquist.

Source: 2004 American National Election Study.

---

[21] Following Zaller, I use a simple information battery to measure political awareness. The NES asked respondents to identify Dick Cheney, Tony Blair, Dennis Hastert, and William Rehnquist. Awareness is measured by the number of correct answers. The distribution was zero, 15 percent; one, 22 percent; two, 35 percent; three, 20 percent; and four, 8 percent.

FIGURE 7.5
Political Awareness and Support for the Iraq War

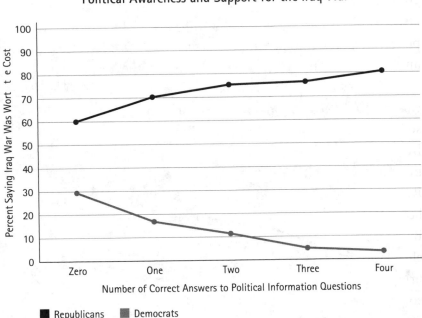

Republicans   Democrats

Note: Respondents were asked to identify Dick Cheney, Tony Blair, Dennis Hastert, and William Rehnquist.
Source: 2004 American National Election Study.

regardless of party, with the most informed respondents showing the smallest partisan difference.

By the 2004 election, in contrast, Bush, Kerry, and other political leaders had become divided along party lines by the Iraq War, and consequently, belief that the venture was worth the cost was related positively to political awareness among Republicans but negatively to it among Democrats (Figure 7.5). Polarization thus increased steeply with political awareness; the least aware Republicans and Democrats were 31 points apart, the most informed,

77 points apart. Partisan differences of opinion regarding the effects of the Iraq War on the terrorist threat to the United States also become greater with awareness (Figure 7.6). Among the least politically informed, party differences on this question are slight; among the most aware, they are huge.

Opinion leadership was of course in evidence long before the election. George W. Bush was without question the dominant source of cues that shaped Republicans' opinions about the war in Iraq, but he was backed by Secretary of State Colin Powell (more broadly esteemed than the president) as well as virtually all Republicans of stature in or out of government. Ordinary Republicans thus had little inducement to break ranks, and they did not. But this raises the question of why solidarity among Republican elites was so high and why it generally survived the collapse of the original case for war. It is at least conceivable that the president's continued rock-solid support among ordinary Republicans had something to do with it: Republican opinion leaders who dissented might well have lost that status.

Among Democrats as well, it is not obvious that opinion leaders always led rather than followed. As noted in Chapter 4, many Democrats in Congress had supported the war, including all prospective presidential aspirants. Indeed, Bush got a larger share of House and Senate Democrats' votes for his war against Iraq than his father had gotten for his Gulf War 12 years earlier, even though support for the second war was significantly lower among ordinary Democrats than it had been for the first.[22] Public delight

---

[22] In five polls taken during the month before the start of the Gulf War in 1991, an average of 53 percent of Democrats supported going to war, with support dipping below 50 percent in only one survey; in 15 polls taken during the month before the start of the Iraq War in 2003, an average of 44 percent Democrats backed going to war, and in only four polls did support for the war exceed 50 percent.

FIGURE 7.6

As a Result of the United States Military Action in Iraq, Do You Think the Threat of Terrorism Against the U.S. has Increased, Decreased, or Stayed the Same?

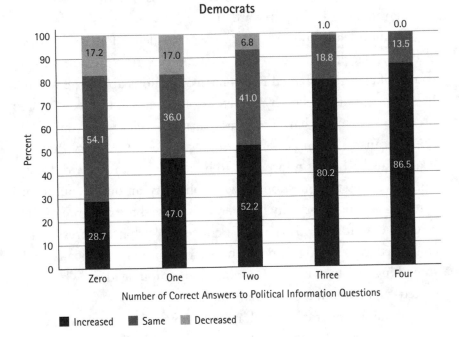

with the American and British forces' rapid success and low casualties in the first month of the war discouraged vocal criticism or expressions of second thoughts among Democratic leaders for a considerable time afterward. No one was sorry to see Saddam gone, and, as noted in Chapter 6, criticizing the invasion invited the retort, "So, you'd rather have Saddam still in power?" Eventually, the persistent chaos and continuing violence, combined with the failure to find WMD or evidence of Saddam's involvement in 9/11, greatly reduced the political risks of questioning the

FIGURE 7.6 *(continued)*

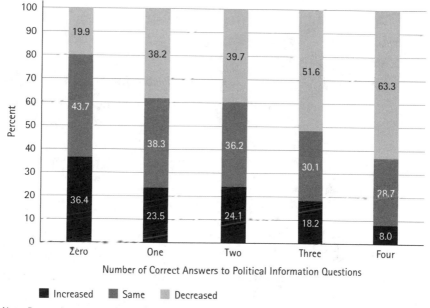

Republicans

Note: Respondents were asked to identify Dick Cheney, Tony Blair, Dennis Hastert, and William Rehnquist.
Source: 2004 American National Election Study.

war's wisdom or necessity, but it was not until Howard Dean found a receptive audience among ordinary Democrats for criticism of Bush's war that it became common among Democratic leaders. Just as in the case of Clinton's impeachment, mainstream Democratic politicians appeared to be taking cues from their followers, not vice versa.[23]

---

[23] Gary C. Jacobson, "Public Opinion and the Impeachment of Bill Clinton," in Philip Cowley, David Denver, Andrew Russell and Lisa Harrison, eds., *British Elections and Parties Review* 10 (London: Frank Cass, 2000): 1–31.

RATIONAL IGNORANCE?

Opinion leadership can be considered a species of delegation: rationally ignorant citizens with neither the time nor inclination to understand the complexities of, for example, foreign policy delegate that task to trusted agents who supposedly command the necessary expertise. Ideally, this process enables people to achieve cognitive efficiency (substituting cheap, simple cues for complex, expensive information) while reaching the same conclusions they would have reached had they been as fully informed as their agents.[24] For the process to work benignly, people are supposed to use freely available information to monitor their agents, compelling them to maintain a minimum level of credibility lest they lose the trust essential to their status as opinion leaders. The example of the Iraq War, however, shows that opinions may be remarkably impervious to discordant information because people with strongly held prior beliefs are so ready to miss or deny the point.

As noted in Chapter 6, the absence of evidence that Iraq possessed WMD and that Saddam Hussein had been involved in 9/11 did not prevent large numbers of Americans, particularly Republicans, from continuing to believe both of these rationales for the war. But a survey taken during the 2004 presidential campaign revealed a level of resistance to dissonant information more striking still. The PIPA/Knowledge Networks Poll conducted in September and October asked not only respondents' opinions about the war's main rationales, but also strictly factual questions

---

[24] Arthur Lupia and Mathew D. McCubbins, *The Democratic Dilemma: Can Citizens Learn What They Need to Know?* (Cambridge, UK: Cambridge University Press, 1998), Chapter 5.

TABLE 7.1
Bush and Kerry Supporters' Beliefs Concerning Justifications for the Iraq War (Percent)

	BUSH SUPPORTERS	KERRY SUPPORTERS
Iraq had actual weapons of mass destruction or a major program for developing them.	72	26
Iraq was directly involved in 9/11	20	8
Iraq gave al-Qaeda substantial support	55	22
Total	75	30
Experts believe now that before the war:		
Iraq had WMD	56	18
Were divided on the question	18	23
Iraq did not have WMD	23	56
Duelfer Report (ordered by President Bush) said:		
Iraq had WMD	19	7
Iraq had major program to build WMD	38	16
Total	57	23
9/11 Commission Report concluded:		
Iraq was directly involved in 9/11	13	7
Iraq gave al-Qaeda substantial support	43	20
Total	56	27

SOURCE: "The Separate Realities of Bush and Kerry Supporters," the PIPA/Knowledge Networks Poll: The American Public on International Issues, at http://zzpat.tripod.com/cvb/pipa.html, accessed November 24, 2004.

about what well-publicized official reports had concluded about their accuracy after the war. Differences between Bush and Kerry supporters were predictably huge on the two basic justifications involving WMD and an al Qaeda connection (see the first two questions in Table 7.1). But substantial differences also persist on strictly factual questions, with Republicans displaying a startling capacity to get them wrong: Only 23 percent recognized that the consensus of experts analyzing postwar information was that Iraq had not possessed WMD immediately prior to the war; 57 percent and 56 percent, respectively, got the Duelfer Report and the 9/11 Commission conclusions exactly backwards. Kerry supporters appear to be considerably better informed, but then the information was more consistent with their biases, and it is notable that from 23 to 41 percent of them also got the factual questions wrong.

Even knowing what was in the official reports did not necessarily convince Bush supporters that the war's premises had been wrong; 18 percent who acknowledged that the Duelfer Report, ordered by Bush from the CIA, had concluded that Iraq had no WMD and no active program to produce them still believed otherwise.[25] The survey also pointed to the explanation for Bush supporters' continuing acceptance of the discredited rationales: They thought that the Bush administration was sticking to them (Table 7.2). Large majorities of Bush and Kerry supporters alike believed that the administration was still asserting claims that the official reports, ostensibly accepted by administration officials as accurate, had concluded were unfounded; smaller majorities even believed that the administration was saying it had found clear evidence of WMD and a close al Qaeda connection. The strong, bipartisan agreement on these perceptions suggests that if the Bush administration had indeed admitted that the original premises for the war were faulty, it had done it so quietly and equivocally that

---

[25] "The Separate Realities of Bush and Kerry Supporters," the PIPA/Knowledge Networks Poll: The American Public on International Issues, 4, at http://zzpat.tripod.com/cvb/pipa.html (accessed November 24, 2004).

TABLE 7.2

Perceptions of the Bush Administration's Statements Concerning the Justifications for the Iraq War (Percent)

	BUSH SUPPORTERS	KERRY SUPPORTERS
Believe Bush administration is saying that prior to war:		
Iraq had WMD	63	58
Iraq had major program to build WMD	19	24
Total	82	82
Believe Bush administration is saying that:		
Iraq was directly involved in 9/11	19	25
Iraq gave al-Qaeda substantial support	56	49
Total	75	74
Believe Bush administration is saying U.S. has found clear evidence Saddam Hussein worked closely with al-Qaeda	55	52

SOURCE: "The Separate Realities of Bush and Kerry Supporters," the PIPA/Knowledge Networks Poll: The American Public on International Issues, at http://zzpat.tripod.com/cvb/pipa.html, accessed November 24, 2004.

most of the public had missed the concession. Bush's categorical refusal to admit any mistake regarding the war, at least in public, thus probably helped keep his supporters loyal at the same time it reinforced the distrust and disdain of his opponents.

The survey also discovered high levels of misinformation among Bush supporters on other questions concerning the war and the election. Only 31 percent (compared to 74 percent of Kerry supporters) recognized that a majority of people surveyed in other countries opposed the Iraq War; only 9 percent acknowledged that most people in other countries preferred Kerry to Bush for president (69 percent of Kerry supporters got it right); 17 percent (compared to 86 percent of Kerry supporters) realized that world opinion of the United States had been made worse by Bush's foreign policies. Bush and Kerry supporters did indeed seem to exist in "separate realities"[26] as a majority of Bush's supporters misperceived facts to keep their beliefs consonant with a commitment to the president. I will have more to say about this in Chapter 9.

MOBILIZING VOTERS

The deep partisan divisions inherited and reinforced by the Bush administration shaped the strategies of both the Bush and Kerry campaigns, which put far more effort into mobilizing their own partisans than in reaching out to the dwindling number of uncommitted voters or to partisans on the other side. Both succeeded. Kerry's campaign actually surpassed its mobilization targets, producing a total Democratic vote 16 percent higher than Al Gore's 2000 total. But Bush's campaign did even better, increasing his total vote by 23 percent over 2000 and delivering him a narrow but unambiguous victory—50.7 percent of the popular vote to Kerry's 48.3 percent.[27] Its most important targets were religious conservatives, notably the five million conservative Christians who Karl Rove, the president's chief strategist, estimated had sat out the 2000 election.[28] Skirting the rules restricting partisan

---

[26] Ibid., pp. 6–7.

[27] According to the 2004 American National Election Study, presidential turnout among Democratic identifiers was 5 percentage points higher than in 2000 and 5.5 points higher than their 1972–2000 average; among Republican identifiers, it was 8.5 points higher than in 2000 and 7.5 points higher than their 1972–2000 average. NES respondents always overstate their participation, but this does not prevent valid cross-election comparisons. The 2004 data are from the American National Election Study advance release (VERSION 20050131, Jan 31, 2005), available at http://www.umich.edu/~nes/studyres/download/nesdatacenter.htm. Earlier data are from the NES 1948–2002 Cumulative Data File available at the same site.

[28] Jackie Calmes and John Harwood, "Bush's Big Priority: Energize Conservative Christian Base" *Wall Street Journal*, August 30, 2004, at http://online.wsj.com/article/0,SB109382546485804152,00.html (accessed August 31, 2004).

activities by tax-exempt organizations, the campaign organized "friendly congregations" and encouraged clergy to carry the Bush message. It was often an easy sell, for many conservative Christian groups were already organizing their own campaigns for the president. Their efforts were aided by the Massachusetts Supreme Court decision giving that state's same-sex couples the right to marry, to which Bush had responded by backing a constitutional amendment outlawing the practice.[29]

Republican strategists were of course fully aware of how strongly religious conservatives had bonded with the president. A pre-election ABC News/*Washington Post* survey that, in addition to the usual political and demographic questions, asked respondents to classify themselves as "very religious," "somewhat religious," or "not religious" revealed just how totally the very religious Republicans (44 percent of the party's identifiers) belonged to the president (Table 7.3). They were most supportive of his war and gave him the highest performance ratings of any subgroup (ranging from 91 percent on his handling of Iraq to 98 percent on his handling of the terrorist threat). They were even overwhelmingly positive about the economy and Bush's handling of it, not the president's strongest suit at this juncture. And they were virtually unanimous in planning to vote for him later in the fall. Very religious respondents among independents and Democrats also usually viewed the president more positively than their less religious counterparts. Very religious Republicans and secular Democrats, together comprising about 20 percent of the respondents in this poll, could scarcely have been more polarized. As to

[29] Alan Cooperman and Thomas B. Edsall, "Evangelicals Say They Led the Charge For the GOP," *Washington Post*, November 8, 2004, A01.

TABLE 7.3

Religiosity and Attitudes Toward George W. Bush and the Iraq War, September, 2004 (Percent)

	REPUBLICANS			INDEPENDENTS			DEMOCRATS		
	Very Religious	Somewhat Religious	Not Religious	Very Religious	Somewhat Religious	Not Religious	Very Religious	Somewhat Religious	Not Religious
Percent in category	43.5	41.4	15.4	27.5	41.6	30.9	31.0	41.1	27.9
Iraq War was worth the cost	86.8	72.9	58.2	61.1	50.3	35.8	25.4	17.3	10.6
Approve Bush's handling of Iraq	91.0	83.6	55.4	61.4	51.5	36.8	17.9	19.6	8.8
Economy excellent or good	85.3	75.0	64.8	47.6	45.9	40.2	21.6	19.4	21.8
Approve Bush's handling of the economy	95.3	85.7	74.4	55.5	40.8	37.6	19.9	13.7	10.4
Approve Bush's handling of terrorist threat	98.1	95.6	67.8	67.8	63.7	59.3	38.4	28.2	20.8
Approve of Bush's job performance	95.9	90.5	59.1	73.0	57.9	34.4	22.6	20.2	9.9
Plan to vote for Bush in November	98.3	96.0	79.4	67.7	48.4	29.4	21.6	15.6	6.0

SOURCE: ABC News/*Washington Post* Poll, September 23–26, 2004.

mobilization, Republicans who identified themselves as very religious in this survey were also the most likely to report having been contacted by organizations supporting Bush (32 percent, compared to 22 percent for somewhat religious, and 11 percent for Republicans who were not religious); among Democrats, secular respondents the more likely to have been contacted by their candidate's supporters (31 percent, compared to 19 percent for other Democrats). The mobilization efforts, then, were skewed toward the extremes on this dimension.

THE VOTE

High turnout was only one manifestation of the polarized electorate in 2004. Surveys taken during the campaign season found that, compared to previous elections, fewer voters were undecided, fewer were open to changing their minds, more supported their candidate strongly, and more thought the election was "extremely important" and that it "really matters who wins."[30] The proportions of respondents in the 2004 National Election Study (NES) who said that there were important differences between the parties, who cared who won, and who tried to influence someone else's vote were the highest ever recorded.[31] The polarized atmosphere and partisan mobilization efforts produced

---

[30] "Choice of President Matters More in 2004," news release, Pew Research Center for the People and the Press, July 8, 2004; "Swing Vote Smaller Than Usual, But Still Sizable," news release, Pew Research Center for the People and the Press, June 24, 2004; "Slight Bush Margin in Final Days of Campaign," news release, Pew Research Center for the People and the Press, October 30, 2004.
[31] Alan I. Abramowitz and Walter J. Stone, "The Bush Effect: Polarization, Turnout, and Activism in the 2004 Presidential Election," presented at the Annual Meeting of the American Political Science Association, Washington, D.C., September 1–4, 2005.

the highest level of party line voting in the 52-year history of the NES, eclipsing the previous record set in 2000. With independents who said they leaned toward one party included as partisans, 89 percent of Democrats and 90.6 percent of Republicans voted for their party's candidates; excluding leaners, the respective figures are 92 percent and 94 percent. Because the proportion of purely independent voters also matched its all-time low in 2004, the proportion of the electorate composed of loyal partisans—84.8 percent—was also the highest the NES ever recorded (the previous record, 81.3 percent, was set in 2000).[32]

The electoral divisions exposed in 2000 (see Chapter 3) reappeared in 2004, and the voting patterns suggest little change in voters' preferences between the two elections. At the House district level, for example, the correlation between the major-party presidential vote in 2000 and 2004 was .98. The exit polls indicated that Bush and Kerry voters had quite different ideas about what issues and candidate characteristics were most important (Figure 7.7). Bush was the strong favorite among those who put terrorism or moral values at the top of their concerns and was a slight favorite among voters caring most about taxes; Kerry was preferred by people who thought education, health care, or the economy was most important. Kerry was also preferred by those most concerned with Iraq. Bush was the overwhelming favorite of voters who thought religious faith was the most important quality in a president, and also dominated among voters who listed strong leadership, clear stands on issues, and honesty as most important. Kerry was preferred by those who believed caring

---

[32] Data are from my own analysis of the 2004 American National Election Study. Exit polls documented equally high levels of party loyalty; see "Election Results" at http://www.cnn.com/ELECTION/2004/pages/results/states/US/P/00/epolls.0.html (accessed November 26, 2004).

FIGURE 7.7
Issues and Character in the 2004 Vote

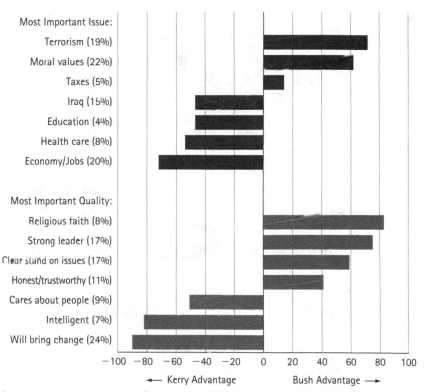

Source: National Exit Poll at http://www.cnn.com/ELECTION/2004/pages/results/states/US/P/00/
epolls.0.html (accessed November 26, 2004).

about people was most important, and he was the overwhelming favorite among those for whom intelligence mattered most. Unfortunately for Kerry, only 7 percent of the electorate put the highest premium on intelligence. His largest margin came from the quarter of the electorate who thought what mattered most was bringing change—that is, those for whom the most important thing was making George W. Bush a one-term president.

Opinions on the Iraq War were, not surprisingly, strongly related to the vote (Figure 7.8). Relative support for Bush and Kerry varied dramatically according to whether or not voters approved of the war, believed it was part of the war on terrorism, had made the United States safer, and thought it was going well.

FIGURE 7.8
Opinions on the Iraq War and the 2004 Vote

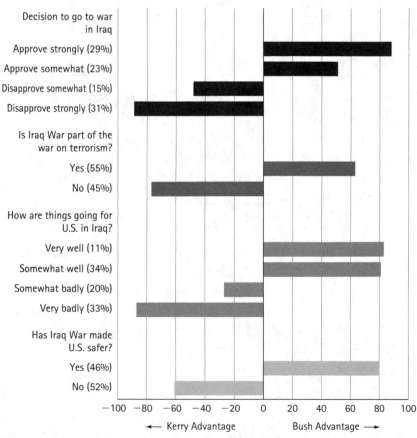

Source: National Exit Poll at http://www.cnn.com/ELECTION/2004/pages/results/states/US/P/00/epolls.0.html (accessed November 26, 2004).

FIGURE 7.9
Support for Iraq War and the Presidential Vote Choice

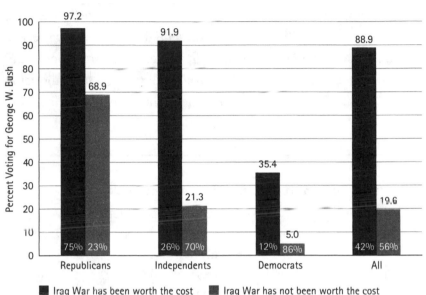

■ Iraq War has been worth the cost   ■ Iraq War has not been worth the cost

Note: The proportion of respondents in category appears at the bottom of the column.
Source: 2004 American National Election Study.

The NES survey also found a tight relationship between support for the war and the presidential vote that remains when party identification is taken into account (Figure 7.9); the relationship was particularly strong for the pure independents.[33] In total, 89 percent of Democrats and 82 percent of Republicans and independents cast a presidential vote consistent with their views on whether or not the Iraq war was worth the cost. It is also worth noting that the Iraq War question was asked in the pre-election wave of the NES survey, whereas the vote question was naturally asked after

---

[33] The question was, "Taking everything into account, do you think the war in Iraq has been worth the cost or not?"

the election, reducing the likelihood that the answer to the former was merely a rationalization of the answer to the latter.

Opinion as to whether the Iraq War was worth the cost remains a strong predictor of the presidential vote when a variety of variables in addition to party identification are taken into account. The estimated coefficient on this variable in the first logit model in Table 7.4 shows its continued potency when party identification,

TABLE 7.4
Multivariate Logit Models of Presidential Voting in 2004

	MODEL 1	MODEL 2	MODEL 3
Iraq War was worth the cost	2.97***	1.85***	1.48***
	(.34)	(.39)	(.43)
Party Identification	.86***	.68***	.65***
	(.09)	(.11)	(.11)
Ideology	.80***	.43	.39
	(.24)	(.27)	(.27)
Income	.17	.34	.36
	(.19)	(.22)	(.23)
Religious service attendance	.21*	.26*	.25*
	(.10)	(.12)	(.12)
Male	−.11	−.11	−.12
	(.30)	(35)	(.35)
African American	−1.44***	−1.62***	−1.67***
	(.42)	(.45)	(.46)
Hispanic	.54	−.33	−.12
	(.50)	(.56)	(.56)

continued

TABLE 7.4 (continued)

	MODEL 1	MODEL 2	MODEL 3
Approve of G.W. Bush's overall performance		2.87***	2.61***
		(.38)	(.39)
Approve of G.W. Bush's handling of Iraq			.95*
			(.44)
Constant	−4.14***	−4.71***	−4.64***
	(.50)	(.60)	(.61)
Log likelihood chi square	683.93	747.41	752.09
Pseudo R-squared	.68	.74	.75
Number of cases	726	726	726

NOTE: The dependent variable is 1 if the respondent voted for Bush, 0 if for Kerry; the Iraq war variable takes the value of 1 if the war was worth it, 0 otherwise; party identification is a 7-point scale from 0 (strong Democrat) to 6 (strong Republican); ideology takes a value of 1 for respondents placing themselves to the right of center on a 7-point liberal-conservative scale, −1 to the left of center, and 0 at the center; income takes the value of 1 if family income falls into the top third, 0 if in the middle third, and −1 if in the bottom third; religious service attendance is 1 = never, 2 = a few times a year, 3 = once or twice a month, 4 = almost every week, 5 = every week; male, African American, and Hispanic take 1 if respondent is in the category, 0 otherwise; the approval variables are scored 1 if respondent approved, 0 if not.
SOURCE: 2004 American National Election Study;
*p < .05, **p < .01, **p < .001.

ideology, income, religious service attendance, gender, and race and ethnicity are controlled. The coefficient indicates that, for example, if values on the other variables predicted a .33 probability of voting for Bush, that probability would increase to .90 if the respondent believed that the Iraq War was worth the cost rather than the contrary; similarly, a .50 initial probability would become .95, and an initial .67 probability would become .97, if the respondent thought the war was worth it. We know that opinions on the war are strongly related to approval of the president overall and of his handling of Iraq in particular and that these variables should also be very strongly related to the vote, but opinion on the war remains a strong predictor of presidential preference even when the first (Model 2) or both (Model 3) of these approval variables are included in the equation. The coefficient on the war opinion variable in Model 3 indicates that if the values of the other variables produced an initial probability of voting for Bush of .33, it would double to .67 if the respondent also thought the war was worth it; under the same condition, a .50 probability would become .81, and a .67 probability would become .89.

Party identification remains the most powerful predictor of the vote in all of these equations, and race always makes a substantial difference, reflecting the low level of regard for Bush (and other Republicans) among African Americans. Religiosity as expressed by service attendance also has a stable independent effect on the vote; for example, other variables remaining unchanged, Model 3's predicted probability of voting for Bush would rise from .33 to .57 if religious attendance were in the highest rather than lowest category. Income, gender, and Hispanic ethnicity, on the other hand, were not significantly related to the vote once the other variables are controlled (although all three are, by themselves, significantly related to it).

Bush's narrow victory was a product of higher Republican turnout and slightly greater party loyalty among Republican identifiers. His advantage over Kerry on the terrorism issue[34] was the

---

[34] For a summary of the polling data on this question, see James E. Campbell, "Why Bush Won the Presidential Election of 2004: Incumbency, Ideology, Terrorism, and Turnout," *Political Science Quarterly* 120 (Summer 2005): 225.

principal source of Democratic defections; the 23 percent of Democrats in the NES survey who approved of Bush's handling of terrorism defected to Bush at a rate 12 times greater than did the 77 percent who did not (32.7 percent compared to 2.6 percent). The Kerry campaign's hesitant response to attacks on his Vietnam War record by the "Swift Boat Veterans for Truth," a 527 group distinguishable from the Bush campaign only by a legal fiction, may have raised doubts about his reliability among enough Democrats nervous about homeland security to cost him the election. Unlike every previous winner except John Kennedy in 1960, Bush ran behind among independents, 48 percent to 49 percent in the exit polls, and 40 percent to 55 percent in the NES study (excluding partisan leaners, 40 to 58 percent). In any close election, every contribution to victory is arguably decisive, but there is no question that the superior turnout and loyalty of Republicans was the *sine qua non* of Bush's reelection.

THE CONGRESS

The intensely partisan presidential contest found echoes in the 2004 House and Senate elections, much to the advantage of Republican candidates, for the unusually high Republican turnout and high levels of party line voting served to magnify the already formidable structural advantage Republicans now enjoy in the battle for congressional seats.[35] The advantage stems from the greater efficiency with which Republican voters are distributed

---

[35] Gary C. Jacobson, "Polarized Politics and the 2004 Congressional and Presidential Elections," *Political Science Quarterly* 120 (Summer 2005): 211.

across districts and states, most clearly evident in the major-party vote for president in 2000. Short-term political forces were evenly balanced that year, and party line voting was the highest it had been in decades, so both the national and district-level presidential vote reflected the electorate's underlying partisan balance with unusual accuracy.[36] The Democrat, Al Gore, won the national popular vote by about 540,000 of the 105 million votes cast. Yet the distribution of these votes across current House districts yields 240 in which Bush won more votes than Gore but only 195 in which Gore outpolled Bush. Part of the reason for this Republican advantage is demographic: Democrats win a disproportionate share of minority and other urban voters, who tend to be concentrated in districts with lopsided Democratic majorities; Republicans hold more districts with narrower majorities, thus "wasting" fewer of their voters.[37] But it is also a product of successful partisan gerrymanders brought off by the Republicans in states where they controlled the redistricting process after the 2000 census.[38] Democrats actually ran stronger in House races in 2004 than they had in 2002,[39] yet the high levels of party polarization and loyalty reinforced the Democrats' structural handicap,

---

[36] Gary C. Jacobson, "A House and Senate Divided: The Clinton Legacy and the Congressional Elections of 2000," *Political Science Quarterly* 116 (Spring 2001): 5–27.

[37] For example, according to the CBS News/*New York Times* Poll of August 20-25, 2004, Democratic identifiers outnumbered Republicans nearly five to one in New York City. See "New York City and the Republican Convention" at http://www.cbsnews.com/htdocs/CBSNews_polls/nyc.pdf (accessed November 6, 2004).

[38] The most important of these states were Florida, Michigan, Ohio, Pennsylvania, and, after 2002, Texas.

[39] Their total vote increase by 1 percent from 48.1 to 49.1; their average district level vote increased by 1.4 percentage points in districts contested in both 2002 and 2004; in nearly two-thirds of these districts, Democrats improved on their 2002 vote.

leaving them no chance of making significant gains. They lost a net three seats but would have gained a like number had it not been for the Republicans' remap of Texas after they took control of the state in 2002.[40] Very few House seats changed party hands in 2004, but 80 percent of them went to the party winning the most presidential votes in the district. The number of districts with split House and presidential outcomes dropped to 59 (14 percent of all seats), lowest in the half-century such data have been available.[41]

Republicans enjoy a similar structural advantage pursuing Senate seats, an edge that was enhanced by the class of seats up for election in 2004. Despite running behind Gore nationally, Bush had carried 30 of the 50 states in 2000, including 22 of the 34 states with Senate contests in 2004. Democrats had to defend ten seats in states Bush had won, including five left open by retirements, all in the South, where support for Democrats has been eroding for several decades (see Chapter 2). Meanwhile, Republicans were defending only three seats in states Gore won. In the end, Republicans won all five of the southern Democratic seats and made a net gain of four; eight of the nine Senate seats that changed party hands conformed to the red state-blue state presidential division. After the election, three-quarters of Senate seats were held by the party whose presidential candidate had taken the state in 2004, the highest level of partisan consistency of this sort in at least five decades.[42]

---

[40] Jacobson, "2004 Elections," pp. 201–202.
[41] Ibid., p. 207.
[42] Jacobson, "2004 Elections," p. 209.

High turnout and high party loyalty, combined with the Republicans' structural advantage and the set of Senate seats contested in 2004, thus served to strengthen the Republican grip on Congress despite the absence of any pro-Republican trend in public opinion. Indeed, the Bush administration's strategy of serving the party's base while in office and putting most of its energies into mobilizing core supporters during the reelection campaign was arguably even more productive for congressional Republicans than it was for the president. A partisan standoff with both sides highly motivated and loyal to their parties guarantees, at present, Republican control of Congress.

The results of the congressional elections promised little mitigation of the intensely partisan atmosphere in which they took place. The turnover of congressional seats pointed in the opposite direction. All six of the Senate Democrats replaced by Republicans had been more moderate than their party's average (based on DW-Nominate scores). Four of the six newly elected Republican senators who had served in the House were more conservative than their party's average in that body. Moreover, the two retiring Republican senators whose seats were won by Democrats had voted to the left of their party's mean. Thus in the Senate, both parties lost moderates and, at least on the Republican side, gained more extreme ideologues. Changes brought about by the House elections had a similar thrust, though the effect was smaller because a much smaller proportion of House seats changed party hands. The five Texas Democrats who were pushed out by redistricting and replaced by Republicans had been more conservative than the average for their party, as was Ralph Hall, who had taken one look at the new lines and decided he was really a Republican. However, the net ideological effect of the other six party turnovers in the House was, by the same standard, neutral.[43]

AFTERMATH

National campaigns always intensify partisan differences, but issues, campaign strategies, and the fact that the election was a referendum on an especially divisive administration engaged in an especially divisive war, magnified their effect in 2004. Bush won reelection by the smallest margin of any president in his tory, and few Democrats were satisfied with the outcome; in one postelection survey asking about feelings rather than opinions, 88 percent of Kerry voters said they felt disappointed; 74 percent, worried; 35 percent, angry; and 29 percent, depressed.[44] The election left the nation as widely divided along party lines in their assessments of the winner as they had been before. As a result, Bush received the lowest overall Gallup job approval rating of any newly reelected president for whom survey data are available, as his near-unanimous approval among Republicans was offset by extraordinarily low approval among Democrats, producing the largest partisan gap (76 percentage points) in the series (Figure 7.10).[45] The 2004 election thus consolidated

---

[43] Ibid., pp. 213–214.

[44] Bush voters, in contrast, felt relieved (90 percent), reassured (90 percent), safer (88 percent), and elated (64 percent); see "Voters Liked Campaign 2004, But Too Much 'Mud-Slinging,'" Research Report, Pew Center for the People and the Press, November 11, 2004, at http://people-press.org/reports/display.php3?ReportID=233 (accessed November 12, 2004).

[45] Note also the downward trend over time in approval by the loser's partisans, another manifestation of the long-term trend in out-party presidential approval discussed in Chapter 2.

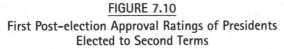

FIGURE 7.10
First Post-election Approval Ratings of Presidents Elected to Second Terms

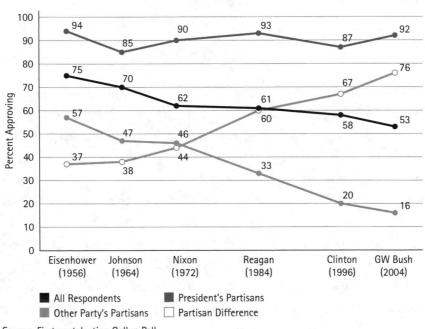

Source: First postelection Gallup Poll.

George W. Bush's status as "a divider, not a uniter," and nothing in the conduct or substance of his campaign suggested that his second term would do anything to change it.

CHAPTER 8

❖

President of Half the People

In his first press conference after winning reelection in 2004, George W. Bush let it be known that he planned an aggressive second-term domestic agenda—partial privatization of Social Security, making the 2001 tax cuts permanent, tax "simplification," cutting social programs, pursuing pro-industry tort reform, energy and environmental policies—that was likely to be even more divisive than his first. "I earned capital in the campaign, political capital," he told reporters, "and now I intend to spend it. It is my style. . . . I've earned capital in this election—and I'm going to spend it for what I told the people I'd spend it on, which is—you've heard the agenda: Social Security and tax reform, moving this economy forward, education, fighting and winning the war on terror."[1] It certainly is his style; despite losing the popular vote in 2000, Bush had acted in his first term as if he had won

---

[1] Dan Froomkin, "Bush Agenda: Bold but Blurry," November 5, 2004, at http://www.washingtonpost.com/wp%2Ddyn/articles/A27833%2D2004Nov5.html (accessed August 12, 2005).

mandate, so it was inconceivable he would do otherwise after his undisputed victory in 2004. Moreover, the election had given him Republican reinforcements in the House and Senate, enlarging his ambitions by making it easier for him to prevail on the Hill, at least as long as Republicans stuck together.

A MANDATE?

All winners like to claim popular mandates, although more often than not, the claim commits the classic logical fallacy, *post hoc, ergo proctor hoc* (after this, therefore because of this). As Bush expressed it, "After hundreds of speeches and three debates and interviews and the whole process, where you keep basically saying the same thing over and over again, that when you win, there is a feeling that the people have spoken and embraced your point of view, and that's what I intend to tell the Congress, that I made it clear what I intend to do as the President, now let's work to—and the people made it clear what they wanted, now let's work together."[2] In the afterglow of victory, such assertions are understandable if empirically dubious,[3] but as Bush's statement makes clear, the claim of a mandate is also tactical, intended to persuade other politicians that their constituents want what the president wants.

But how much political capital did Bush actually gain from the election? And what popular mandate did he receive, other

---

[2] Ibid.
[3] One systematic analysis identified only three "mandate elections" since 1960: 1964, 1980, and 1994. See David A. M. Peterson, Lawrence W. Grossback, James A. Stimson, and Amy Gangl, "Congressional Response to Mandate Elections," *American Journal of Political Science* 47 (July 2003): 416–417.

than to continue keeping terrorists at bay? The answer to the first question is, not much, if any at all. The election left Americans as evenly and widely divided along party lines in their opinions of the president as they had been before it (recall Figures 1.2 and 7.10). The president's high job approval ratings among Republicans, and their high turnout and loyalty at the polls, left no doubt that he had amassed a generous stock of political capital among his own partisans. But there was little postelection softening of Democratic hostility, and his approval among independents remained well below 50 percent. In terms of popular approval, Bush was actually in a stronger position after his first election than after his second. In the first quarter of his first term, Bush's job approval rating averaged 89 percent among Republicans, 55 percent among independents, and 32 percent among Democrats; in the first quarter of his second term, the comparable averages were 90 percent, 43 percent, and 18 percent, respectively.[4] If "political capital" means popular support that can be drawn upon to win legislative victories,[5] Bush's was in a currency honored only in Republican territory.

Neither is there much plausible evidence of a mandate for Bush's domestic agenda. Had terrorism not been in the picture and the election hinged on domestic issues, Kerry would almost certainly have won. Asked specifically about mandates in *Time Magazine*/SRBI Poll taken in December 2004, only 33 percent of respondents said Bush had won a mandate to partially privatize

---

[4] Calculated from the data in Figure 1.2.
[5] And popular support does help in this regard; see Gary C. Jacobson, "Partisan Polarization in Presidential Support: The Electoral Connection," *Congress and the Presidency* 30 (Spring 2003): 29.

Social Security, and only 38 percent said he had won a mandate to change the tax structure.[6] Majority support for his Social Security and tax proposals was limited to Republicans.[7] Again, if he had a mandate, it was from only his own partisans.

As a practical matter, however, neither of these things would matter for the second term as long as the president could count on overwhelming support from ordinary Republicans and, consequently, the Republicans on the Hill. The first term had demonstrated that playing to the base could be a successful legislative strategy; Democrats could be ignored or co-opted with minor concessions as long as Republican leaders kept the troops together, as they usually did. If Republicans were to split, however, Bush could not expect much help from Democrats. Quite the opposite: The hostility of their core supporters to the president, along with his tepid support among independents, left Congressional Democrats with little incentive to help Bush in any way and every reason to obstruct administration proposals for which their electoral constituencies expressed little enthusiasm. The prime example is, of course, Bush's effort to reform Social Security.

THE CAMPAIGN TO REVAMP
SOCIAL SECURITY

The campaign for Social Security "reform" during Bush's second term repeated many of the patterns set in the first term, but its results so far offer a telling illustration of the potential liabilities

---

[6] "Post-election Political Study," *Time* Magazine/SRBI, December 13–14, 2004, at http://www.srbi.com/time-dec152004.pdf (accessed August 10, 2005).
[7] See "The George W. Bush Presidency: Four More Years," CBS News/*New York Times* Poll, January 14–18, 2005, at http://www.cbsnews.com/htdocs/CBSNews_polls/bush_back.pdf (accessed January 30, 2005).

of being a "divider." The decision to take on the nation's most venerable and popular middle-class entitlement program was characteristically bold. Moving Social Security reform to the top of his agenda after the election, Bush presented himself as a leader who dared to touch the lethal "third-rail of American politics" when other politicians lacked the courage.[8] He then went public with an elaborate campaign, orchestrated by Karl Rove, to drum up support for action that began with a highly-publicized "60 stops in 60 days"[9] tour of the country. The tour, which eventually extended beyond the planned 60 days, took Bush to a series of local meetings where he spoke before carefully-screened audiences to carefully-screened panelists who could be depended on to stay on message. The message was that the Social Security system was in crisis, on its way to bankruptcy in fewer than 40 years, and younger workers would eventually be stiffed. Bush's one positive proposal for changing the system, highlighted at every juncture, was to allow workers to put up to one-third of their Social Security contribution into an investment account they would own and control. Returns from these investments would, under optimistic scenarios, more than offset the reduction in the Social Security benefits to which people who opted for private accounts would otherwise be entitled.

The problem was that private accounts (Bush and then the entire Republican establishment took to calling them "personal" accounts after the adjective got a better reaction from focus

---

[8] See, for example, the White House's transcript of his address to the American Society of Newspaper Editors Convention on April 15, 2005, at http://www.whitehouse.gov/news/releases/2005/04/2005 0414-4.html (accessed August 12, 2005). The "third-rail" metaphor refers to the electrified third-rail on subway lines: "Touch it and you die."

[9] This was the administration's title for the campaign; see http://www.treas.gov/press/releases/js2287.htm (accessed August 28, 2005); the number of stops never reached 60.

groups[10]) did nothing to address Social Security's solvency "crisis." Indeed, they would make it worse by taking money out of the system and adding an estimated $2 trillion in transition costs to the national debt. Actually solving the crisis would require something the president avoided mentioning as long as possible: cutting benefits or raising the age of eligibility (from the start, Bush had ruled out the third option for making the arithmetic work, raising Social Security taxes). For most of his 60-day blitz, Bush refused to offer any specifics beyond advocating partial privatization while challenging his Democratic critics to put their ideas on the table. They refused to bite. Other than rejecting private accounts, indeed, demanding that they be taken off the table before they discussed anything, Democrats offered nothing. And why would they? Any effective step toward making the system solvent was guaranteed to be unpopular. Republicans controlled the agenda and everything else, so let them take the lead. Just as the Republican minority had made sure that only Democrats' fingerprints were on the unpopular budget-balancing provisions included in Bill Clinton's 1993 budget,[11] Democrats in Congress saw no reason to shield Republicans from the heat for proposing the painful steps required to make the Social Security system solvent.

The careful vetting of audiences and participants left no doubt that the Social Security meetings were strictly marketing exercises

---

[10] Liberal Texas columnist Molly Ivins wrote an amusing column on the switch; in order to avoid being convicted of liberal bias for using the old term once Bush had abandoned it (which Republican strategist Frank Luntz actually said would be justified), she said, "I shall refer to them as 'the accounts formerly known as private.'" Molly Ivins, "'Private accounts' versus 'personal accounts,'" *The Free Press*, January 27, 2005, at http://www.freepress.org/columns/display/1/2005/1052 (accessed August 12, 2005).
[11] Not a single Republican in either chamber voted for Clinton's 1993 budget, which aimed to reduce the projected deficit by $500 billion over the ensuing five years through a combination of politically-unpopular tax increases and spending reductions.

designed for local news media; the president did not come to listen but to persuade. As he put it at one of the meetings, "In my line of work you got to keep repeating things over and over and over again for the truth to sink in, to kind of catapult the propaganda."[12] And as a sales campaign, "Strengthening Social Security" again played fast and loose with the truth. Bush kept talking about how the system would be "bankrupt" by 2042 without mentioning that this meant only that available funds would cover 70–75 percent of currently-promised benefits rather than the whole amount and that these benefits would still be appreciably higher in real terms than present-day retirees receive.[13] He did not correct panelists who took "bankruptcy" to mean that no money at all would be left in the program for younger workers, a common misperception the administration never tried to dispel.[14] He avoided mentioning any costs—either to workers whose benefits would be reduced, to the nation's fiscal health, or to future recipients if the system were really to be made actuarially sound. In talking up private retirement accounts as a step toward an "ownership society," the president glossed over the fact that the accounts would be subject to stringent mandatory guidelines over how the money in the accounts could be invested and accessed.[15] The campaign relied on two mutually exclusive economic scenarios

---

[12] "Remarks by President Bush in a Conversation on Strengthening Social Security," Greece, New York, March 24, 2005, PR Newswire at http://www.prnewswire.com/cgi-bin/stories.pl?ACCT=109&STORY=/www/story/05-24-2005/0003685801&EDATE=, (accessed August 11, 2005).
[13] Scheduled benefits rise faster than inflation because they are indexed to wages, not prices.
[14] In the February 24–28 CBS News/New York Times Poll, 46 percent of respondents thought that by bankruptcy, Bush meant there would be no money at all; 40 percent thought he meant reduced benefits; at http://www.pollingreport.com/social2.htm (accessed August 12, 2005).
[15] "Bush's State of the Union: Social Security "Bankruptcy?" FactCheck.org, February 3, 2005, at http://www.factcheck.org/article305.html (accessed August 12, 2005).

for its central components: slow economic growth (an average of 1.9 percent over 75 years) to generate the "crisis," and, at the same time, investments appreciating at 6.5 percent per year (after inflation) to make the private accounts a better deal than the current system. As critics pointed out, in no plausible economic model could both scenarios be true.[16]

WHY THE CAMPAIGN FAILED

Bush's Social Security road show succeeded in raising public awareness of the program's long-term problems, but it failed signally to generate support for the president's proposals or for the president himself. Part of the reason is that the administration could not control the terms of debate. Critics were quick to point out what they saw as the flaws in the administration's claims and harped on Bush's refusal, for several months, to propose any concrete changes in the system that actually addressed the "bankruptcy" threat. The town meetings got as much attention from national news reporters for their artifice as for their message. Democrats and their allied interest groups mounted an energetic defense of the New Deal's greatest and most popular achievement in op-ed pieces, blogs, and TV ads.

More important, large portions of the public, cool to both the singer and the song, formed a receptive audience for critics of

---

[16] If the economy did well enough to support such high investment returns, the Social Security shortfall would disappear; if it grew at the pace projected by the system's trustees, investments could not deliver returns that would make private accounts superior; see Paul Krugman, "Many Unhappy Returns," *New York Times*, February 1, 2005, at http://www.pkarchive.org/column/020105.html (accessed August 12, 2005).

Bush's proposals. Before the president began his traveling campaign for it, most Americans liked the idea of investing some of their Social Security contributions in the stock and bond markets. At the time Bush put his proposal at the top of his second term agenda, most polls found the public split fairly evenly on the question, but with considerable variation depending on question wording. No matter how the question was asked, however, support for the idea declined during Bush's national campaign for it. Seven variants of the question were asked three or more times between December 2004 and June 2005; for six of the seven variants, support declined between the first and last survey in the series by between 4 and 7 percentage points; for the seventh variant, there was no change. Overall, support for Bush's proposal fell from an average of 46.1 percent to an average of 41.7 from the first to the last of these polls.[17]

The devil was, as always, in the details. When people were asked if they supported the idea of private accounts without mention of any of the costs, they divided nearly evenly, with an average of about 45 percent supporting the idea.[18] When asked if they backed the idea if it were accompanied by a reduction in guaranteed future benefits, average support dropped to 39 percent.[19] In surveys that specified that the cut in guaranteed benefits could be up to one-third, matching the proportion of Social Security taxes diverted into private accounts, support dropped to an average of

---

[17] From data in CBS News/*New York Times*, ABC News/*Washington Post*, NBC/*Wall Street Journal*, Gallup, and Pew Center for the People and Press polls, at http://www.pollingreport.com/social/htm (accessed August 12, 2005).

[18] In 31 polls asking the question in this form, an average 45.2 percent support and 46.6 percent opposed the idea; support ranged from 35 percent to 56 percent with a standard deviation of 5.3; see Ibid.

[19] From 11 polls, with an average of 38.6 supporting (standard deviation, 7.3), 54.6 opposing; see Ibid.

22 percent.[20] And if the program were to add $2 trillion to the national debt over the next ten years, on average only 27 percent of respondents favored it.[21] Both of these latter two conditions were part of the package, so over time, as more people came to understand what establishing the private accounts would entail, support for the idea declined. So, too, did approval of the president's handling of the Social Security issue, which by early August 2005 was down to about 30 percent, recovering a bit only after Bush stopped talking about it (Figure 8.1). His job performance rating on this issue consistently fell well below his ratings in other major issue domains (for comparison, see Figure 4.4).

The campaign also ran up against the reality that people who were not already Bush loyalists did not believe the president's proposals for reforming the system were offered in good faith. Asked in January 2005, who they thought Bush was "trying to help more, average Americans or Wall Street investment companies," 75 percent of Democrats and 54 percent of independents answered "Wall Street."[22] Asked in May if the president's real agenda was to "save and strengthen Social Security" or to "dismantle Social Security as we know it," 76 percent of Democrats and 54 percent of independents chose "dismantle."[23] Asked in June

---

[20] From three polls, with an average of 21.7 percent supporting (standard deviation 0.6), 69.0 percent opposing; see Ibid.

[21] From four polls, with an average of 27 supporting (standard deviation, 13), 64 percent opposing; support in three of these four ranged from 17 to 21 percent; the fourth was an outlier (46 percent); see Ibid.

[22] Only 19 percent of Republicans expressed this view; 73 percent said "ordinary Americans." See "The George W. Bush Presidency: Four More Years," CBS News/*New York Times* Poll, January 14–18, 2005, p. 20.

[23] Only 16 percent of Republicans picked "dismantle," 72 percent chose "save and strengthen." See "Why So Many People Oppose the President's Social Security Proposals," *The Harris Poll #41*, May 13, 2005 at http://www.harrisinteractive/com/harris_/poll/index.asp?PID=570 (accessed May 13, 2005).

FIGURE 8.1
Approval of GWB's Handling of Social Security Since his Reelection

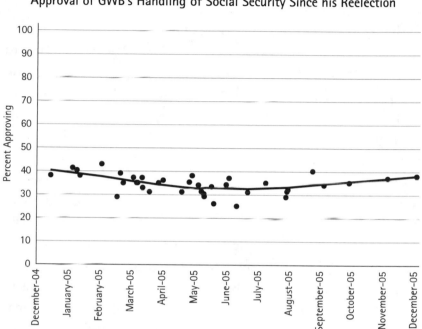

Sources: ABC News/*Washington Post*, CBS News/*New York Times*, AP/IPSOS, Harris, Gallup, Pew Center for the People and Press, *Newsweek*, and *Time* polls, most at http://www.pollingreport.com/social/htm and, in some cases, the poll's own wesbite.

if they were confident or uneasy about "Bush's ability to make the right decisions about Social Security," 88 percent of Democrats and 70 percent of independents said they were "uneasy."[24]

Some of this cynicism may have reflected public statements by some of Bush's allies in the campaign who really did want to

---

[24] One third of Republicans were also "uneasy," while 59 percent were "confident"; see "The President, Social Security, and Iraq," CBS News/*New York Times* Poll, June 10–15, 2005, p. 4.

dismantle Social Security.[25] And although the causal linkages are hopelessly entangled, some of it is also almost certainly a legacy of the Iraq War. At least support for the president's ideas on Social Security was strongly related to opinions on whether the war was worth the cost and whether the administration was deliberately deceptive in making the case for it (Figure 8.2). Regardless of party, respondents who believed they were misled on the war or who thought it was a bad idea were much less likely to support the president's Social Security proposals. Only 37 percent of all respondents in this poll voiced support for the president's plan; it was backed by 64 percent of those who thought the United States had done the right thing in going to war in Iraq but by only 13 percent who thought the war was a mistake. Of course, critics of Bush's Social Security plans were fond of pointing out what they claimed were parallels between the misleading campaign to drum up support for the Iraq War and the equally deceptive effort to "catapult the propaganda" to win public backing for privatizing Social Security; the polling data suggest that this contention resonated with a substantial segment of the public.

As Figure 8.2 indicates, Republicans were considerably more supportive of Bush's proposal than were Democrats—no shock here—and over time, partisan differences widened.[26] Partisan dif-

---

[25] For example, Stephen Moore, former president of the Club for Growth, an antitax group backing Bush's plans for private accounts, was widely quoted when he said, "Social Security is the soft underbelly of the welfare state. If you can jab your spear through that, you can undermine the whole welfare state." See John Tierney, "Can Anyone Unseat FDR?" *New York Times*, January 23, 2005, at http://www.nytimes.com/2005/01/23/weekinreview/23tier.html?ex=1264136400&en=9bc1372a4e3f80 22&ei=5090&partner=rssuserland (accessed August 15, 2005).

[26] Ask by the CBS News/*New York Times* Poll in January 2005 if they thought "allowing individuals to invest a portion of their Social Security taxes on their own is good idea or a bad idea," 58 percent of Republicans and 30 percent of Democrats said it was a good idea. Asked the same question in June, 70 percent of Republicans but only 26 percent of Democrats said it was a good idea (support among independents also dropped 4 points, from 48 percent to 44 percent); see, "The George W. Bush Presidency: Four More Years," CBS News/*New York Times* Poll, January 14–18, 2005, p. 20, and "The President, Social Security, and Iraq," CBS News/*New York Times* Poll, June 10–15, 2005, p. 4.

FIGURE 8.2
Opinions on the Iraq War and Social Security Reform

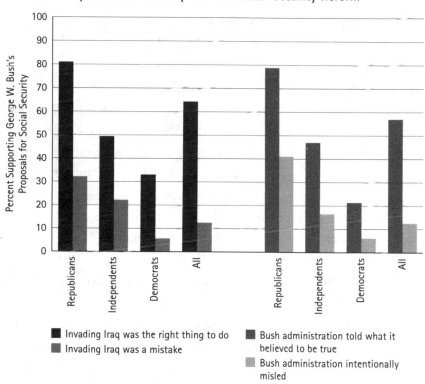

Source: ABC News/*Washington Post* Poll, March 10–13, 2005.

ferences were also larger when it was labeled Bush's plan rather than simply described. In the survey that was the basis of Figure 8.2, 42 percent of Democrats supported "a plan in which people who chose to could invest some of their Social Security contributions in the stock market" but only 11 percent said they supported "George W. Bush's proposals on Social Security"; 83 percent said they opposed his proposals, 59 percent "strongly." In the same survey, 85 percent of Democrats and 59 percent of independents also said that the more they heard about Bush's proposals, the less they liked them. Among Republicans, 77 percent backed the stock market option, 73 percent supported the president's proposals, and 64 percent said that the more they heard about the proposals, the more they liked them.

Republicans were generally supportive of the president's ideas for Social Security, but not by margins large enough to offset the strong Democratic opposition to any proposal with Bush's name attached to it. Furthermore, when the downside of privatizing part of the system was mentioned—cuts in scheduled benefits, adding to the national debt—most Republicans no longer supported the idea.[27] Even conservative Christians were less helpful to the president than usual, supporting his Social Security proposals at rates only a few points higher than did other Republicans.[28] Approval of Bush's handling of the Social Security issue among Republicans was also well below his ratings for other policy domains; in six surveys taken between March and August 2005, an average of 60 percent of Republicans approved of Bush's handling of Social Security, compared to 76 percent on the economy, 77 percent on Iraq, and 87 percent on terrorism and 87 percent overall during the same period.[29] Among Democrats, Bush's average approval rating on Social Security was in single digits, 9 percent, and among independents, it was 24 percent.[30] It is not hard to fathom why congressional Democrats saw no reason to follow the president's

---

[27] See the CBS News/New York Times polls, January 14–18, May 20–24, and June 10–15, 2005.
[28] In the ABC News/Washington Post Poll taken March 10–13, born-again/Evangelical Republicans supported private accounts at the same level as other Republicans; in the June 2–5 survey, their level of support was 4 points higher. Their approval of Bush's handling of the issue was also 4 to 5 points higher in these polls.
[29] Computed from data in Figures 1.2, 1.6, 1.7, and 1.8.
[30] ABC News/Washington Post polls, March 10–13, April 21–24, and June 2–5, 2005; CBS News/New York Times polls, May 20–24, June 10–15, and July 29–August 2, 2005.

lead on this issue and why it made many Republicans in Congress very nervous.

THE BIPARTISAN CONSENSUS

Ironically, there actually was a bipartisan public consensus on what to do (or, more accurately, what not to do) about Social Security. The difficulty for politicians was that the consensus opposed virtually all of the changes that might assure the program's long-term solvency. In the March, 2005 ABC News/*Washington Post* Poll, for example, majorities of Republicans, Democrats, and independents said they opposed increasing the Social Security tax rate, raising the retirement age for receiving full benefits, further reducing benefits for early retirees, reducing guaranteed benefits for future retirees, or changing the formula for calculating benefits to reduce their rate of growth. The only proposal that won majority support—again across party lines—was collecting Social Security tax on all wages, not just the first $90,000. Unfortunately, that would not raise enough money to solve the problem. In the face of such numbers, Bush's strategy of avoiding specifics aside from promoting the upside potential of private accounts for many months is understandable, as was the Republicans insistence that reform had to have bipartisan support to proceed.

At the end of April, under pressure to fill out his proposal, Bush sought to win over some Democrats by suggesting that reductions in promised future benefits be calibrated to fall heaviest on highest income groups and not at all on the lowest. Or, as he spun it, "I propose a Social Security system in the future where benefits for low-income workers will grow faster than benefits for people who are better off."[31] The idea by itself was attractive to ordinary Democrats, although a bit less so to Republicans. When the Pew Center Poll described such a policy to half their sample without mentioning it was Bush's idea, 54 percent of Democrats and 47 percent of Republicans favored it. But when it was described to the other half sample as Bush's proposal, it drew support from 62 percent of Republicans but only 34 percent of Democrats. Thus the Bush cue cut sharply both ways, boosting Republican's support by 15 points but reducing Democrat's by 20. Support also dropped 12 points among independents, from 55 to 43 percent, and similarly overall, from 53 percent to 45, when the proposal was identified as the president's.[32] Being a divider, then, could have its downside.

OTHER ISSUES

The president had greater success with other parts of the agenda where he could count on stronger Republican support. In the first eight months of Bush's second term, Congress enacted a bankruptcy overhaul bill, class-action tort reform, and an energy bill the administration had been pursuing since the beginning of Bush's presidency, and it ratified the Central American Free Trade

---

[31] Richard W. Stevenson and Elizabeth Bumiller, "Bush Cites Plan That Would Cut Social Security," *New York Times*, April 29, 2005, at http://www.nytimes.com/2005/04/29/politics/29bush.html? (accessed August 11, 2005).
[32] "Economy, Iraq Weighing Down Bush Popularity," Survey Report, Pew Center for the People and The Press, May 19, 2005, at http://people-press.org/reports/display.php3?ReportID=244us (accessed May 19, 2005).

Agreement (CAFTA). All were notable victories for the administration. The first two were won with unanimous or near-unanimous support from congressional Republicans, and the minority of Democratic votes they received (beyond the handful of Senate votes needed to preclude a filibuster) were superfluous.[33] The energy bill needed a bit more Democratic support to pass because of Republican defectors (31 in the House, 6 in the Senate); this was achieved by a judicious distribution of pork and the omission of a provision opening the Alaskan National Wildlife Refuge to drilling (which was to be accomplished by an end run using the budget resolution, which is not subject to filibuster). CAFTA was the closest call; it passed the House by a single vote after the count was delayed to allow a few more Republican arms to be twisted; Democrats were much less supportive than they have been of previous free trade agreements, but the 15 who voted for it were just enough to offset the 27 Republicans who resisted the pressure and defected. None of these was a great popular victory, but all of them were welcomed by core Republican supporters in the corporate sector, who were the prime beneficiaries.

THE TERRI SCHIAVO CASE

The president ran into a bit more trouble trying to please his other pillar of support, religious conservatives. The legal struggle between the husband and parents of Terri Schiavo, a Florida woman who had been in a persistent vegetative state for 15 years,

---

[33] There was only a single Republican vote against either bill in either chamber.

over whether to remove a feeding tube that was keeping her alive
had emerged as an issue of great symbolic importance to religious
conservatives, who viewed hers as a right-to-life case. Responding
to their outcries, Congress passed a law giving federal courts juris-
diction to intervene to take the case from the state courts, which
had repeatedly sided with the husband and finally ordered the
tube removed. President Bush took the rare step of interrupting
his vacation in Texas to fly back to Washington to sign the
legislation, which he later celebrated as bipartisanship in action:
"Democrats and Republicans in Congress came together last
night to give Terri Schiavo's parents another opportunity to save
their daughter's life."[34] The vote was in fact fairly bipartisan; in
the House, 97 percent of Republicans and 47 percent of Democrats who cast votes supported the measure (the measure passed
the Senate by voice vote).

The public's reaction was also bipartisan: majorities of
Republicans as well as Democrats thought Congress and the president had had no business intervening. Most people could imagine
themselves facing this kind of wrenching decision some day, and
the last thing they would want was to have a federal case made of
it.[35] Polls taken at the time found from 70 to 82 percent of
respondents saying that the action was "not right," "inappropri-

---

[34] "Bush signs law letting parents seek restoration of feeding tube," CNN.com, March 22, 2005, at
http://www.cnn.com/2005/LAW/03/21/schiavo/ (accessed August 18, 2005).
[35] Given a choice of who should make such decisions, only 9 percent of respondents to the CBS
News/*New York Times* Poll of March 21–22, 2005 said "federal government;" 13 percent said "state
government," and 75 percent said the government should stay out. See "The Terri Schiavo Case," CBS
News Poll report, March 23, 2005, at http://www.realclearpolitics.com/Polls/cbs_schiavo.pdf (accessed
August 18, 2005).

ate," and that Congress and the president "should have stayed out." Partisan differences on these questions were small, and a majority of Republicans (as large as 72 percent in one survey) panned the action. Majorities nearly as large (from 65 percent to 74 percent) said that Congress and Bush had been motivated by political advantage, with only 13 to 25 percent saying they acted on principle or out of real concern for Schiavo.[36] Even half of the Republicans viewed the move as politically motivated, although Democrats were much more uniformly cynical.

The extraordinary intervention by Republican congressional leaders and the president in the Schiavo case underlined the powerful influence of religious conservatives in their party's coalition. It suggested that the real political capital accumulated in the 2004 election belonged to conservative Christian activists who could claim, not implausibly, that their efforts had kept Bush in the White House. It also suggested the difficulties a payback could pose for Republican politicians who, in scrambling to respond to a vocal and passionate minority of key supporters, failed badly to anticipate how the rest of their coalition, not to mention the rest of the electorate, might react. And it reinforced the image of Republicans in Washington as either right-wing religious zealots or their thralls.[37]

---

[36] Pew Center for the People and the Press, *Time*, CBS News/*New York Times*, ABC News/*Washington Post*, Harris, and Gallup Polls reported at the surveys reported at http://pollingreport.com/news.htm#Schiavo (accessed August 18, 2005).

[37] In October 2005, another component of the Republican base, Washington's conservative lobbyists and pundits, showed its political muscle—and Bush's dependence on his party's right wing—by derailing Bush's nomination of his friend and White House counsel, Harriet Miers, to the Supreme Court. Four days after she withdrew, Bush nominated Samuel Alito, a staunchly conservative judge much more to their liking.

THE IRAQ WAR, AGAIN

George W. Bush's approval ratings slipped a bit after the Schiavo affair (see Figure 1.1), and some observers suggested a connection,[38] but the more serious problem he faced was the lack of visible progress in Iraq. As the conflict dragged on and the bombings and American casualties showed no signs of slacking off, even some Republican politicians began questioning the administration's strategy and policies.[39] Public support for the administration's strategy, however, changed little between the 2004 election and the summer of 2005. Retrospective views of the war became more negative in the fall (Figures 6.1 and 6.2), but Republicans, at least, continued to support the action by a large if slightly diminished majority (Figure 6.3). Opinions on how the war was going were quite stable (Figure 8.3). Reflecting the administration's claims that progress was being made, Republicans were far more optimistic than Democrats or independents (Figure 8.4), but these partisan gaps had developed in early 2004 and had not widened since. Conflicting reports and the high degree of uncertainty about the direction of developments in Iraq again created conditions where partisan biases dominated people's response to these questions.

Support for staying the course was also quite stable during the first 11 months of Bush's second term, although it showed signs

---

[38] Bush's approval ratings on handling the Schiavo case were 31, 34, and 41 percent in the three polls that asked this question. See http://pollingreport.com/news.htm#Schiavo (accessed August 18, 2005).
[39] See, for example, the comments of Republican senators Chuck Hagel and Trent Lott in Josh Meyer, "Republican Senator Says U.S. Needs Iraq Exit Strategy Now," *Los Angeles Times,* August 22, 2005, at http://www.latimes.com/news/nationworld/iraq/la-fg-usiraq22aug22,0,2949443.story?coll=la-home-headlines (accessed August 22, 2005).

FIGURE 8.3
How Well is the War in Iraq Going?

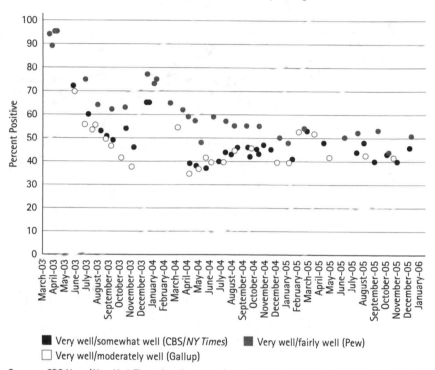

Very well/somewhat well (CBS/*NY Times*)   ■ Very well/fairly well (Pew)
□ Very well/moderately well (Gallup)

Sources: CBS News/*New York Times,* Pew Research Center for the People and Press, and Gallup Polls, at http://pollingreport.com/iraq.htm (accessed December 18, 2005).

of diminishing after Hurricane Katrina (Figure 8.5; Katrina's effects are discussed in Chapter 9). Its expressed level depended on question wording. Questions giving the alternatives of staying until the situation in Iraq has stabilized or withdrawing troops "as soon as possible" or "immediately" produced the highest levels of support, usually above 50 percent (the black markers in Figure 8.5), while questions that gave the option of withdrawing

FIGURE 8.4
Evaluations of How Well the War in Iraq is Going, by Party

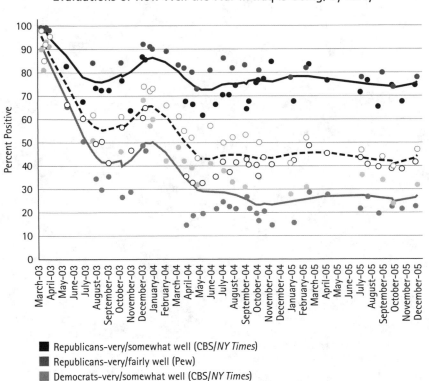

Republicans-very/somewhat well (CBS/*NY Times*)
Republicans-very/fairly well (Pew)
Democrats-very/somewhat well (CBS/*NY Times*)
Democrats-very/fairly well (Pew)
Independents-very/somewhat well (CBS/*NY Times*)
Independents-very/fairly well (Pew)

FIGURE 8.5
Support for Keeping U.S. Troops in Iraq

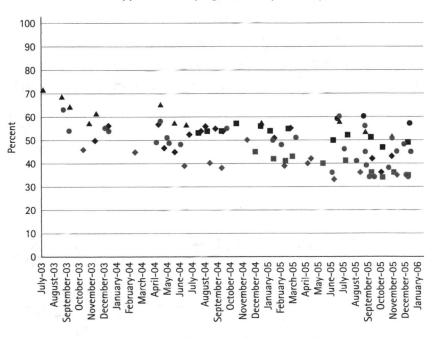

- ◆ Stay as long as it takes to make Iraq a stable democracy, or withdraw troops as soon as possible
- ■ Keep U.S. troops in Iraq until situation has stabilized, or bring troops home as soon as possible
- ▲ Keep troops until civil order restored despite U.S. casualties, or withdraw forces even if civil order is not restored
- ● Keep U.S. troops in Iraq until situation has stabilized, or bring troops home immediately
- ◆ Keep troops in Iraq until there is a stable government, or bring most troops home next year
- ● Send more troops/same as now or withdraw some/all troops
- ■ Maintain troop level to secure peace and stability, or reduce number of troops since elections have been held

Sources: ABC News/*Washington Post,* CBS News/*New York Times,* Pew Center for the People and Press, IPSOS, Harris, Gallup, and NBC News/*Wall Street Journal* polls at http://www.pollingreport.com/iraq.htm (accessed December 18, 2005).

some or most troops or doing so "next year" found a larger proportion wanting to bring troops home even if stability had yet to be achieved (the gray markers in Figure 8.5). Even among Democrats, support for staying the course did not decline much until after Katrina (Figure 8.6), and support for seeing the war through was on average twice as high as support for having gone

FIGURE 8.6
Support of Keeping U.S. Troops in Iraq, by Party

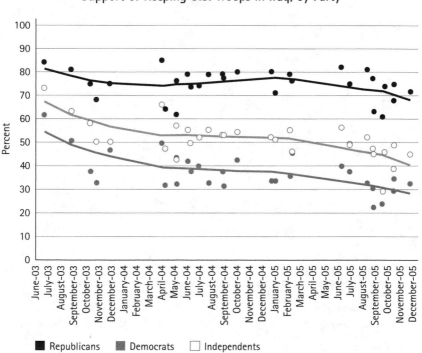

Sources: ABC News/*Washington Post*, CBS News/*New York Times*, and Pew Center for the People and the Press polls.

to war in the first place, a sign that Kerry's dilemma continued to sustain the president's cause: even if the invasion had been a bad idea, the United States could not now precipitously abandon Iraq without risking disaster.[40] If not before the war, Iraq was now a staging and breeding ground for anti-American Islamic terrorists, justifying continuing U.S. involvement. Invoking the potent memory of 9/11, Bush thus sought to shore up support for his policies by continually reiterating that, as he put it in his August 20, 2005, radio address, "We're fighting the terrorists in Afghanistan, Iraq, and around the world, striking them in foreign lands before they can attack us here at home."[41] Retrospective approval of the war and support for keeping U.S. troops in Iraq, after edging lower in some of the surveys taken in the fall of 2005, rebounded a few points in December in response to Bush's renewed public defense of the war (featuring all the old arguments) aimed at reversing the erosion of support for staying the course.[42]

The president's problem—and source of grumbling among Republican politicians—was that the effectiveness of the war effort was coming into question. All along, majorities of the

---

[40] Among independents, support for staying the course was on average about 10 percentage points higher than retrospective approval of the invasion (52 percent to 42 percent); among Republicans, there was no difference (about 80 percent in both cases). In late 2005, House Republicans took to exploiting the Democrats' dilemma by offering resolutions calling for immediate withdrawal from Iraq in an attempt to reduce the options to either abandoning Iraq or supporting the president's current approach.

[41] "President's Radio Address," August 20, 2005, at http://www.whitehouse.gov/news/releases/2005/08/20050820.html (accessed August 22, 2005).

[42] Dana Milbank, "Repititous, Yes, But They Didn't Cut and Run," *Washington Post*, December 15, 2005, A19.

public were not persuaded that the Bush administration had a
clear plan for achieving its goals in Iraq, regardless of how these
goals were stated (Figure 8.7). Americans were particularly skeptical that Bush had a clear plan for getting U.S. troops out (the
darker open circle markers). Even Republicans expressed less
than overwhelming faith that the administration had a coherent

FIGURE 8.7
Does the Bush Administration Have a Clear Plan for Iraq?

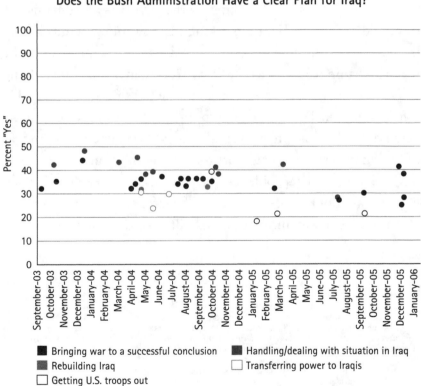

Sources: ABC News/*Washington Post*, CBS News/*New York Times*, Pew Center for the People and the
Press, and National Annenberg Election Study surveys.

strategy for achieving its goals in Iraq; among Democrats, that faith was close to nonexistent (Figure 8.8).

The president's conception and style of leadership made it difficult to deal with such sentiments. Whether or not he ever entertained doubts about the rightness of his decision to invade Iraq or the soundness of his advisors' strategy for winning the war—Bush

FIGURE 8.8
Does the Bush Administration Have a Clear Plan for Iraq? (by Party)

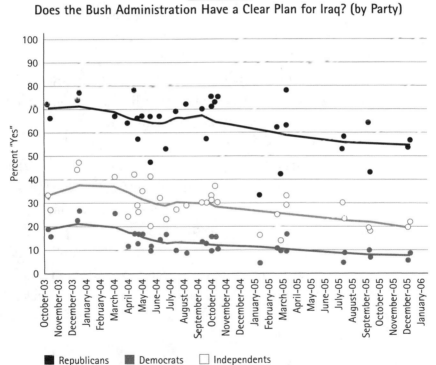

■ Republicans   ■ Democrats   □ Independents

Sources: ABC News/*Washington Post*, CBS News/*New York Times*, and Pew Center for the People and the Press polls.

claimed he had not[43]—he could never admit mistakes or second thoughts because doing so would contradict his idea of leadership. As he told Bob Woodward, "A president has got to be the calcium in the backbone. If I weaken, the whole team weakens. If I'm doubtful, I can assure you that there will be a lot of doubt. If my confidence level declines, it will send ripples throughout the whole organization."[44] The need to display resolution and confidence required continual upbeat pronouncements that, in the face of the bad news regularly coming out of Iraq in the months following Bush's second inauguration, seemed increasingly detached from reality. Vice President Dick Cheney's assertion in late May that the insurgency was "in its last throes" was not credible even to Republicans.[45] Expressing confidence and optimism with any credibility became something of a challenge for Bush and his spokespersons. As part of his December 2005 campaign to rally support for remaining in Iraq, the president thus sought to strengthen his credibility by a rare voluntary acknowledgement of mistakes in prewar intelligence and postwar tactics while continuing to insist that "given Saddam's history and the lessons of September 11, my decision to remove Saddam Hussein was the right decision."[46]

Perhaps more ominous for the president, the public was becoming increasingly doubtful that the Iraq War was making the United States more rather than less secure from terrorist attacks.

[43] Bob Woodward, *Plan of Attack* (New York: Simon and Schuster, 2004), p. 420.
[44] Bob Woodward, *Bush at War* (New York: Simon and Schuster, 2002), p. 259.
[45] In the June 23–26 ABC News/*Washington Post* Poll, only 42 percent of Republicans said the insurgency was "on its last legs"; 55 percent said it was not, as did 68 percent of Democrats and 70 percent of independents (analysis by author).
[46] Warren Vieth, "Bush Admits Mistakes but Defends War," *Los Angeles Times,* December 15, 2005, A1.

As usual, different question wordings produce (in this case modestly) different distributions of opinion, but the overall trend is clearly downward, with a notable dip after the terrorist bombings of the London Underground in June (Figure 8.9). These surveys do not tell us whether people believed the risk of terrorism would

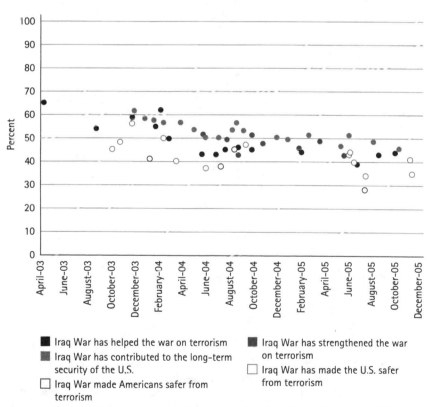

FIGURE 8.9
The Effect of the Iraq War on Terrorism and U.S. Security

Sources: ABC News/*Washington Post*, Pew Center for the People and Press, Harris, Gallup, *Time*, and *Newsweek* polls at http://www.pollingreport.com/iraq.htm (accessed December 18, 2005).

be even greater if the United States pulled out of Iraq, but they do indicate an erosion of belief in the administration's most important remaining rationale for staying there. The usual partisan differences emerge on these questions, although they are not quite as wide as on many of the other questions regarding the war (Figure 8.10).

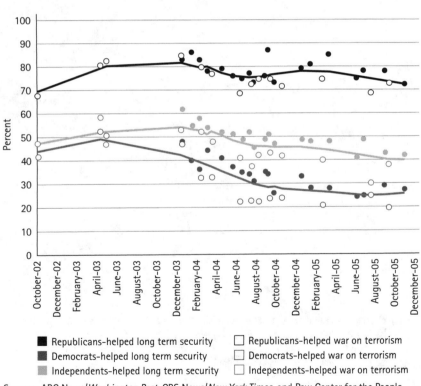

FIGURE 8.10

The Effect of the Iraq War on Terrorism and U.S. Security (by Party)

■ Republicans–helped long term security   ☐ Republicans–helped war on terrorism

■ Democrats–helped long term security   ☐ Democrats–helped war on terrorism

■ Independents–helped long term security   ☐ Independents–helped war on terrorism

Sources: ABC News/*Washington Post*, CBS News/*New York Times*, and Pew Center for the People and the Press polls.

UNWAVERING CHRISTIAN
CONSERVATIVES

As Figures 8.4, 8.6, 8.8, and Figures 8.10 indicate, the continuing high levels of support from ordinary Republicans have so far kept the Iraq War from turning into a complete political liability for the Bush administration. And among Republicans, conservative Christians have been the most steadfast in following the president. Some evidence for this was presented earlier (Figures 6.17 and 6.18). Table 8.1 offers an additional perspective on the extraordinary support white, born-again/Evangelical Christians continued to give to the president's Iraq policies while doubts were rising elsewhere in the public, even among other Republicans. The data are from an ABC News/*Washington Post* survey taken in late June 2005, focusing on the Iraq War; the table includes the response distributions of Democrats for comparison and as a reminder of how large partisan differences have become on these questions.

Nearly nine in ten white, born-again Christians offered retrospective support for the war; they were more likely than other Republicans to find the number of American casualties acceptable, to believe the war has helped U.S. security, to express optimism about developments in Iraq, and to favor staying the course. Almost half agreed with Cheney that the insurgency was on its last legs. On most of these questions, the difference between born-again/Evangelical Christians and other Republicans is statistically significant at p < .05.[47] In this survey, about 42 percent of Republicans put

---

[47] With the number of cases here (290 Republicans in the survey out of a total sample of 920), any difference of approximately 9 percentage points or more is a significant p < .05.

TABLE 8.1
Religiosity and Attitudes Toward the Iraq War, June 2005 (Percent)

	WHITE BORN-AGAIN/ EVANGELICAL CHRISTIAN REPUBLICANS	OTHERS REPUBLICANS	DEMOCRATS
1. Considering everything, do you think the United States did the right thing in going to war with Iraq or do you think it was a mistake?			
Right thing	89.7	81.2	22.7
2. All in all, considering the costs to the United States versus the benefits to the United States, do you think the war with Iraq was worth fighting, or not?			
Worth the cost	88.5	71.3	25.2
3. Again thinking about the goals versus the costs of the war, so far in your opinion has there been an acceptable or unacceptable number of U.S. military casualties in Iraq?			
Acceptable	63.7	47.8	13.5
4. Do you think the war with Iraq has or has not contributed to the long-term security of the United States?			
Yes	84.4	73.1	35.2
5. Do you think the United States has gotten bogged down in Iraq, or do you think the United States is making good progress in Iraq?			
Making good progress	70.8	60.7	17.9
6. Do you think the United States should keep its military forces in Iraq until civil order is restored there, even if that means continued U.S. military casualties; or, do you think the United States should withdraw its military forces from Iraq in order to avoid further U.S. military casualties, even if that means civil order is not restored there?			
Keep forces in Iraq	86.6	78.4	40.0
7. Overall how do you think things are going for the United States in Iraq at this time—very well, well, badly or very badly?			
Very well or well	86.2	74.8	24.5
8. How confident are you that Iraq will have a stable, democratic government a year from now—very confident, somewhat confident, not too confident or not confident at all?			
Very or somewhat confident	67.6	60.3	24.7

continued

TABLE 8.1 *(continued)*

	WHITE BORN-AGAIN/ EVANGELICAL CHRISTIAN REPUBLICANS	OTHERS REPUBLICANS	DEMOCRATS

9. Do you think the United States is or is not making significant progress toward restoring civil order in Iraq?

Making significant progress	79.0	74.2	30.6

10. Do you think the number of U.S. military forces in Iraq should be increased, decreased, or kept about the same?

Increases or kept the same	88.8	84.0	44.6

11. Do you think the anti-government insurgency in Iraq is on its last legs?

Yes	48.3	37.8	29.1

SOURCE: ABC News/*Washington Post* Poll, June 23–26, 2005.

themselves in the first group, so their contribution to continued general Republican support for the president's Iraq policies was considerable. So, then, was their contribution to the wide partisan differences on questions relating to the war.

The steady, overwhelming support for U.S. involvement in Iraq provided by Bush's core Republican constituents gave the administration a good deal of leeway in coping with the insurgents while trying to help Iraqi allies impose order and establish a viable representative government. As long as ordinary Republicans remained supportive, any pressure to withdraw American forces before the new regime was securely in place would be resistible. Through 2005, Republicans remained largely optimistic about Iraq and were likely to remain so as long as there were enough markers of progress, such as the parliamentary elections held in December, to counter any sense that Iraq has become another

Vietnam-like quagmire. Unless conditions in Iraq were to deterio-
rate palpably, the Bush administration should be able to count on
sufficient patience from its core supporters to continue its effort
to redeem what has threatened to become a political debacle of
the first magnitude.

The Bush administration could not, on the other hand, count
on broad political support for other preemptive military actions.
One (at least temporary) legacy of the Iraq War has been to make
Democrats more dovish and Republicans more hawkish. A Pew
Center study found that the proportion of Democrats agreeing
with the statement, "Good diplomacy is the best way to ensure
peace," had risen from 62 percent in 1999 to 76 percent in 2004;
among Republicans, the proportion agreeing had fallen from
46 percent to 32 percent. The share of Republicans agreeing that
"we should all be willing to fight for our country whether it is
right or wrong" had risen from 59 to 66 percent, while the proportion of Democrats agreeing with this sentiment had fallen from
45 percent to 33 percent.[48] Barring a direct attack on the United
States or its close allies, mobilizing bipartisan support for invading
anyone will not be easy when distrust of the administration among
Democrats runs so high.

CONCLUSION

Nothing in George W. Bush's second-term policies, objectives, or
strategies promises any significant narrowing of the wide partisan

---

[48] Pew Research Center for the People and the Press, "Politics and Values in a 51%–48% Nation," news
release, January 24, 2005, accessed at http://people-press.org/reports/display.php3?ReportID=236
(accessed January 28, 2005).

divisions generated by his first administration—on the contrary. His domestic agenda is largely a conservative Republican wish list with little cross-party appeal; congressional Democrats, stiffened by their own supporters' overwhelming disapproval of the president and his policies, have every incentive to remain in opposition. The Iraq War continues to generate the widest partisan divisions ever recorded for such a military action. In all likelihood, only a dramatic improvement that allows a U.S. withdrawal would soften Democrats' negative views of the enterprise, and only a dramatic setback would seriously erode Republican support for it. Neither seems likely at this juncture, but neither can be ruled out; recent history has delivered too many surprises to allow certainty about such matters. Barring such developments, however, the Iraq War will continue to divide the country, for there is little prospect of any change in administration policy. Having declared Iraq the main front in the war on terrorism, it is unimaginable, politically or psychologically, that Bush could disengage short of something that could be portrayed as victory, for doing so would be to concede failure on his presidency's defining mission.

Republicans in Congress may be nervous about touching the "third rail" without bipartisan cover and in the fall of 2005 were showing signs of worry about ebbing public support for the Iraq War—it was hard to ignore the Ohio by-election in which an anti-war, anti-Bush Democrat who was a veteran of the Iraq War came close to winning a solidly Republican House district[49]—but it is difficult to imagine them initiating a movement toward the political

---

[49] The Democrat won 48.3 percent of the vote in a district in which the departing Republican incumbent had never won less than 70 percent of the vote and which had given George W. Bush 64 percent of its votes in 2004.

center. A highly polarized, highly partisan citizenry serves their electoral purposes well (see Chapter 7), so they would have no reason to reach across the aisle even if they were not held back by their own conservative principles and supporters. Only if ordinary Republicans were to turn against the Bush administration in significant numbers would they come under any pressure to distance themselves from the president, and that has not happened at any point during Bush's tenure so far.

George W. Bush, then, seemed destined to remain a polarizing figure presiding over a polarized nation through the remainder of his presidency, at least barring some new horror that unifies Americans in the manner of 9/11. And under that scenario, it would be the terrorists rather than Bush who would be the "uniters." Whether he could have bridged the partisan divide, and whether he even cares that he has not (except pragmatically, as in pursuit of Social Security reform), is one of several remaining questions and issues I take up in the next, and final, chapter. I also consider whether Hurricane Katrina's devastation of the New Orleans and the Gulf Coast in late August 2005, and the Bush administration's response to the disaster, might have had any prospect of shaking up the public's increasingly ossified opinions about the president.

CHAPTER 9

❖

Conclusions and Speculations

G eorge W. Bush chose the Texas House of Representatives as the venue for his December 13, 2000, victory address because, he said on the occasion, "It had been home to bipartisan cooperation. The spirit of cooperation we have seen in this hall is what is needed in Washington, D.C."[1] No doubt the president was sincere in wanting to be a "uniter, not a divider," as he had been in Texas. The question was, on whose terms? The answer turned out to be, on his terms. Bipartisan cooperation emerged on issues where Democrats' preferences were basically compatible with Bush's preferences: the education bill, the prescription drug benefit, legislative responses to 9/11. When they were not, Bush pursued a conservative Republican agenda, which could have won bipartisan support only via the abject capitulation of congressional Democrats.

---

[1] Quoted in Fred I. Greenstein, "The Leadership Style of George W. Bush," in Greenstein, *Bush Presidency*, p. 6.

With both chambers of Congress and the federal regulatory apparatus in Republican hands, and with the wartime conditions created by 9/11 to augment presidential power, Bush did not need significant Democratic support to achieve a number of notable changes in public policy—on taxes, energy policy, regulation, tort liability, and trade policy—that were welcomed by his conservative Republican base. And mobilizing that base rather than reaching out to Democrats or the dwindling ranks of the uncommitted was a successful electoral strategy in both 2002 and 2004. In contrast to his experience in Texas, where Democrats controlled one or both houses of the legislature during his term as governor, Bush as president did not need to be a "uniter" to achieve many of his main goals, and the goals were clearly more important to him than the unity. Bipartisanship was a means to win policy changes, not an end in itself, and thus dispensable if unneeded or unduly confining.

Combined with the historical currents he inherited, his peculiar road to the White House, and the problematic nature of the Iraq War, Bush's style, agenda, and tactics ultimately provoked the most divergent partisan assessments of any president since the advent of regular polling on the president's job performance. It is impossible to gauge precisely the relative contribution of each of these factors, but it seems safe to conclude that the uniquely divisive character of the Iraq War (Chapter 6) is the primary reason that Bush overtook Ronald Reagan and Bill Clinton to become the most polarizing president on record (Figure 1.4).

Just how reflexive partisan responses to Bush had become was underlined by public evaluations of the administration's response to devastation caused by Hurricane Katrina in late August 2005. Natural disasters are usually occasions for national unity. After Katrina, and after what was universally regarded as slow and inept official response to the humanitarian crisis it spawned,[2] the public immediately split along party lines in assessing the president's performance in responding to the disaster. An ABC News/*Washington Post* poll taken five days after the hurricane hit found 74 percent of Republicans but only 17 percent of Democrats approving of Bush's handling of the crisis.[3] A Gallup Poll taken a few days later after the hurricane found 69 percent of Republicans saying the president had done a "great" or "good" job in responding to the hurricane and flooding of New Orleans, and 66 percent of Democrats saying he had done a "bad" or "terrible" job. Only 10 percent of Republicans rated Bush's response negatively, and only 10 percent of Democrats rated it positively.[4] Beyond provoking familiar partisan reactions, Katrina's aftermath handed Bush a new and unexpected agenda; I consider some potential consequences for the remainder of his presidency later in this chapter.

---

[2] In a CBS News Poll taken September 6–7, 2005, 77 percent said the federal government could have responded "much better" to the hurricane and 80 percent said it could have moved faster. See CBS News Poll, "The Aftermath of Katrina," at http://www.cbsnews.com/stories/2005/09/08/opinion/polls/main824591.shtml, (accessed September 8, 2005).

[3] Dan Balz, "For Bush, A Deepening Divide," *Washington Post*, September 7, 2005, p. A19.

[4] Independents sided with the Democrats, 47 percent negative, 29 percent positive. The remaining respondents said the response was neither good nor bad. See David W. Moore, "Public Skeptical New Orleans Will Recover," Gallup News Service, September 7, 2005, at http://gallup.com/, (accessed September 7, 2005). In the Zogby America Poll taken a couple of days later, 67 percent of Republicans rated Bush's handling of Katrina as "excellent" or "good," while 71 percent of Democrats rated it "poor." Another 18 percent of Democrats rated his performance as "fair"; only 10 percent rated it as "excellent" or "good." See Zogby America Poll, September 5–6, 2005 at http://pollingreport.com/disasters.htm, (accessed September 8, 2005).

DOES BUSH CARE?

Does it matter to Bush that Americans are so deeply divided along party lines over his presidency? It assuredly beats having a bipartisan consensus on a *negative* view of his performance; the wide partisan gap means that, unlike some of his predecessors (see Figure 1.3), Bush has retained the support of at least his own partisans. Does it matter that so many Democrats take such a dim view of his presidency? No doubt it matters pragmatically, as, for example, when overwhelming opposition of ordinary Democrats to Social Security reforms labeled as the president's denies congressional Republicans the bipartisan cover they would need to risk touching the "third rail." But there is no reason to believe it would otherwise matter to this president. In his own words, "I really don't care what polls and focus groups say. What I care about is doing what I think is right."[5] When a reporter at his October 2005 press conference noted that "85 percent of the Republicans approve of the job you're doing, but only 15 percent of the Democrats approve of the job you're doing" and asked, "What is it about that the Democrats find so objectionable?" Bush was dismissive: "Ask the pollsters. My job is to lead and to solve problems."[6]

This does not mean that he and his political advisors, notably Karl Rove, are not avid consumers of data from polls and focus groups; administration pollsters conduct extensive public opinion research, although, to maintain the fiction that Bush is a leader

---

[5] Kathryn Dunn Tenpas, "Words vs. Deeds: President George W. Bush and Polling," *The Brookings Review* (Summer 2003): 32.

[6] "President Holds Press Conference," White House news release, October 4, 2005, at http://www.whitehouse.gov/news/releases/2005/10/20051004-1.html.

who disdains polling, largely out of sight of the press or public.[7] But the research is aimed at finding out how best to market policies, not to discover what the public wants (or at least think it wants). Mass opinion is something to be molded and led, not followed.

The Bush administration is of course not the least unique in this regard. Every administration seeks to shape public opinion to further its policy goals; if it does not, it risks abandoning the field to opponents mobilizing the public against them. But the Bush administration has been unusual in its desire to make major policy changes for which there is little popular demand and in its routine reliance on deceptive rhetoric to drum up enough public support to get its way in Congress. For a president who likes to present himself as something of a populist, Bush's conception of leadership is decidedly elitist: He knows what's right for the American people and insists on pushing for it even if most of them might prefer otherwise. His policies have often been elitist in a more material sense as well, delivering major benefits to wealthy individuals and corporations with scant regard to their effects on less affluent or less well-connected Americans. I do not assume cynicism here; Bush appears to believe sincerely in the current Republican orthodoxy that ensuring the prosperity of the wealthy while weakening the social safety net is the road to betterment for all. It not only provides more capital for capitalists to invest in productive enterprises (old-fashioned trickle-down economics), but it also compels people to take greater responsibility for assuring their

---

[7] Ibid.; Joshua Green, "The Other War Room," *Washington Monthly* (April 2002), at http://www.washingtonmonthly.com/features/2001/0204.green.html (accessed August 12, 2004).

own economic well being, thereby strengthening their moral character. Help for the needy who remain is best delivered by private, faith-based charities, which, unlike government agencies, can insist on conformity to traditional social norms as a condition of assistance.

That Bush has achieved as much as he has on the domestic side is testimony to the skill with which he and his strategists have managed to feed and exploit people's "unenlightened self-interest."[8] For example, the mystery of why popular majorities favor repealing an estate tax that only about 2 percent of families will ever pay becomes less mysterious when we find nearly half the public believing that "most families have to pay" and only one-third knowing that "only a few families have to pay." Among the 57 percent who said they favored repeal, 69 percent said one reason was: "It might affect YOU some day."[9] The administration's rhetoric about saving the family farm or small business from the "death tax," regardless of how misleading,[10] faces little skepticism among people so grossly misinformed. Under such circumstances, careful manipulation of language to frame the debate and to define relevant "facts" can be a potent tactic.

Its potency, however, depends strongly on the existing beliefs and attitudes of the audience and the exclusion of alternative frames and facts. Bush has been least successful when trying to

---

[8] Larry Bartels, "Homer Gets a Tax Cut: Inequality and Public Policy in the American Mind," *Perspectives on Politics* 3 (March 2005): 21.
[9] NPR/Kaiser Family Foundation/ John F. Kennedy School of Government Poll, August 2003, quoted in ibid.
[10] The American Farm Bureau Federation, lobbying for the estate tax repeal, could not cite a single instance of a family farm lost because of the estate tax; see David Clay Johnston, "Talk of Lost Farms Reflects Muddle of Estate Tax Debate," *New York Times*, April 8, 2001.

shape public opinion on matters where people have firm prior beliefs or some personal familiarity with the issue at hand. Social Security is a prime example. Hurricane Katrina is another; the administration's upbeat assertions of progress in its immediate aftermath made no headway against the scenes of destruction and desperation Americans could see on their television screens. The public's response to the Schiavo affair also suggests that opinions on deeply personal, directly experienced or readily imaginable matters remain resistant to opinion leadership. The Bush administration has been most successful when it has been able to define reality in ways consistent with people's prior beliefs in domains where a rationally ignorant public normally defers to supposedly better-informed opinion leaders, as in the lead-up to the Iraq invasion. Most of the time, however, Bush has succeeded spectacularly in persuading Republicans, especially the party's conservative Christian faction, to accept his vision and leadership but has failed to sway more than a small proportion of Democrats and somewhat larger minority of independents to see reality his way.

COMPETING REALITIES

I use the term "reality" here advisedly; one of the intriguing features of the Bush administration is its implicit premise that, for all practical political purposes, perceptions *are* reality, and that reality can therefore be shaped to its convenience. There is a certain irony in discovering that a president and administration who profess firm belief in divinely-ordained absolutes are, operationally, post-modern social constructionists. And not only of perceptions;

journalist Ron Suskind reported the following dialogue with a "senior advisor to Bush":

> The aide said that guys like me were "in what we call the reality-based community," which he defined as people who "believe solutions emerge from judicious study of discernable reality." I nodded and murmured something about enlightenment principles and empiricism. He cut me off. "That's not the way the world really works anymore," he continued. "We're an empire now, and when we act, we create our own reality. And while you're studying reality—judiciously, as you will—we'll act again, creating other new realities, which you can study too, and that's how things will sort out. We're history's actors . . . and you, all of you, will be left to just study what we do."[11]

The Bush administration's policies certainly created their own reality in Iraq, but plainly not the one intended: An imagined terrorist hotbed with links to Osama bin Laden and al Qaeda was turned into a real one. The task of realizing a democratic, stable, peaceful Middle Eastern nation that respects the human rights of its citizens has proven far more difficult than the war's advocates anticipated. Rival realities arising from Iraqi history, religion, and culture keep getting in the way. The "reality-based community" has reasserted itself, and its "judicious study of discernable reality" in Iraq has led to widespread criticism of the decision to go to war and a loss of trust in George W. Bush's leadership in that community and among citizens who share its perspectives. Bush's support has remained firm, however, among those whose notions

---

[11] Ron Suskind, "Without a Doubt." *New York Times*, October 17, 2004, Section 6, p. 44.

of reality derive from a priori beliefs that are simply not open to empirical refutation. Certainly there are "reality-based" defenders of the president and his invasion of Iraq, but it is hard to imagine that Bush would have retained as much support as he has, especially among Republicans, without the tenacious loyalty of religious conservatives for whom faith in the president has been largely impervious to changing events or new information.

Many of Bush's Democratic detractors have their own strong predispositions, but the magnitude of the rally to his side after 9/11, and the smaller rallies coinciding with the onset of the Iraq War and the capture of Saddam Hussein (Table 1.2), indicate that, at one time anyway, changed circumstances could change their opinions of the president. This may no longer be the case. Democrats' views of reality, shaped most powerfully by the Iraq War and its disillusioning aftermath but also influenced by other actions of the administration, now including its response to Hurricane Katrina, has come to include the perception that the president is indifferent to their concerns,[12] incompetent,[13] and not to be trusted (see Chapters 6 and 8). The reflexive reaction to Bush among Democrats and most independents has become skepticism rather than faith. Of course this, too, may lead to misconceptions. For

---

[12] In the October, 2005 CBS News/*New York Times* Poll, the proportion of Democrats saying Bush did not share their priorities for the country hit 87 percent; among independents, it was 71 percent; 69 percent of Republicans held the opposite view; at http://www.cbsnews.com/stories/2005/10/06/opinion/polls/main924485.shtml (accessed October 6, 2005). In their October 2004 poll, 84 percent of Democrats had said that Bush "did not understand the needs and problems of people like yourself"; 84 percent of Republicans said he did. See "Into the Home Stretch," October 14–17, 2004, at http://www.cbsnews.com/sections/opinion/polls/main500160.shtml (accessed October 25, 2004).
[13] A CBS News/*New York Times* Poll taken in the wake of Hurricane Katrina found 75 percent of Democrats expressing little or no confidence in Bush's ability to handle a crisis (only 12 percent of Republicans held this view); 76 percent said he did not have strong qualities of leadership (only 15 percent of Republicans concurred); see "The Aftermath of Katrina," September 6–7, 2005, at http://www.cbsnews.com/htdocs/CBSNews_polls/hurricane.pdf (accessed September 9, 2005).

example, although the president and his team hyped the case well beyond what the evidence had warranted, there is little reason to doubt that they really believed Saddam Hussein possessed WMD and was busy trying to make more. Most Democrats, however, had by the beginning of Bush's second term come to believe that he and his team were either "mostly lying" about WMD (39 percent) or were "hiding important elements of what they knew" (47 percent) to justify invading Iraq.[14] For some, skepticism has elided into conspiracy theories; the idea that the real purpose of invading Iraq was to control its oilfields and fatten Halliburton's bottom line also has its adherents among Bush's critics; a few even suggest that the U.S. government had a hand in 9/11.[15]

More broadly, most Democrats failed to notice, or at least acknowledge, the improved performance of the economy after 2002 (Figure 9.1).[16] Here is an instance where the views of Republicans have varied in response to changing circumstances, while those of Democrats have not. Class differences in the party coalitions may have something to do with this gap—economic circumstances improved more for upper- than for lower-income groups[17]—but not enough to account for such sharply divergent

---

[14] "The George W. Bush Presidency: Four More Years," CBS News/*New York Times* Poll, January 14–18, 2005, at http://www.cbsnews.com/htdocs/CBSNews_polls (accessed January 31, 2005).

[15] "Getting Agnostic About 9/11," *Los Angeles Times Magazine*, August 28, 2005, p. 6. Halliburton, an energy services conglomerate headed by Dick Cheney before he became vice president, has received billions of dollars in government contracts for work in Iraq.

[16] In 2004, for example, the GDP grew by 4.2 percent in real terms, and per-capita disposable income grew by 3.4 percent, and unemployment averaged only 5.5 percent, down from 6.0 percent in 2003.

[17] A Gallup Study found that in polls taken December 2002 through March 2003 there was no difference across income groups in responses to a question about whether it was a good or a bad time to be looking for a job; 79 percent of both the lowest and highest income groups said it was a bad time; responses to the same question in March–July, 2005 polls found a 21 point gap between the top and bottom income groups, with 48 percent of the "$75,000+" category saying it was a good time, compared to 27 percent of the "less than $20,000" category. This may well reflect real differences in the job market, but it may also be linked directly to partisanship; the partisan gap on this question was 11 points in the first period, 38 points in the second.

FIGURE 9.1
Rating of the Economy, 2001–2005

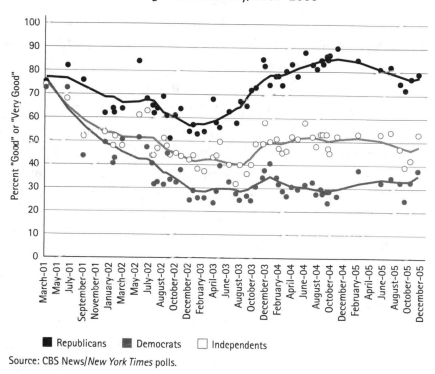

Republicans Democrats Independents

Source: CBS News/*New York Times* polls.

readings of economic conditions by ordinary Democrats and Republicans.

THE NEWS MEDIA

If Republicans and Democrats tend to maintain separate views of reality, one contributing factor may be the increasingly fragmented and ideologically diverse sources of news they now draw on for information. For example, a study by Steven Kull and his associates, based on three polls taken between June and September 2003, found that perceptions of factual aspects of the Iraq War varied significantly according to the source respondents relied on for national news. They examined the frequency with which respondents held three specific misconceptions about the Iraq War: "Clear evidence that Saddam Hussein was working closely with al Qaeda has been *found*," that "weapons of mass destruction have been *found* in Iraq," and that "world opinion *favored* the United States going to war with Iraq."[18] Levels of misperception on these questions were strongly related to the respondent's source of news (Figure 9.2). People informed by the Fox network reported the highest incidence of misperception (averaging 45 percent across the three questions), while the NPR/PBS audience reported the least (11 percent). The CBS audience was the second most, and consumers of print media the second least error-prone, with the audience for other sources falling in between.

Kull and his coauthors also offer evidence that these results are not entirely the consequence of people choosing sources compatible with their partisan or ideological preconceptions. Even when party identification and support for Bush's reelection were controlled (along with a battery of additional demographic variables, including education), news sources had a large and significant effect on the incidence of misperception, with the Fox audience again having the highest probability of getting it wrong, and NPR/PBS audiences having the lowest.[19] Moreover, those Fox watchers who said they followed the news "very closely" were the most misinformed on all three questions. For consumers of print media, in contrast, accuracy increased significantly with increasing attentiveness to

---

[18] Steven Kull, Clay Ramsay, and Evan Lewis, "Misperceptions, the Media, and the Iraq War," *Political Science Quarterly* 118 (Winter, 2003–2004): 575; emphasis in the original.
[19] Ibid., pp. 589–590.

FIGURE 9.2
News Source and Misperceptions About the War in Iraq

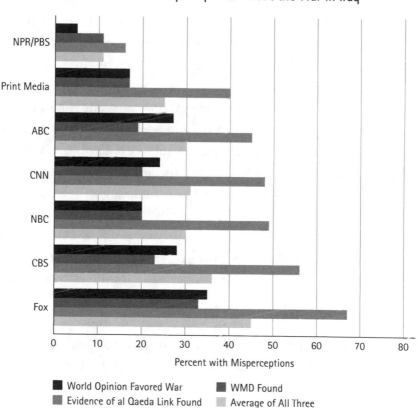

Source: Stephen Kull, Clay Ramsay, and Evan Lewis, "Misperceptions, the Media, and the Iraq War,"
Political Science Quarterly 118 (Winter 2003–2004): 569–598.

news.[20] Not surprisingly, the number of misperceptions was related
monotonically to support for the war, which ranged from 23 percent
among those holding no misperceptions to 86 percent among those
holding all three.[21] The direction of causation between support for

---

[20] For other media there was little or no effect. See ibid., p. 586.
[21] Ibid., p. 580.

the war and beliefs expressed in response to these questions remains, of course, thoroughly ambiguous.

Although the news source effects found by this study cannot be explained away by audience self-selection, people do clearly tend to choose news outlets whose biases, such as they are, seem to fit their own. Republicans and conservatives are overrepresented in the Fox News audience, Democrats and liberals are overrepresented in the public radio and television news audiences and among readers of magazines like the *New Yorker, Harper's,* and the *Atlantic.* Audiences for specific commentators are even more skewed; 77 percent of Rush Limbaugh's listeners and 72 percent of Bill O'Reilly's viewers call themselves conservatives (about double the proportion in the general public).[22] Democrats outnumbered Republicans almost six to one among those who said they had seen Michael Moore's caustic anti-Bush "documentary," *Fahrenheit 9/11.*[23] There is no way to measure the precise effect of selective attention to news and opinion sources that reinforce rather than challenge partisan and ideological biases, but it is likely to have made at least a modest contribution to the public's polarized responses to the president and his administration's policies.

Finally, the Bush administration's disdainful treatment of the Washington press corps, which it sees as dominated by "reality-based" liberals posing tendentious questions designed to undermine

---

[22] "News Audiences Increasingly Politicized," Pew Research Center for the People and the Press, news release, June 8, 2004, 14–15, at http://people-press.org/reports/display.php3?ReportID=215 (accessed July 7, 2005).

[23] "Fahrenheit 9/11 Viewers and Limbaugh Listeners About Equal in Size Even Though They Perceive Two Different Nations, Annenberg Data Show," National Annenberg Election Study, news release, August 3, 2004, at http://www.annenbergpublicpolicycenter.org/naes/2004_03_fahrenheit_08-03_pr.pdf (accessed August 10, 2004).

its carefully constructed messages, has both reflected and reinforced the idea that all sources are biased and all information carries a partisan, ideological spin. Stone-walling reporters and fanning popular distrust of mainstream news media are logical tactics for an administration intent on conveying its own constructions of reality, unmediated, to the public. It is probably impossible to determine what, if anything, the Bush administration's practices have had to do with it, but Americans have become increasingly distrustful of the major news media since 2000, with the shift twice as large among Republicans (who were much more distrustful to begin with) as among Democrats.[24] On a related question, the share of Republicans saying the press was "too critical of America" grew from 42 percent to 67 percent between the July 2002 and June 2005 Pew Center polls; in contrast, the share of Democrats taking this view change little (it fell from 26 percent to 24 percent), opening yet another substantial partisan gap in political perceptions.[25]

HURRICANE KATRINA

Nature's implacable reality in the form of Hurricane Katrina, and the raw scenes of material and human devastation that followed, posed a stark challenge to the entire tenor of George W. Bush's presidency. No upbeat spin or show of confidence could offset televised images and stories of bodies floating in the flooded

---

[24] "News Audiences Increasingly Politicized," overview.
[25] "Public More Critical of Press, But Goodwill Persists," Pew Research Center for the People and the Press, news release, June 6, 2005, at http://people-press.org/reports/display.php3?ReportID=248 (accessed July 8, 2005).

streets of New Orleans, of hungry and thirsty refugees neglected for days, of fires and looting in abandoned neighborhoods. No amount of blame leveled at state and local officials, however well deserved, or at citizens of New Orleans themselves, could hide the fact that the federal government's response had been slow, disorganized, badly informed, poorly led, and, for an inexcusably long time, ineffectual. For once, the president had to admit his own and his appointees' mistakes, for to claim otherwise would have marked him as delusional. Worse for Bush, the failure was in a domain that was supposed to be his strong suit, homeland security; the government's flawed response to Katrina raised pointed questions about how well prepared the United States was, fully four years after 9/11, to deal with the consequences of a major terrorist attack. Katrina also brought issues of race, class, and poverty to the forefront, for among the worse hit and slowest to receive help were African Americans from New Orleans' poorest neighborhoods. Most of the victims were not part of the Republican coalition nor of the class served by the Bush administration's usual domestic policies; any serious step to address their needs would require a major shift in its legislative agenda. So, of course, would the task of rebuilding so much of the Gulf Coast.

Katrina delivered an exogenous shock to the political system potentially large enough to shake up the partisan divisions that had hardened during Bush's first term. It does not seem likely at this writing that it will have this effect, but it is too early to know for certain. Democratic leaders saw no reason to restrain their criticism of the administration's shaky performance in the crisis; administration critics linked it to other policies they opposed, including Bush's Iraq policy (arguing that it had crippled the government's response by thinning the ranks of the National Guard back home), his stance on global warming, and his budget priorities. Republicans reflexively counterattacked, accusing Democrats of "playing the blame game" while themselves trying to shift the blame to mostly Democratic state and local officials. Issues of race and class also quickly became the grist of partisan debate, as did the question of who—Congress? An independent commission? The White House?—would investigate the government's failures.[26]

As noted earlier, the first public reactions to the administration's performance split sharply along party lines, and this did not change in subsequent months. Bush's overall performance ratings dipped to the lowest of his presidency; more important, his ratings among Republicans fell enough to worry administration strategists (Figure 1.2), although they actually remained quite high, around 80 percent, and the decline was smaller among the party's conservative core than among more moderate Republicans.[27] His approval ratings also dropped among independents, and among Democrats it hit record lows, averaging a mere 8 percent in the four October 2005 Gallup polls. Perhaps more worrisome for the administration, support for keeping troops in Iraq also fell in some polls (Figures 8.5 and 8.6) as domestic needs took priority in respondents' minds.[28] The public's preferred way

[26] Isaiah J. Poole, "Partisan Finger-Pointing over Katrina," *CQ Weekly* (September 12, 2005): 2414–2415.

[27] A Pew Center for the People and the Press poll measured Bush's support among Republicans as falling from 88 percent to 79 percent between July and September 2005. Among conservative Republicans, it fell from 91 percent to 84 percent; among others, from 81 percent to 70 percent. See http://people-press .org/reports/tables/255.pdf (accessed September 19, 2005). In the 17 Gallup and CBS News/*New York Times* polls used for Figure 1.4 taken after Katrina, Bush's approval averaged 82 percent among Republicans, down only 4 points from the June–August average of 86 percent.

[28] "Iraq and Its Impact Back Home," CBS News/*New York Times* Poll, September 9–13, 2005 at http://www.cbs.news.com/htdocs/CBSNews_polls/Iraq_916.pdf (accessed September 19, 2005).

to pay for reconstruction was, by a wide margin over any other option, to cut spending for the war in Iraq.[29]

The modest decline in Republican approval and unambiguous evidence that a large majority of Americans, leaders and ordinary citizens alike, were critical of Bush's initial response to Katrina's devastation prompted the administration to change its approach. In a nationally-televised speech on September 15, the president acknowledged his administration's failures and took formal responsibility. He also acknowledged the class and racial disparities exposed by the disaster. And he sought to reclaim the initiative by proposing a hugely expensive federal program to completely rebuild New Orleans and the devastated Gulf Coast region, restoring communities and upgrading the poorest areas.[30] Such a massive if unspecified undertaking enjoyed broad public support[31] and, in theory, should have been more to the taste of Democrats than of Republicans. But its details held the potential for Gulf reconstruction to become yet another arena for bitter partisan conflict.

Small government and fiscal conservatives were appalled by what sounded to them like the kind of New Deal-type big-spending program they had been fighting against for decades. In response, the president, while promising to spend "whatever it

---

[29] In the September 16–19, 2005 CNN/USA Today/Gallup Poll, 54 percent took this option; 17 percent wanted to raise taxes, 6 percent wanted to cut domestic spending, and 15 percent wanted to increase the deficit, at http://pollingreport.com/disasters.htm (accessed September 21, 2005).
[30] "President Discusses Hurricane Relief in Address to the Nation," White House press release, September 15, 2005, at http://www.whitehouse.gov/news/releases/2005/09/20050915-8.html (accessed September 19, 2005).
[31] For example, asked if the proposed $200 billion to be appropriated by Congress for rebuilding was the right amount, 52 percent of respondents to an Associated Press/Ipsos poll (taken September 16–18, 2005) said it was the right amount, 15 percent said it was too little, and only 24 percent said it was too much; see http://pollingreport.com/disasters.htm (accessed October 6, 2005).

takes" on reconstruction, also vowed that he would not raise taxes to pay for it but would rely on unspecified offsetting spending cuts in other programs; his chief economic advisor admitted that most of the estimated $200 billion for reconstruction would be borrowed,[32] the debt to be passed on, then, like the cost of the Iraq War, to future generations. This stance made it almost certain that the partisan budgetary battles that have been a central component of national politics since the Reagan administration would reemerge in post-Katrina politics.

There were also signs that the administration would try to use reconstruction as an opportunity to further its conservative agenda: vouchers for displaced students to pay for private and religious schooling, suspension of environmental regulations and prevailing-wage requirements, tax breaks for businesses large and small, and funds for faith-based charities were all on the table. The rumor that Karl Rove had been put in charge of reconstruction plans fueled suspicion that "the administration will consider conservative ideological gains as a paramount consideration" in carrying them out.[33] This approach would be consistent with the administration's track record, and insofar is it is pursued, would no doubt provoke the usual polarized response from politicians and the public. Bush and his advisors have always cared more about pleasing core Republican constituencies than about broadening his appeal, and despite the president's nod to Americans outside

---

[32] "Press Briefing by Scott McClellan; Claude Allen, Assistant to the President for Domestic Policy; and Al Hubbard, Assistant to the President for Economic Policy and Director, National Economic Council," White House press release, September 16, 2005, at http://www.whitehouse.gov/news/releases/2005/09/20050916-6.html (accessed September 19, 2005).

[33] Dan Froomkin, "Mr. Big Government," *Washington Post* on-line edition, September 16, 2005, at http://www.washingtonpost.com/wp-dyn/content/blog/2005/09/16/BL2005091601005.htm (accessed September 19, 2005).

the Republican tent after Katrina, it seemed unlikely that this would change, especially considering that the Republican base was about all Bush had left when Katrina hit.

Still, partisan conflict is to a considerable degree agenda-driven, and a massive reconstruction program for the Gulf region is inherently less divisive than the administration's ideas for reforming Social Security, Medicaid, or the tax system. If the focus remained on reconstruction, and ideological conflict over its details could be kept in check, partisan strife in Washington might decline and partisan divisions among ordinary citizens might become less pronounced. But in light of George W. Bush's long-term political objectives and conception of leadership, and with three more years in office, a commitment to staying the course in Iraq, and the prospect of the 2006 midterm in which mobilizing the Republican base will once again appear to be the party's best strategic option, it is difficult to imagine that he would not return to the ambitions outlined at the beginning of his second term. If so he will continue to be the most divisive national leader in the half-century that polls have regularly gauged popular assessments of the president.

AFTER BUSH

If George W. Bush's leadership style, policy goals, decisions, and political strategies have contributed materially to an unusually high level of partisan disunity in the United States, will his departure from the White House after the 2008 elections reduce partisan tensions and divisions? The answer depends of course in part on who succeeds him, under what circumstances and with what agenda; an election pitting John McCain against, say, Mark Warner (the moderate former governor of Virginia) would have rather different implications for party polarization than one pitting Pennsylvania Republican Rick Santorum (arguably the Senate's most ardent social conservative) against Hillary Clinton. But regardless of whether the next president's leadership style and objectives are less divisive than Bush's, both enduring political conflicts and the current configuration of party coalitions are likely to fuel high levels of partisan conflict for the foreseeable future. Tax and budget disputes, to pick one inescapable example, can only become more contentious as deficits rise and the baby boomers begin drawing Medicare and Social Security. Republican politicians will not willingly abandon the anti-tax orthodoxy that has defined their party since the Reagan administration; and Democrats will not surrender on the middle-class entitlement programs that have been their bread-and-butter since the New Deal without an all-out fight.

Moreover, the cultural divide between the two party coalitions is likely to persist, and the divisive social issues that make it salient are not going away anytime soon. The study of religion and political behavior in 2004 conducted by James L. Guth and his associates, using a refined version of their religiosity categories outlined in Chapter 2, revealed just how sharply religiosity now divides the parties (Figure 9.3).[34] Regardless of

---

[34] James L. Guth, Lyman A. Kellstedt, Corwin E. Smidt, and John C. Green, "Religious Mobilization in the 2004 Presidential Election," paper delivered at the Annual Meeting of the American Political Science Association, September 1–4, 2005.

FIGURE 9.3
Religiosity and Party Identification, 2004

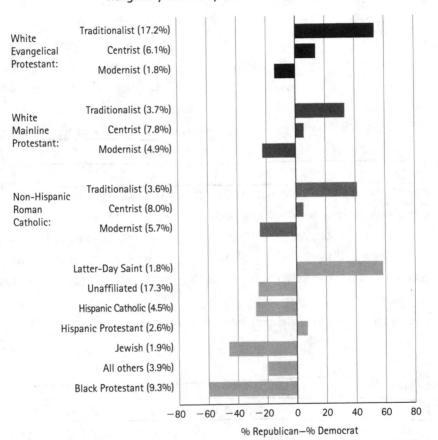

Source: James Guth, Lyman A. Kellstedt, Corwin E. Schmidt, and John C. Green, "Religious Mobilization in the 2004 Presidential Election," presented at the 2005 Annual Meeting of the American Political Science Association, Washington, D.C., September 1–4, Table 3.

denomination, religious traditionalists—defined by orthodox or fundamentalist beliefs, regular participation, and identification with religious movements—are overwhelmingly Republican. Of the 26 percent of their respondents who are classified as religious traditionalists or Latter-day Saints (LDS/Mormons), 69 percent identify themselves as Republicans, only 20 percent as Democrats. Of the 36 percent who are modernist in religion, unaffiliated, Jewish, or in the residual "other" category, 50 percent are Democrats, only 25 percent are Republicans. Democrats hold a wide lead among minorities (except Hispanic Protestants); religious centrists (22 percent of respondents) give Republicans an edge, 45 percent to 38 percent.

Restated in terms of the party coalitions, 45 percent of Republicans are religious traditionalists or LDS; only 22 percent are from the modernist/unaffiliated/Jewish/other categories; 25 percent are religious centrists, only 8 percent, minorities of any kind. In contrast, 44 percent of Democrats are from the modernist, et al., category; 24 percent are minorities, 20 percent are religious centrists, and only 13 percent are religious traditionalists or LDS. Thus the largest factions in each party are at polar opposites on the religious/cultural divide, and the parties also have very different ethnic compositions. Issues touching on these divisions—abortion, same-sex marriage, stem-cell research, creationism in science classes, assisted suicide, sex education, faith-based delivery of social services, affirmative action, immigration—are thus guaranteed to provoke sharp partisan differences long after the current administration is history.

George W. Bush has placed himself squarely on one side of the divide, and this has brought him a solid, so far nearly unshakable base of support in his party's dominant faction. But reliance on that base has also limited his ability to try to reach beyond it to recapture disaffected Democrats and independents. Future Republican presidential candidates and presidents are likely to face similar dilemmas, as will Democrats who want to expand their appeal beyond secular modernists, liberals, and minority voters—something they will have to do to have any chance of retaking power in Washington. With the partisan configurations and policy conflicts now in place, the question is whether anyone can succeed in winning either party's presidential nomination and still become "a uniter, not a divider."

APPENDIX

Data Sources and Question Wordings

The survey data reported in this book were culled from a wide variety of sources; many of them are cited where appropriate, but some figures are based on data from so many sources that it was infeasible to list them all. Except for certain questions regarding the Iraq War, I used only surveys that sampled the adult population rather than registered or likely voters. My initial source for data on the distribution of responses for entire samples was PollingReport.com, an indispensable archive, updated daily, of survey results from all of the major commercial polling organizations. PollingReport.com reports findings from, among others, the ABC News/*Washington Post,* CBS/*New York Times,* Gallup (sometimes reported as Gallup/CNN/*USA Today*), NBC News/*Wall Street Journal,* Pew Research Center for the People and the Press, *Newsweek, Los Angeles Times, Time,* CNN/*Time,*

Associated Press/IPSOS, Harris, Fox News, Democracy Corps, Quinnipaic College, *Investor's Business Daily,* and Zogby Polls. Data from all of these polls were the basis for one or more of the figures displayed in this book.

PollingReport.com does not routinely report results broken down by party identification, although it occasionally supplies these figures. For such information, I relied regularly on the CBS News/*New York Times* Poll reports that are linked to the news stories of their polls (click on the "learn more" icon), ABC News/*Washington Post*'s Poll Vault, the Pew Research Center for the People and the Press news releases, and more irregularly on other surveys reported in news stories or available on-line by the poll's sponsoring organization. I also subscribed to a Gallup service that provides demographic breakdowns on the presidential approval question. Some of the partisan breakdowns (and other findings) came from my own analyses of surveys from the CBS/*New York Times,* ABC News/*Washington Post,* and Pew Center polls. The first two are archived at the Interuniversity Consortium for Political and Social Research (ICPSR), although with lags of a year or more; the third can be downloaded (again with a lag) from the Pew Center's website. I also analyzed data from the American National Election Studies,[1] and got additional figures from the National Annenberg Election Survey, the PIPA/Knowledge Networks Poll, the 2000 and 2004 Exit polls, and other published sources cited in the text.

---

[1] Specifically, I analyzed data from The National Election Studies, THE 2004 NATIONAL ELECTION STUDY [dataset]. Ann Arbor, MI: University of Michigan, Center for Political Studies [producer and distributor] and the 1948–2002 NES Cumulative Data file.

THE IRAQ WAR QUESTIONS

It is infeasible to present the actual wordings of every question asked in the thousands of surveys I used to create the figures, but I have included such information when I thought it necessary. The widest assortment of questions sought to tap support for the Iraq War, and I list them below. For analyses reported in Figures 6.2 and 6.4, I combined responses of closely related questions into a smaller number of categories. Here is the full range of questions (sources in parentheses):

I. Before the War:

Do you approve or disapprove of the United States taking military action against Iraq to try to remove Saddam Hussein from power? (CBS News/*New York Times*)

Do you support or oppose U.S. military action to remove Iraqi President Saddam Hussein? (Fox News)

Would you favor or oppose having U.S. forces take military action against Iraq to force Saddam Hussein from power? (ABC News/*Washington Post*)

Would you favor or oppose invading Iraq with U.S. ground troops in an attempt to remove Saddam Hussein from power? (Gallup)

Would you favor or oppose taking military action in Iraq to end Saddam Hussein's rule? (Pew Research Center for the People and the Press)

Would you favor or oppose sending American troops back to the Persian Gulf in order to remove Saddam Hussein from power in Iraq? (Gallup)

Do you think that the United States should or should not take military action to remove Saddam Hussein from power in Iraq? (ABC News/*Washington Post*)

Do you think that the United States should or should not take military action against Iraq and Saddam Hussein? (NBC News/*Wall Street Journal*)

Do you think the United States should take military action in order to remove Saddam Hussein from power in Iraq, or not? (*Los Angeles Times*)

Do you think removing Saddam Hussein from power is worth the potential loss of American life and the other costs of attacking Iraq, or not? (CBS News/*New York Times*)

Would you support or oppose the United States going to war with Iraq? (ABC News/*Washington Post*)

Would you support or oppose a U.S. invasion of Iraq with ground troops? (ABC News/*Washington Post*)

Would you support using military force against Iraq, or not? (*Newsweek*)

Currently, would you strongly support, somewhat support, somewhat oppose, or strongly oppose a war against Iraq? (Zogby)

Do you favor or oppose taking U.S. military action against Iraq? (*Chicago Tribune*)

II. After the War Began:

Do you support or oppose the Bush Administration's decision to take military action against Iraq at this time? (*Los Angeles Times*)

Do you support or oppose the United States having gone to war with Iraq? (ABC News/*Washington Post*)

Do you approve or disapprove of the United States' decision to go to war with Iraq in March 2003? (CNN/Gallup)

Looking back, do you think the United States did the right thing in taking military action against Iraq, or should the U.S. have stayed out? (CBS News/*New York Times*)

Considering everything, do you think the United States did the right thing in going to war with Iraq or do you think it was a mistake? (ABC News/*Washington Post*)

Do you think the U.S. made the right decision or the wrong decision in using military force against Iraq? (Pew Research Center for the People and the Press)

Do you think going to war with Iraq was the right thing for the United States to do or the wrong thing? (Fox News, Quinnipiac College)

From what you know now, do think the United States did the right thing in taking military action against Iraq last year, or not? (*Newsweek*)

Do you think the United States was right or wrong in going to war with Iraq? (*Time*)

Do you think the U.S. made the right decision or the wrong decision in going to war against Iraq? (PIPA/Knowledge Networks)

All in all, considering the costs to the United States versus the benefits to the United States, do you think the war in Iraq was worth fighting or not? (ABC News/*Washington Post*)

All in all, do you think it was worth going to war in Iraq, or not? (Gallup)

All in all, do you think the situation in Iraq was worth going to war over, or not? (National Annenberg Election Survey, *Los Angeles Times*)

All things considered, do you think the United States going to war with Iraq has been worth it or not? (Fox News)

Generally speaking, do you think the outcome of the war in Iraq has been worth the cost in U.S. military lives, or not? (*Los Angeles Times*)

Do you think the result of the war was worth the loss of American life and other costs of attacking Iraq, or not? (CBS News/*New York Times*)

In your view, is the war against Iraq worth the toll it has taken in American lives and other kinds of costs, or isn't the war worth these costs? (*Time*)

When it comes to the war in Iraq, do you think that removing Saddam Hussein from power was or was not worth the number of U.S. military casualties and the financial cost of the war? (NBC News/*Wall Street Journal*)

Do you think removing Saddam Hussein from power was worth the loss of American life and other costs of attacking Iraq, or not? (CBS News/*New York Times*)

Generally speaking, do you think the outcome of the war in Iraq has been worth the financial cost to the U.S., or not? (*Los Angeles Times*)

In view of the developments since we first sent our troops to Iraq, do you think the United States made a mistake in sending troops to Iraq, or not? (Gallup)

Generally speaking, do you support or oppose the U.S. military action in Iraq? (*Investor's Business Daily*)

Do you favor or oppose the U.S. war with Iraq? (Gallup)

Do you support or oppose the United States taking military action to disarm Iraq and remove Iraqi President Saddam Hussein? (Fox News)

Do you think that the United States should or should not have taken military action to remove Saddam Hussein from power in Iraq? (NBC News/*Wall Street Journal*)

In general, do you approve or disapprove of current military policy in Iraq? (*Time*)

Do you approve or disapprove of the United States' current occupation of Iraq? (CBS News/*New York Times*)

Do you support or oppose the current U.S. military presence in Iraq? (ABC News/*Washington Post*)

Index

Numbers preceded by an n indicate footnote number.